Diet of Despair

A book about Eating Disorders for Young People and their Families

by

Anna Paterson

Illustrated by Philippa Drakeford

Paul Chapman Publishing
A SAGE Publications Company
1 Oliver's Yard
55 City Road
London EC1Y 1SP

SAGE Publications Inc.
2455 Teller Road
Thousand Oaks, California 91320
SAGE Publications India Pvt Ltd
B-42, Panchsheel Enclave
Post Box 4109
New Delhi 110 017

Paterson, Anna

Diet of despair
: a book about
eating
                  616.
                  852
1805099

Commissioned and edited by George Robinson
Book and cover design: Barbara Maines from an idea suggested by Simon Teff

ISBN 978-1-873942-19-2

Printed on paper from sustainable resources
Printed in Great Britain by Cromwell Press Ltd

Anna with her fiancé Simon - December 2001

Biography

"Diet Of Despair" is Anna Paterson's second book. Her first book "Anorexic" (Westworld International, 2000) was an autobiographical account of her 14 year struggle with anorexia. Anna is now recovered and spends her time trying to help other eating disorder sufferers who contact her daily. She works to raise awareness about the reality of these illnesses and is regularly asked to speak about her experiences. Anna is currently completing her third book "Running On Empty", a novel about eating disorders for young people. She lives with her fiancé Simon, who helps her with all aspects of her work including editing her books and they are currently saving up for their first house.

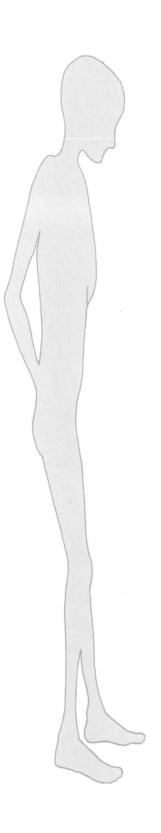

I want to thank Simon for his tireless support and help with this book every step of the way. I now think he knows as much about eating disorders as I do.

I also want to thank my very dear friend Mike Robeson for all the invaluable help he has given me whilst I was writing this book.

Contents

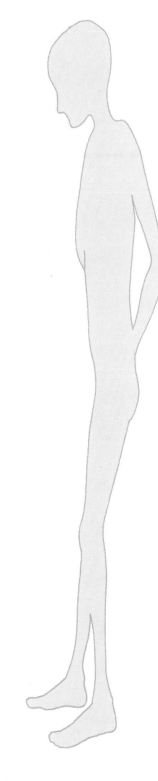

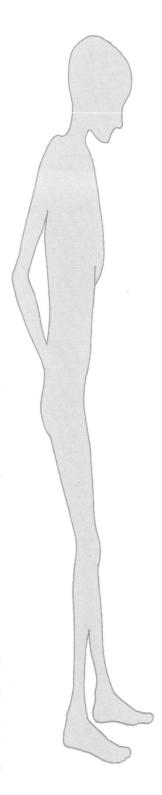

Introduction

Eating disorders such as anorexia nervosa and bulimia nervosa are a growing problem in today's society and the age of sufferers is getting younger. Many people believe that eating disorders are just 'out of control' diets but there is much more to them than that. They are not actually about food and weight at all. They are about self-esteem and confidence, as well as abuse, control and communication within families.

With this book, I am hoping to help young people who are struggling to understand and recover from an eating disorder. I am not a doctor or a counsellor but I have a great deal of personal experience in this area. I suffered from anorexia nervosa for over 14 years and have been in recovery since 1999. I am now at a healthy weight and no longer feel afraid of food. However, I do understand how desperately lonely, frightened and confused you can feel when you have these illnesses.

I have also tried to learn all that I could about these disorders and have talked with many people suffering from anorexia nervosa, bulimia nervosa and other eating disorders. I want to use the knowledge I now have to try and help people recover. I know what helped me to fight my anorexia and I have tried to include all this information in the book. It **is** possible to beat your eating disorder but first you have to understand the illness and why it developed. I hope that with this book I can help you to learn more about these frightening illnesses. As I have discovered, it is not always an easy battle to win but it is such a worthwhile one.

I would strongly advise anyone who is reading this book and thinks that they may have an eating disorder to talk to an adult they trust. Before you start the diet and exercise plans or any of the therapy exercises in this book, it is wise to contact your doctor and make sure that they feel it is safe for you to begin. Eating disorders are very dangerous illnesses and many young people die from them. It is vital that a doctor is involved in your recovery.

I have described anorexia and bulimia in the greatest detail in this book, although other eating disorders are mentioned. If you are suffering from compulsive eating, you may find it helpful to read the sections on bulimia, as these will also give you some practical tips and solutions for beating your own illness.

Throughout the book you will find personal diary extracts and therapy exercises. These describe my experiences of anorexia in more detail. I spent a number of years in therapy and have learned many helpful tips for recovery. I have shared these and explained how they can help you beat your eating disorder too. I will describe specific events in more detail later on in the book but before you start reading, let me briefly outline my own story.

7

My Story

From the age of three, I was mentally and sometimes physically abused by my Grandmother. She treated me badly in many different ways, repeatedly telling me that I was worthless, unloveable, ugly and fat even though I was none of these. She constantly played cruel tricks on me (such as force feeding me and abandoning me in shops) and gradually my self-esteem was destroyed. Many horrific memories remain, including the time when I was seven years old and my Grandmother forced me to walk through the Chamber of Horrors in Madame Tussauds. She told me that I was a revolting person and belonged in this place with all the other disfigured and damaged faces.

I saw my Grandmother every day in an attempt to protect my Mother. My Mother suffered from migraines and I realised that these headaches became worse whenever my Grandmother treated her badly. Quickly I learned that I could stop my Grandmother from being cruel to my Mother if I took all the abuse instead. I was too frightened to ever tell my parents about my Grandmother's ill treatment because she said that she would kill my parents if I spoke out about it, so I stayed quiet.

My Grandmother often told me that I was a failure and said that I would never do well at school. This caused me to work even harder at my studies and I would always complete my homework the night it was set. Even though my Gran didn't live with us, she was often in the kitchen with my Mother when I returned from school and I became afraid of going home. I began to join in all the after-school activities available, including swimming, hockey, computer studies and gymnastics. I was wearing myself out though and by the age of 13, my body was no longer able to cope with all the abuse and hard work and it began to shut down.

I developed 'glandular fever' and after many months of illness was admitted to the children's ward of our local hospital. My Grandmother visited me every day and continued to whisper cruel words to me. At the same time, she told the doctors and nurses that she believed my parents were abusing me. The doctors decided to stop my parents from visiting so frequently and instead encouraged my Gran to visit more often. I became very unhappy and stopped eating, so the doctors prescribed adult doses of anti-depressant drugs.

Almost immediately, these powerful drugs caused me to start hallucinating. The doctors thought I was telling them lies to avoid doing my homework and just increased the dosage of the pills. The hallucinations became more frequent and I couldn't look at a page or blank wall without horrific images appearing before my eyes. A few days later another problem developed and I found that I was losing the ability to read and write. When I looked at a page of writing, the words began to swim and move around so that sentences became meaningless.

It took my parents a number of days to convince the doctors that I was telling the truth about my condition and the pills were stopped but the damage had already been done. After I left hospital, I slowly taught myself to read again with the help of a piece of card that isolated just a few words at a time. Over the next two years I became used to reading and writing in this way and took all my 'O' level classes during this period. It wasn't until I began my 'A' level studies that I was able to read and write normally again.

By the time I was 17 we were having serious family problems. To help with her migraines, my Mother had been on tranquilizers since I was six years old. Now, 11 years later, she was taking a massive cocktail of them together with some very strong painkillers. She had disappeared into her own fantasy world and was writing strange poetry and letters to the singer John Denver. My Grandmother told me that my parents' marriage was in trouble and that they were going to get divorced. She said that this was all my fault.

It was then that I decided I had to disappear. I felt worthless and as if all I did was cause problems. I believed that I no longer deserved food and so stopped eating. I didn't feel this was enough punishment though and also began to seriously self-harm. Trapped in an impossible situation, I realised I was developing anorexia.

For the next four years my weight slowly dropped. I managed to keep my illness under control while my life was relatively calm but as soon as there was any extra stress, that dormant monster anorexia reared its head again. I left college at 19 because I was bullied by a 'friend' and instead started work in a solicitors' office. The first three months were fine but in time my boss began to treat me badly. My Gran's treatment had led me to believe that I deserved to be abused by anyone and he soon realised he could sexually harass and humiliate me. This behaviour continued for over two years.

By the age of 21 I was very ill. Two days after my twenty-first birthday, my parents told me that I was ruining their lives and making them both ill. The guilt I felt was tremendous but I simply couldn't eat, even for them. I felt totally controlled by an anorexic 'voice' in my head that sounded just like my Grandmother. It told me I was fat and ugly and had to starve myself. It yelled loudly every time I ate, repeatedly telling me I was a very bad person. I was now completely obsessed with food and did everything possible to avoid eating. Unable to force myself to eat, I grew extremely weak and had to give up my job as a legal secretary.

My parents took me to our family doctor who was horrified by my weight loss and immediately sent me to see a psychiatrist at our local hospital. She diagnosed anorexia nervosa and I felt as if my deepest darkest secret had been discovered. I felt ashamed and very alone. I had to agree to see a psychiatric nurse once a week but the shame I felt left me unable to share my true thoughts and feelings with her. Misled by my confusing answers to her questions, the nurse disagreed with the original diagnosis and started to treat me for the illness M.E. (chronic fatigue syndrome).

Relieved that the nurse no longer believed I was suffering from anorexia, I fell even deeper into the illness becoming more withdrawn every day. Just after Christmas I felt so desperate and alone that I attempted suicide. Halfway through the attempt, I realised that my Mother would return home to find my dead body and I just couldn't hurt her in that way. I felt that I had already caused her enough pain by what I believed to be my 'selfish' behaviour. I put away the knife and bandaged my bleeding wrist.

Later that year, my Father retired from his job and we all moved to Cornwall to try and escape from my Grandmother. I managed to avoid doctors for three months but eventually we had to join the local health centre. The doctor I saw was horrified by my condition. During my physical examination, the nurse had discovered that I was trying to cheat the scales and they realised that my weight was now at a life-threatening level.

After just three months in my new home, I was confronted by two doctors who wanted to admit me to hospital. I tried to beg them to allow me to stay at home but my Mother said that she could no longer cope and I was admitted to my first psychiatric hospital. I was put on complete bed rest because my weight was so low that the doctors were scared that I could have a heart attack at any time. I should have been safe in the hospital but my Grandmother still managed to reach me there. She sent me letters telling me that my parents did not love me and asking why I didn't just let myself die? Instead of showing the doctors this evidence of her abuse, just as my Gran had instructed, I carefully tore up the letters and hid them at the bottom of my waste bin.

After a month, I had gained six pounds and managed to convince the doctors to discharge me. I began weekly therapy that increased to daily therapy as my weight slowly began to fall again. I had left hospital determined that the anorexia would never win again but after a few weeks at home, it had regained control and the 'voice' was louder than ever. I was once again lying and cheating so that I could lose weight. I hated myself every time I pretended I'd eaten or hidden some food but I felt I had to obey that 'voice'. My parents tried to force me to eat more but this just led me to become even more cunning and secretive.

One horrific day, two years after my release from hospital, I managed to totally block the drainage system in our Cornish home. I can still remember the complete terror I felt when I heard my Father's words: *"She's really done it this time! I don't want to call her my daughter any longer!"* My Mother was equally angry and said that she didn't believe my Father would ever forgive me. I vowed never to hide food or cheat the scales again but anorexia is a very powerful illness and that whispering 'voice' in my head soon took back control.

Three years after the first hospital admission, my weight had dropped to its lowest ever. I was seeing a psychiatric nurse every day and he was measuring out tiny portions of food for me to eat but my body could no longer process solid food. Even though I was eating, I was losing more weight every day. I tried to fool the doctors into believing I was heavier than I really was but eventually my tricks were discovered and I found myself back in hospital again. This time I was admitted to an eating disorders unit 200 miles from my home, where I was told that I was now just hours away from death.

Looking in the bathroom mirror for the first time since my illness had begun, I saw how I really looked. I was a walking skeleton, with my skin stretched tight over bones. My face had become a skull and when I smiled, it looked like I was wearing a horror mask. For that brief period of time I could understand why everyone was so worried.

The hospital saved my life and I stayed there for six months, working hard at therapy sessions each day. I wasn't completely honest with the doctors though, as the anorexic 'voice' in my head was still very powerful. I had learned so much therapy over the years that I was just repeating it back to them without feeling anything. My occupational therapist did realise what I was doing though and decided to play me the REM song "Everybody Hurts". As I heard the lyrics about holding on and never giving up, I broke down for the first time and started to talk very vaguely about my Grandmother's abuse. When I was discharged from the hospital a few months later, I was physically better but mentally and emotionally I was still very ill.

For the next five years, I lived at home with my parents. The confidence I had developed in hospital slowly began to disappear. I had been able to talk and joke with anyone in the hospital but once I was home, I started to hide in my anorexic shell again. Gradually my weight dropped once more, although I managed to maintain it at a level just high enough to keep me out of hospital. I started my own needlework business but this just gave me another safe reason to stay hidden at home. I led a very isolated life, seeing only my therapists. The few times I went out were with my parents and we lived a very controlled, timetabled existence. I was an adult woman, living the life of a child.

At the age of 29 I felt that my life would never change. I believed that I would always have anorexia and although it stopped me from doing so much, I could see no other options. The loneliness eventually became too much to bear and I joined a pen pal club. Through this group I met Simon, who I soon learned also suffered from low self-esteem. For the first time in my life, I felt able to tell someone about the abuse and my anorexia. This was the real start of my

recovery because Simon was able to show me that I was not the terrible person my Grandmother had always told me I was. Slowly I began to realise that I did not need to punish myself by starvation and self-harming. I learned to trust Simon's view of my body rather than my own distorted anorexic view.

Simon was the first person to show me unconditional love and after a few months, we became engaged. With Simon's help, my recovery continued and I am now living a fulfilled happy and healthy life. Recovery is not easy or quick and the fact that Simon was willing to stand by me however long this took gave me the courage I needed to keep making progress.

I decided to share my experiences in the hope that I could help other sufferers beat their eating disorders. I wrote my autobiography and soon found that many people wrote to me to share their own experiences. I began to realise just how huge a problem eating disorders were for young people and how little practical information and advice there was available. This is why I have shared my knowledge and experience of eating disorders and how to recover from them in this book. I hope that this will be a useful guide to help sufferers and their friends and families to fight these killer diseases.

Part One

Learning About Eating Disorders

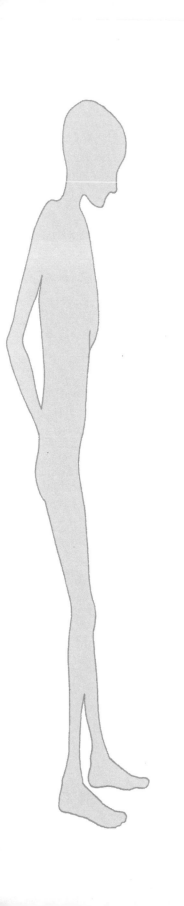

Chapter 1

What Is Anorexia Nervosa?

Summary

Anorexia nervosa is a growing problem amongst people in today's society. This chapter describes the feelings and symptoms associated with this illness.

Anorexia nervosa is the best known of all the eating disorders. Many people believe it is a fairly new illness that has only recently become a problem but this is not the case. Anorexia has been around for at least 300 years although it is only now that people are really starting to understand this illness. Most sufferers are female but there are also a growing number of men suffering from this disorder.

Anorexia is a very secretive illness and anorexics often feel ashamed of their behaviour and try to pretend that there is nothing wrong. However, it is obvious when someone is suffering from this disorder because it involves severe weight loss. This weight loss can be so extreme that sufferers may die of starvation. The faster the weight loss, the more dangerous the illness, because the body has no time to adjust and a sufferer can die when their heart simply stops beating.

Weight loss however is not the only symptom of anorexia. There are other signs that someone is suffering from this illness. People with anorexia seem to lose confidence and start to become quieter and more withdrawn than usual, often isolating themselves from their friends and family. They become totally preoccupied with thoughts of food because their body is starving and their mind can focus on nothing but eating. Sufferers find they want to cook complicated meals and then sit and watch the rest of their family eat, while they have nothing. They may also watch cookery programmes on television or read recipe books. Even though they are starving and desperately want to eat, they avoid food at all costs and can seem angry or frightened if offered a meal or snack.

The sufferer has a terrible fear of becoming fat and cannot see how thin they really are. They often start to wear many layers of baggy clothing, not only because they want to hide their body but also because they are very cold. As they are eating no food, they have no fuel to keep their body warm and their feet and hands can turn blue. A fine covering of dark hair called **lanugo** starts to grow on the sufferer's chest, stomach, arms and face. This is the body's way of trying to keep itself warm.

Foods that were once favourites are quickly dropped from the diet. Many sufferers suddenly turn vegetarian in an attempt to avoid certain fatty foods (like red meat) and excuses are constantly given for not eating. Over time, the sufferer grows more frail and their skin becomes pale, with deep black shadows appearing under their eyes.

Rules and rituals begin to develop around food. Meal times can last hours and sufferers may cut their food up into very tiny pieces. I can remember slowly eating peas just one at a time. Sometimes anorexics will not actually eat in front of other people at all and shut themselves away to eat just the small amount of food they allow themselves.

Anorexics often divide into two groups - 'safe' and 'unsafe'. The 'safe' foods are those which contain very few calories (a **calorie** is a unit of energy). An 'unsafe' food is one that is higher in calories and which may contain fat and sugar.

Anorexia often develops during **puberty**, when a young person's body starts to change. These changes can affect both boys and girls but again it is mostly girls who suffer problems. The amount of fat in a child's body increases during puberty and some young girls cannot cope with this change. They may also feel unable to accept that they are becoming an adult because that will mean new responsibilities, which can seem very scary. When anorexia develops and weight drops below a certain level for girls, their periods often stop or become irregular. This means that the sufferer has returned to a child-like state.

Anorexics often feel physically very ill since their bodies are trying to function without any food. Fainting and dizziness are common problems and anaemia is another side effect of anorexia. **Anaemia** occurs when there is not enough iron in the blood. This means that the sufferer often feels short of breath and very light headed. Restlessness at night (**insomnia**) and muscle spasms often occur. They can develop **constipation** (which is when someone has trouble passing faeces) because they are just not eating enough food to keep their bowels working properly. This leads many anorexics to turn to **laxatives** (a medicine that causes the bowels to empty more often) and they can become addicted to them very quickly.

There are many emotional as well as physical changes that occur when someone develops anorexia nervosa. They may find it hard to concentrate and as a person's weight drops, their brain shrinks in size too. Sufferers often feel moody and irritable and may become snappy with friends and family. Depression is also a common problem that is associated with anorexia and other eating disorders.

Over time, doctors and researchers have noticed that there seem to be some distinct characteristics that many anorexics share. They often appear to be high achievers and always try to get good grades at school. I know that this was certainly true for me. I always tried to get 'A' grades and felt disappointed with anything lower. Like many other anorexics, I felt a strong need to be perfect. I would rewrite whole essays if I had made just one spelling mistake.

Many anorexics are people pleasers. They feel afraid of conflict and try to agree with everyone, rather than argue or put forward their own point of view. They want people to approve of them all the time and feel uncomfortable if they upset anyone. It may be that this behaviour has developed because of their home situation. Perhaps they feel that their parents are very controlling and weight loss is the only way they can gain some control over their life.

Anorexia nervosa is an illness about control. The sufferer feels in control when they restrict the amount of food they eat but the reality is very different. The illness is actually in control of the sufferer because once a person starts down the anorexic road, it is very difficult to turn things around without a lot of help, encouragement, support and love. Anorexia is an addiction and to feel good, the sufferer needs to cut down on more and more food every day. A lot of anorexics also try to exercise as much as possible, often running everywhere rather than walking normally.

Anorexia nervosa is sometimes called the 'slimmer's disease'. I believe this is an unfair description because it is very rare for people to develop anorexia simply because of a desire to lose weight. At least 75% of the people who develop this illness have never been overweight and so there have to be other reasons why these disorders start.

In my case, at the age of 17, I simply felt that I did not deserve to eat food any longer. I had been mentally abused by my Grandmother from the age of three. I believed that I took up too much space in the world and felt I had to lose weight and disappear.

Anorexia is an illness of low self-esteem. Sufferers often feel that they are worthless, horrible people and that no one could ever like them. They believe that they deserve pain instead of happiness. They deny themselves pleasures that other people take for granted and feel guilty if they buy anything nice.

If you have found that bells have been ringing in your head as you read this chapter, try and answer the following questions honestly:

- Do you feel afraid of eating certain foods?
- Do you love cooking meals for other people but rarely eat them yourself?
- Do you skip meals and try to go whole days without eating?
- Do you feel alone, frightened, irritable or miserable and unable to talk to anyone in confidence?
- When you look in the mirror, do you see a fat person even though people tell you that you are thin?
- Do you often watch cookery programmes and read recipe books?
- Do you weigh yourself on the bathroom scales very often?

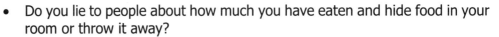

- Do you lie to people about how much you have eaten and hide food in your room or throw it away?
- Do you exercise in secret?
- Do you keep notes of how much you eat and panic if it is more than you had allowed yourself?
- Do you feel guilty whenever you eat?
- Do you suffer from physical problems? Headaches? Muscles pains? Tiredness? Dizziness? Restlessness? Insomnia? Constipation?
- Do you try to achieve high grades and feel a failure if you do not achieve perfect scores?
- Do you avoid going out with friends in case you have to eat a meal with them?
- Do you have trouble concentrating?
- Do you feel happy when you lose weight and miserable if you gain any?
- Do you know how many calories each food contains?
- Are you unhappy with certain parts of your body, such as your stomach, thighs or bottom?
- Do you feel the need to punish yourself if you gain weight or eat extra food?
- Do you ever harm yourself on purpose because you feel you are a bad person?
- Do you feel horrible if your stomach is full after a meal?
- Do you ever hear a "voice" in your head, which tells you that you are a bad person?

If you answer "Yes" to many of these questions then you may well have the eating disorder anorexia nervosa. Please continue reading this book to learn more about this illness and also talk with a doctor or an adult that you trust. Try to share the worries you are having about food and eating.

I would like to end this chapter with an entry from my personal diaries, which shows just how complicated anorexia can be:

Sunday January 5th 1997
I feel very confused and upset today. I had to buy a new pair of jeans because mine are falling apart. I decided to look through a catalogue because I just don't feel able to buy them from a shop. I had to measure myself and was so convinced that I would be a huge size. I took my measurements and went back to the catalogue to see which size I was. The chart didn't even have my measurements though because I was just too skinny but I CANNOT believe that. How can I be thin when I feel so FAT? I feel such an incredible pig every time I eat and hate myself whenever I put food into my mouth. It feels like such a wrong thing to do.

Chapter 2

What Is Bulimia Nervosa?

Summary

Bulimia nervosa is also an increasingly common disorder. This chapter describes the feelings and symptoms associated with this illness.

Even if you have heard of anorexia nervosa, you may not have heard of **bulimia nervosa**. Although more people suffer from bulimia than anorexia, it was only medically recognised as an illness in 1979. Bulimia is common although it is difficult to obtain accurate figures since it is such a hidden illness. It is estimated that a quarter of women aged between 18 and 40 suffer from this disorder, although the age of sufferers is getting younger all the time. Bulimia is an illness suffered mostly by women. Over 90% of all sufferers are female. Awareness of this illness is gradually spreading and it has become a popular topic for the media, as many famous actresses and pop stars have bravely admitted they suffer from the disorder.

Like anorexia, bulimia is a very secretive illness but unlike anorexia, it can be hidden from the outside world since sufferers are frequently a normal weight. Many anorexics fear that they will turn from anorexia to bulimia as they recover and start eating. Although some people suffer from both bulimia and anorexia, they are in fact two separate illnesses and research has shown that one does not necessarily lead to the other. Certainly in my case, I suffered from anorexia for fourteen years but never had any bulimic episodes.

Bulimia usually develops later than anorexia. Whereas anorexia is often present in young girls aged between 10 and 16, bulimia rarely takes hold until the late teens.

Unlike anorexics, who maintain a strict control over their food intake, bulimics find it harder to limit the amount of food they eat. Quite often, feelings of hunger cause them to binge on large quantities of the food they so desperately want. This is the food that they have denied themselves while on their 'restricted' diet. It is usually high in fat and sugar such as chocolate, cookies and crisps. A binge can last for a long time but on average, bulimics say they binge for around two hours. During that time a large amount of food can be eaten, for example as much as 30,000 calories during just one binge. This is the equivalent of about 15 days food.

Many bulimics say they feel totally out of control during a binge and simply force extra food into their mouths without even tasting what they are eating. It is not unheard of for bulimics to eat frozen or uncooked food, stale food from dustbins or even pet food.

Following a binge, bulimics usually suffer tremendous guilt as well as physical pain from the large amounts of food they have eaten. This guilt, together with a fear of gaining weight, leads the sufferer to find ways of getting rid of the food they have so recently eaten. Self-induced vomiting is common and is when sufferers force themselves to be sick. Some people may take medicines called **emetics** to make themselves vomit. This is a VERY dangerous thing to do and MUST be avoided. Another method used to dispose of the food is purging. This is when bulimics take laxatives and/or **diuretics** (which increase the number of times a person passes urine) to cause food and drink to pass through their body much faster.

Both vomiting and purging are extremely dangerous ways of 'dieting' and can lead to serious medical problems or even death. I will describe the terrible effects of both purging and vomiting in detail later in this book.

Like anorexics, bulimics also turn to over-exercising and starving as ways of keeping their food intake under control. However, as time passes their hunger grows so strong that once again they find themselves bingeing and vomiting. The majority of bulimics try to follow a strict diet plan but cravings for favourite foods can trigger them into a massive binge. Often bulimics fall into a period of chaotic eating when they are either bingeing and vomiting or starving. One behaviour leads to the other and a vicious cycle is started. The bulimic binges and vomits, which leads them to feel so guilty that they stop eating altogether, which is known as fasting. **Fasting** (another word for 'starving') causes a person to become so hungry they cannot resist the need for food, which leads to a binge and so the cycle continues.

Binges can be on the spur of the moment when a person is no longer able to resist food, or they can be planned. Bulimics sometimes plan a special binge, days in advance. They may travel to shops well outside their usual area so that no one sees them buying large amounts of food. They may go from shop to shop, buying a little of their favourite food in each one so that they do not attract attention. Some bulimics will just buy convenience foods, such as chips, crisps or chocolate. Others will use every pan in the house, cooking enough food for a large family.

Bingeing often takes place in the evening when a sufferer is alone. Bingeing and vomiting are a sufferer's way of dealing with their problems through food. They are no longer thinking about their problems but instead all their time, energy and thoughts are centred on what they can eat.

There are many factors that can lead a bulimic to binge. These can range from boredom and loneliness through to problems at school or work, weight changes, money worries, disappointments, friendship/relationship troubles or special times of the year - such as birthdays or Christmas.

Many bulimics are afraid of treatment because it involves eating a normal diet. They believe that if they eat without their usual 'methods' of control, they will put on large amounts of weight. Bulimics often feel ashamed of the way they behave but their fear of becoming fat means that they cannot stop the vomiting or laxative abuse.

Although bulimia nervosa is the most hidden of all the eating disorders, there are telltale signs that show a person is suffering from this illness. Their skin often has a pale green tinge due to the constant vomiting. Teeth can also suffer and frequent dental appointments may be needed. When a person vomits, their teeth come into contact with stomach acid, which is very harmful. Tooth enamel is gradually worn away until the teeth themselves start to decay. Many sufferers brush their teeth immediately after vomiting, to remove any telltale smell on their breath. However, this is unwise because it spreads the acid around all the teeth. Rinsing with antiseptic mouthwash or fresh water is considered a safer option although this is still unlikely to stop the decay caused by vomiting.

Small red spots appearing around the eyes due to broken blood vessels are another sign of bulimia. A puffiness of the cheeks (often known as "chipmunk cheeks") can occur because of the constant vomiting. The sufferer's throat is usually sore and mouth ulcers can form. Stomach and bowel problems may also be very common, due to both the vomiting and purging. In addition, the sufferer's hair often starts to fall out although doctors are unsure why. As with anorexia, there are also long-term effects such as bone damage caused by a change in the level of female hormones in the body. Bulimia can affect a woman's monthly period and it may become heavier and irregular.

Another clue that a person may be bulimic is their constant need to visit the bathroom after a meal. Some bulimics will even visit the bathroom during a meal because of their fear of the food they have eaten. Bulimics may frequently say they need a shower or may spend a long time in the bathroom at strange hours, to allow themselves to vomit without being heard.

Unfortunately, practical problems can also arise from bulimia. There are many stories of drains being blocked because of the volume of food a person may be vomiting. Some bulimics may binge and vomit up to ten times a day and over time, they will feel more and more physically ill. Vomiting places a great strain on the sufferer. Their heart races and they start to shiver, sweat and feel weak and tired.

Depression, moodiness and irritability are also symptoms of bulimia. Obviously there are exceptions to every rule but there are certain characteristics bulimics tend to have. They are often bubbly, warm and social people but can change when they are trying to cope with their feelings after a binge. They may become irrational, angry, withdrawn or depressed. This means they often have stormy relationships with friends and family, as their moods can prevent people getting close to them.

Bulimics often feel confused about their feelings and emotions. They no longer eat simply because they are hungry but to fill an emotional need instead. For them there are only extremes. They are either totally empty and starving hungry, or uncomfortably full following a binge. Recovery from bulimia is all about learning to eat a normal amount each day without feeling a need to vomit.

Bulimics may often believe that they have found the perfect solution to weight loss by learning how to vomit. They believe they can eat as much as they want and never put on any weight. However, vomiting or purging are not the 'perfect solutions' that they may at first appear to be. Our bodies adapt to find new ways around each problem. In this case, the salivary glands in a sufferer's throat start to absorb calories while the food is still being chewed. This explains why a person may be vomiting everything they eat but their weight still remains the same. Laxatives do not help with weight loss either. They work on the lower bowel and by the time food has reached this point in a person's body, all of the calories have already been absorbed.

Unlike anorexics, who seem to find total control and escape in their illness, bulimics may turn to other addictions for further relief. Alcohol and drugs are sometimes tried as an 'escape' when feelings of distress and panic take over. Many bulimics may also try slimming drugs to boost their weight loss or tranquillisers to calm themselves down. Both of these drugs are addictive and will cause extra problems.

Money worries can also be a sign that a person is suffering from bulimia nervosa. Food costs a lot of money and a student with bulimia may resort to shoplifting to obtain enough food to satisfy their binges.

If you are worried about whether you or someone you know has an eating disorder such as bulimia nervosa, try answering the following questions:

- Do you feel uncomfortable eating in front of others and always try to eat less?
- Do you secretly buy lots of your favourite 'forbidden' foods and binge when you are alone?
- Do you ever vomit to get rid of the food you have eaten?
- Do you take laxatives as another way to get rid of food from your body?
- Do you attempt to starve yourself following a binge?
- Do you often exercise for hours on end because you feel guilty about the food that you ate?

- Are you normally at a healthy weight but experience constant weight changes, depending on how much you are bingeing, vomiting or fasting?
- Do you often have a sore throat and puffiness around the jaw and cheeks?
- Do you frequently need to see a dentist?
- Do you find yourself planning binges?
- Do you often buy your food in many different shops so that no one notices?
- Do you experience strong cravings for food, which lead you to binge?
- Do you have times when you can think about nothing but food?
- If something goes wrong in your life, do you turn to food as an escape and a way to block out the pain?
- Do you hide food wrappers in the rubbish so that no one can see how much you have eaten?
- Do you suffer from mood swings?
- Do you feel very sad or lonely at times, although you pretend to be cheerful for everyone else?
- Have you ever used alcohol, cigarettes or drugs of any kind for extra relief from emotional pain?
- Do you use breath mints and mouthwash to try to stop anyone from knowing that you vomit?
- Do you suffer from constipation and/or other digestion problems such as stomach pain?
- Are you terrified of becoming fat?
- Do you feel very ashamed of your behaviour with food?
- Have you tried diet pills?
- Does food rule your life and control your moods?

If you answer "Yes" to many of these questions then you may be suffering from bulimia nervosa and should see a doctor. Many bulimics feel too ashamed to talk to anyone about their problems because they believe a doctor will find their behaviour disgusting. Bulimia is an illness like any other and doctors should understand and not blame their patients for being ill. Please DO talk with someone about your behaviour because as with anorexia, bulimia will not simply disappear overnight if you pretend it is not there.

I would like to close this chapter with a poem written by a young woman suffering from an eating disorder.

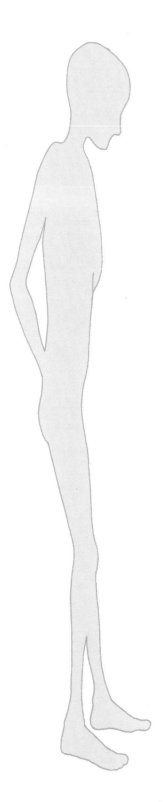

"Bulimia"
by Nicola

As I lean over
I punish myself
But not with a slap
Or a burn or a belt

But by purging myself
Releasing the pain
So I can feel something
Feel human again

My soul it cries out
But my eyes remain dry
As my throat clenches up
And my mind wonders why

As my fingers they reach
And scratch at the skin
Not just of my throat
But my heart deep within

24

Chapter 3

Are There Any Other Eating Disorders?

Summary
In this chapter, other eating disorders such as bulimarexia, binge eating, compulsive exercise disorder and ED-NOS are described and explained.

There are a lot of people who suffer from problems with food, who are not fully anorexic or bulimic. They do not have all the symptoms of these two illnesses but still find that food controls their life in many ways. Thoughts of food, weight and body size affect them daily and because of this, they have chaotic eating habits. People in this group are often said to have an "**ED-NOS**", which stands for "Eating Disorders Not Otherwise Specified".

It is possible that people with an ED-NOS are developing a more serious eating disorder, such as anorexia or bulimia. It is therefore important not to dismiss any problems with food as just something that a person will "grow out of" in time. Food worries are often a sign of larger problems that a person may be unable to talk about and they should not simply be ignored by parents, friends or relatives. If the problems around food are dealt with at an early stage, then full-blown anorexia or bulimia may be prevented.

The following are some examples of ED-NOS that have been identified:

- A woman or young girl who has all of the symptoms of anorexia nervosa but is still having monthly periods.
- A sufferer who has all the symptoms of anorexia including weight loss but their weight is still normal for their height.
- A sufferer who has all the symptoms of bulimia nervosa except that the bingeing and vomiting (or laxative abuse) takes place less than twice a week.
- A sufferer's weight is normal for their height but they vomit after eating even a small amount of food.
- A person who chews and spits out large amounts of food rather than swallowing them.
- Binge eating disorder (or 'compulsive eating').
- Bulimarexia.
- Compulsive exercising (or 'activity disorder').

Binge Eating Disorder (often also referred to as "Compulsive Eating")

Many people turn to food as a comfort when they are feeling miserable. This "comfort eating" can eventually become a **binge eating disorder**, as a person turns to food to escape the problems in their life. Binge eating is not about hunger but is a way of trying to escape from anxieties or worries.

Men are more likely to suffer from compulsive eating than any other eating disorder. Binge eating can also begin at any time in a person's life and can start in childhood but is often not recognised until adulthood.

Like bulimics, people suffering from binge eating disorders eat large quantities of food in a short space of time. They feel out of control and unable to stop the bingeing. Feelings of disgust and shame about their behaviour mean they always binge alone, often hiding empty food packets so that no one discovers their secret. However, unlike bulimics, people who binge-eat do not try to get rid of the food they have eaten. They do not vomit, take laxatives or other medicines such as emetics (to make themselves sick) or diuretics.

Some compulsive eaters don't binge but just nibble all day on high calorie, comfort food such as cookies and cakes. They may often not have meals with their family at all and so appear never to eat much. They might however be overweight due to the high calorie content of the food they eat and so may always be dieting.

There are many health risks linked to compulsive eating, as with other eating disorders. Often, the bingeing leads to obesity and all the problems linked with this, such as diabetes. (These problems are described in Chapter 5). In some rare cases, a person's stomach can actually burst due to the vast amount of food that has been eaten. As with other eating disorders, depression and moodiness are very common, especially after a binge. Between 10% and 40% of all obese people binge often enough to be described as having a binge eating disorder.

If you think you may have a binge eating disorder, try answering these questions:

- Do you eat large amounts of food very quickly?
- Do you eat until you feel uncomfortably full?
- Do you eat in secret because you are ashamed of your behaviour?
- Do you try new diets every week but always end up bingeing on high calorie food instead?
- Do you feel irritated and disgusted with yourself after a binge?
- Do you tend to avoid exercise?
- Do you feel bad about having eaten but DON'T resort to vomiting or purging?
- Do you hate your body?
- Do you eat because you are feeling miserable?

- Do you feel uncomfortable eating with other people?
- Are you overweight?

If you answer "Yes" to many of these questions, you may well have a binge eating disorder. It is very important that you talk with a doctor about these problems as soon as possible.

Bulimarexia

Another illness that is becoming more recognised is **bulimarexia**. As the name suggests, it combines both bulimia and anorexia. Someone who suffers from bulimarexia has the symptoms of anorexia and a low weight but they also vomit like bulimics. Feelings of hunger become more than the sufferer can bear and they finally allow themselves some food, even though this is often only a very small amount. To keep their weight really low, bulimarexics then vomit everything they eat, however little. Their diet will be very limited. I know bulimarexics who will eat just fruit, vegetables, diet yoghurt and bagels but even these foods are often too frightening and a sufferer will still vomit after eating them.

Bulimarexia is the most dangerous of all the eating disorders because it combines severe dieting and vomiting. Sufferers are starving their body and making themselves sick, which puts a great strain on their heart and all the other major organs in their body. Bingeing is also very dangerous for someone who has been limiting the amount of food they eat. Their stomach shrinks when they starve themselves and sudden bingeing can over-fill their now tiny stomach. However, it is not only the physical changes that are painful and distressing. Anorexics who binge feel as though they have finally lost the only control that they had in their lives. This feeling of lost control can lead to serious depression or thoughts of suicide.

Although the illnesses of anorexia and bulimarexia are very similar, there are some differences. Bulimarexics desperately want to have the same control over food that anorexics have but they cannot totally deny their needs and they feel failures because of this.

Compulsive Exercising or Activity Disorder

As the name suggests, this disorder involves **compulsive exercising** and is more common among men than women. Exercise is a necessary part of a healthy life but if the exercising becomes an obsession, then the benefits are lost and it can become an illness. We live in a society that seems obsessed with thin, toned bodies and many people feel that they have to look like this. Gyms are full of people working out during their lunch times and evenings. It can reach a point where people begin to change their lives to fit in even more time for exercising. This can lead them to give up friendships, relationships and their social life. When a person has a compulsive exercising disorder, they find that they are no longer able to keep still. Their whole life is focused on always staying active.

Exercise can become an addiction because it often makes people feel good. When we exercise, chemicals called **endorphins** are released into our brain and these give us a natural 'high' that makes us feel happy. People can enjoy this feeling so much that they return to exercising again and again.

There are certain sports that can encourage people to develop problems with food or exercise. Activities like ballet, gymnastics, ice skating, running, swimming, horse racing and diving are high-risk sports because body size and shape is important. People who take part in these sports often feel they have to keep their weight low. I have spoken with some very slim ballet dancers who have been told that they must lose weight or leave the company. Pressure is put on them to keep to a lower than normal weight. Once a person tries to do that, they may start looking for unnatural ways to control their eating and it is possible they can slip into an eating disorder.

It is common for women or girls who over-exercise to find that their periods stop. They are also at risk from stress fractures and osteoporosis because they are putting too much pressure on their bones. **Osteoporosis** is an illness which develops later in a person's life. A sufferer's bones thin, becoming hollow and fragile, and they can easily break.

Compulsive exercisers don't stop for injuries and will continue to play sports or go to the gym, even though they may have damaged ankles or knees. I know a gymnast who continued to train on a broken ankle. This shows a total obsession with exercise since she must have been in great pain.

People who suffer from a compulsive exercise disorder also often have the symptoms of the other eating disorders. They may be obsessed with their weight, body shape and the amount they eat. Some also take laxatives and will binge and vomit. They may eat special diet formulas or have a very limited diet - for example just fruit, vegetables, rice and grains.

Often the people who have this illness are high achievers. They are frequently independent and successful people who feel they have to be "perfect". Like eating disorder sufferers, compulsive exercisers use their illness to make themselves feel good. They only feel worthwhile if they have managed to complete the full amount of exercise they set for themselves each day.

They also use exercise as a way of controlling feelings and emotions. It helps to block out their problems and the outside world for a while. I have a friend who has a very stressful job. He recently started going to the gym as a way to relax at the end of a busy day. He discovered that working on the exercise machines took his mind away from work problems and within a week, he was going every night to the gym to get his daily 'fix'. He was no longer using the gym as a way to relax or become healthy but simply as a way to shut out his problems.

Over time, people who compulsively exercise lose their control and find that it is the exercising that actually controls them. Just as food dominates the life of an anorexic, exercise can become a total obsession and a person can suffer withdrawal if they do not do their regular daily amount.

People who over-exercise daily experience many physical symptoms. They will continue to exercise, even when they have used up all their energy. Muscles will ache and eventually their speed and performance during exercise will fall. They find it harder to concentrate and changes begin to happen in their body. The only way to reverse these changes is for the exerciser to rest completely but for some compulsive exercisers that feels impossible.

If you feel that you or someone you know has a compulsive exercising disorder, try answering these questions:

- Do you feel that you have to exercise every day?
- Do you plan long and complicated exercise routines, which involve even more exercises as time passes?
- Have you stopped seeing your friends, just so that you can spend more time exercising?
- Do you feel that you must not eat high calorie foods?
- If you eat a high calorie food, do you always make sure that you do extra exercise?
- Do you constantly set yourself higher exercise targets to reach and feel a failure if you do not achieve them?
- Do you only allow yourself to eat if you have exercised?
- Do you tell yourself that you are lazy and will get fat if you don't exercise every day?
- Do you feel physically ill at times but force yourself to continue exercising anyway?

If you have answered "Yes" to many of these questions, you may have a problem with over-exercising. It is not easy to suddenly give up exercising, since people do experience feelings of withdrawal. I would strongly advise that you talk to a doctor and ask for help and advice. It is very possible to give up both eating disorders and compulsive exercising, and I will give you some helpful suggestions about how to do this later on in the book. It is also important that a doctor knows about your problem. Physical damage can be done to our bodies by eating and exercise disorders, and it is vital that you have a check-up if you feel that you may be suffering from one of these illnesses.

Chapter 4

Do Boys And Men Get Eating Disorders?

Summary

Many people think that eating disorders only affect women and girls. This chapter shows how men and boys can also suffer from these illnesses.

Although it is mostly women who suffer from eating disorders, the numbers of men with anorexia, bulimia and ED-NOS are slowly increasing. Eating disorders seem to develop later for men than women and most men do not have problems with food until they are adults. This could be because during puberty, girls tend to develop their natural curves by putting on 'fat' whereas boys become more muscular. Girls can find the changes frightening but boys usually like the differences in their body and often don't have any problems with their weight until their teenage years or early 20's.

It is estimated that men make up only 5 - 10% of all eating disorder sufferers but this figure could be higher. Men are less likely to admit to their eating disorder since they see it as a female illness. Feelings of shame about their problems can stop them from getting the help they need. However, even when they do admit to their illness, the help they need isn't always there.

Although men do suffer from anorexia and bulimia, their illnesses are often based around compulsive exercising rather than just food. Unlike women, who will read recipe books and watch cookery programmes, men often spend much of their time exercising. The media often give the impression that men should be lean and muscular. Although extreme thinness is not considered attractive, men are made to feel that being overweight is also bad. Boys who are very thin can get teased, and may try to build up their muscles by lifting weights. It is possible that this focus on exercise can grow into a compulsive exercising disorder. At the opposite end of the scale, men who feel they are not thin enough may start to diet. These diets can also get out of control though and then anorexia or bulimia can develop.

There are a number of reasons why some men turn to eating disorders. It could be that they were overweight as children and were bullied and teased as a result. More commonly though, men will turn to drink, drugs or even physical violence to solve their problems. This may be why the number of men with eating disorders is so low.

Some sports do encourage thinness, and men who struggle to keep their weight low may turn to dangerous ways of dieting. Sports such as horse riding, athletics and gymnastics all need light bodies for success. Jockeys (who race horses for a living) have to keep their weight very low and many will starve themselves for days before races.

Modelling and acting are two other jobs where looks, size and body shape are important. Men in high profile jobs where appearance is important (such as sales and marketing) may also feel pressured to keep their weight low. Men in the military are another group at risk of developing eating disorders because they are required to keep their weight below a certain level. Research has shown that large numbers of men in the military services suffer from eating problems. In an attempt to reach the standard weight and fitness level needed, they often try diet pills, laxatives, fasting and vomiting. Over time, some men found they could only keep their weight at a low enough level if they continued with this behaviour and their eating disorder began.

Watching a parent suffer from weight related health problems is another reason why certain men develop eating disorders. Being overweight can cause heart and blood pressure problems, and a child who has watched a parent suffer a heart attack can start dieting out of fear that this will happen to them too.

More men suffer from bulimia than anorexia. Some studies estimate that between 10 - 15% of bulimia sufferers are male (whereas only 5% of anorexia sufferers are men). Even more common amongst men are binge-eating disorders, with over 40% of sufferers being male. People were surprised when a top American footballer bravely admitted to having bulimia. The cruel comments and pressure from coaches to keep his weight low had led him into the disorder. Another famous bulimic is Elton John, who works in the music business where there is a lot of pressure to stay 'young' and 'beautiful'.

It is very important that boys or men with eating disorders do not feel ashamed. Often in our culture, men are brought up to believe it is wrong to cry or talk about their problems and emotions. The first step to recovering from an eating disorder comes when a sufferer can share their worries. It is NOT wrong to admit to feeling scared or worried. Most men shut down on their emotions in an attempt to appear 'strong'. This is not actually being strong though. A person who can be honest about their problems shows real strength. Eating disorders are dangerous illnesses and it is important to talk with a doctor about your fears and worries.

It is also important that boys do not give up on their dreams because of the false images that our society puts forward. Appearance is definitely NOT the most important quality a person can have. Talent, ability and character are always far more important.

Chapter 5

What are the Dangers of Eating Disorders?

Summary
Often the sufferers of eating disorders are not aware of the damage they are doing to their body. This chapter examines the health risks and long-term dangers of these disorders.

Eating disorders are very serious illnesses. Many people find it too frightening to learn about the dangers but it is very important to face the truth. Recovery from an eating disorder can only take place when you understand the damage that you are doing to yourself and say: "I WANT to get better". Each of the eating disorders has many dangers, although often the problems overlap between the different illnesses.

Anorexia nervosa

Anorexia is not a comfortable illness to have. If you have anorexia, you are starving your body and will suffer all the symptoms of starvation. Many anorexics say that nothing bad can ever happen to them. Even if they feel ill, they don't take it seriously and believe that they cannot die from their illness. Unfortunately, this is just another aspect of the disorder. Approximately 20% of all anorexics die from their disorders, which is a very high figure for mental health illnesses. It is very important for you to know that you may not receive ANY warning that you could die.

Many changes take place in our body when we are anorexic. I have talked with anorexic sufferers of all ages and we have each had slightly different experiences. Some of the changes that take place are unseen and extremely dangerous. These are the changes that happen inside your body - to organs such as the heart, brain and kidneys. Illnesses like **pneumonia** (an infection of the lungs caused by bacteria) can also develop because when you have anorexia, your body can no longer fight infections and a simple cold can quickly become very serious.

The Heart, Brain and Kidneys

Anorexic behaviour (starving, vomiting and taking pills such as laxatives) affects the **electrolyte** levels in the body. Electrolytes are chemicals such as sodium, potassium, magnesium and chloride. These are often called salts. These chemicals help control our heart rate. If a person has taken laxatives, vomited or cut down on the amount they eat and drink, they can suffer from dehydration. **Dehydration** occurs when you have lost a lot of water from your body and it can no longer function properly. When someone is dehydrated, their level of potassium is lowered and this affects their heart. Their heart rate changes, becoming either slower or faster. These changes are extremely dangerous and can lead to heart attacks.

Dehydration also affects the kidneys. The kidneys clean and filter the blood. They produce nearly 200 litres of fluid each day. Most of this is returned to the body but some is lost as urine when we go to the toilet. If a person does not drink enough or takes laxatives or diuretics, they can suffer from kidney stones or kidney failure. Kidney stones are a painful condition where small crystals form in the kidney. Kidney failure is when the kidneys stop working altogether and a person needs to have **dialysis** (where a machine does the work of the kidneys). If the kidneys fail and dialysis does not begin, a person can die.

The brain is affected by the electrolyte levels in our body and sudden changes can lead to fits. The heart and brain can also change in size when a person is anorexic. The heart is a muscle and it begins to shrink if a person doesn't eat enough food. Anorexia affected my heart and I had to stay in bed for over a month. I was not allowed to walk around because any movement could have put too much strain on my heart and led to a heart attack. The brain also becomes smaller when people starve themselves and I needed to have a lot of tests to see if my brain had changed in size.

The human body is very adaptable and it changes to try to protect itself. We need to eat food to keep our hearts beating, to keep breathing and to keep blood pumping around our bodies. When you do not give your body enough food, the **metabolism** (the way the body uses food to keep itself functioning) slows right down. A person's heartbeat also slows and their pulse rate drops, so that their body only carries out the most vital functions.

The Stomach

When a person is anorexic, their stomach shrinks and becomes much smaller. This means that even when they eat just a small amount of food, they feel full and bloated. As they are eating so little, their bowels don't work properly and they suffer from constipation. When this happened to me, I started taking laxatives so that I would be able to go to the toilet again. However, this was a very dangerous thing for me to do because laxatives are addictive. Our bodies become dependent on them and after a while, you can no longer empty your bowels without their help. Over time, if you continue to take too many laxatives, the bowel can stop working altogether. This is called **atonic colon** and a person may have to visit a doctor two or three times a week for enemas**. Enemas** are when a liquid (soap or olive oil) is passed through a tube into the rectum, and they are needed when someone is suffering from severe constipation. Hopefully, after a few months the bowel starts to work on its own again but unfortunately this does not always happen.

Laxatives are dangerous medicines and should only ever be used under doctor's orders. They can ruin the bowel - it can become torn and surgery may be needed to repair the damage. Some anorexics will take huge numbers of laxatives every day and they risk losing their whole bowel. It can actually pass out of a person's body while they are on the toilet and emergency surgery will be needed.

Laxatives are also not an effective way of losing weight. All they do is cause the body to lose lots of water. Laxatives work on the lower bowel and once food has arrived there, all the calories have already been used by the body. All the sufferer is really doing is speeding up the removal of waste products from the body. If a person takes too many laxatives without drinking enough water, they can cause a dangerous blockage in their bowel. Anyone taking laxatives is likely to suffer from stomach pains.

Other changes that occur with anorexia

- For women, monthly periods stop. This is called **amenorrhea**. This happens because there are no longer enough female hormones in their body.
- Hands and feet will be very cold due to poor blood circulation. Both the hands and feet may turn blue with cold and it is possible that **chilblains** (itchy painful red swellings) will form.
- Soft, light hair called lanugo grows on the sufferer's body in an attempt to keep them warm - especially on their face, chest, arms, stomach and back.
- Muscles start to disappear and a sufferer feels weak and tired.
- Skin becomes very flaky and dry, and sufferers look pale and grey.
- Sufferers may lose hair from their heads.
- Blood pressure can become low.
- Some anorexics also suffer from **stomach ulcers** - breaks in the lining of the stomach that can cause great pain.
- Lack of food can lead to dizziness and fainting.
- Sufferers find it hard to sleep because lack of food makes them restless and they often have bad dreams.
- Sufferers may become very sensitive to light and sound. Both bright lights and loud noises physically hurt their eyes and ears.
- Bones start to thin and lose their density. This leads to a risk of osteoporosis in later years.

- A blood disorder called anaemia can develop when red and white blood cells are not made fast enough. As a result, less oxygen is carried to the lungs and breathing becomes more difficult.

It is frightening to see how many dangers and physical problems you could suffer from if you have anorexia. Anorexia is a painful and distressing illness. I suffered with many of the above symptoms and felt scared and alone. If you have noticed any of the symptoms that mentioned in this chapter, PLEASE see your doctor.

A Diagram of the Internal Organs of the Human Body.

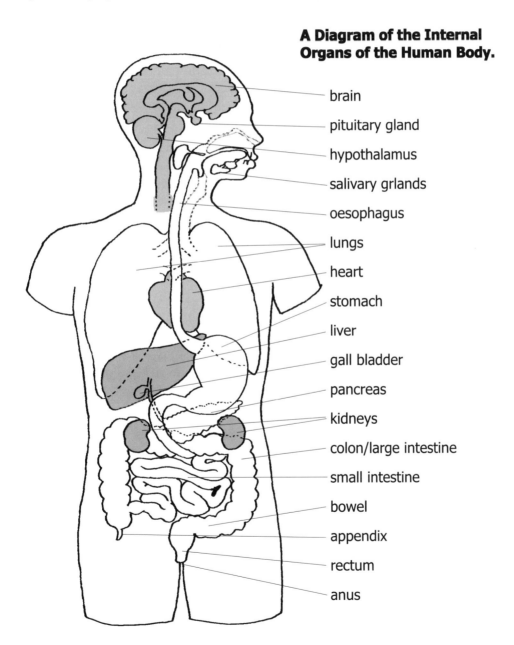

- brain
- pituitary gland
- hypothalamus
- salivary grlands
- oesophagus
- lungs
- heart
- stomach
- liver
- gall bladder
- pancreas
- kidneys
- colon/large intestine
- small intestine
- bowel
- appendix
- rectum
- anus

Bulimia nervosa

Many of the symptoms I have mentioned for anorexia are also side effects of bulimia. There are some different problems that arise from bulimia though, because the sufferer also binges and vomits. The heart problems described earlier in this chapter are often even more of a problem for bulimics. The vomiting causes dehydration which upsets the electrolyte balance of the body. The constant vomiting puts bulimics at risk of a heart attack at any time. Heart **palpitations** (a light fluttering feeling in the sufferer's chest) are common for many bulimics.

There are specific problems when certain electrolytes are missing from the body. When potassium is low, the bulimic is thirsty all the time and suffers muscle cramps and pain, especially in their hands and feet. They feel tired, find it hard to concentrate and heart problems are likely.

When magnesium is low, the nervous system is affected. They feel depressed, restless and confused. They may see or hear things that are not really there. A person may also start to tremble and have epileptic fits. **Epilepsy** is a brain disorder that leads a person to have fits, during which the sufferer falls to the ground and their muscles go into spasm causing them to twitch. It will also affect breathing and a person's lips may turn blue.

If you have any of the symptoms that I have just described, it is vital that you see a doctor as soon as possible. These chemical disturbances are VERY dangerous and the symptoms must not be ignored.

Some bulimics take emetics, which cause them to vomit. Some of these medicines can seriously damage the heart. Vomiting is not only dangerous but it DOES NOT lead to long term weight loss. Bulimics think that they lose all the food they have recently eaten when they vomit. However, only a small amount of the food eaten is actually lost from the body. The risks of vomiting are huge and the more a person vomits, the more their body wants food. This is a natural reaction because the stomach does not think it is being given enough food and craves more.

Teeth are ruined by vomiting. Stomach acid can destroy tooth enamel, causing holes and cracks to form. The front teeth of bulimics are especially at risk. Bright white teeth become dull and brown. If you also drink diet fizzy drinks, this can make the problem even worse since these may cause further damage. Vomiting can ruin your stomach and throat as well. Many bulimics vomit blood because of small rips and tears that occur when they make themselves sick. Some bulimics suffer massive internal bleeds that can lead to death.

Bulimics often have swollen cheeks and puffy faces due to the vomiting. This can be very painful and makes a sufferer feel fat and bloated, which leads to more bingeing and vomiting. The swelling is caused by the glands just below the jaw producing too much saliva. As a bulimic eats huge quantities of sweet foods during a binge, these glands produce the saliva that is needed to start digestion. The glands also are irritated by the acid during vomiting and they become very inflamed and painful.

Like anorexics, bulimics may also take laxatives and all the dangers described above apply for them too. Bingeing, vomiting and taking laxatives can be exhausting and puts a strain on the sufferer's body. They will feel weak, tired and unable to concentrate, and may have headaches and feel dizzy. The skin of a bulimic often looks green, blotchy and sometimes very flushed. Dry patches are common and serious acne is a problem suffered by many bulimics.

Anaemia is common for both bulimics and anorexics. Anaemia is often caused by a lack of iron, which is a mineral our bodies need to function properly. If you are suffering from anaemia, you may feel tired, weak and short of breath whenever you do any exercise. You are probably not eating enough iron-rich foods such as red meat (particularly liver), beans, cereal and bread and it is very important to see a doctor so that you can begin treatment with iron tablets.

Diet or slimming pills are frequently taken by bulimics and these are dangerous too. Doctors used to prescribe diet pills to people who were very overweight. These pills were often amphetamines. **Amphetamines** cause a person to feel wide-awake and restless at first. Before long though, they will begin to feel tired and depressed. They start to crave more of the pills and soon become addicted. They suffer side effects such as shaking, heart palpitations and sleeplessness. Doctors no longer prescribe these diet pills as they are very dangerous.

Today the most common slimming pills are **appetite-suppressants**. These are pills that stop a person from feeling hungry. Once again though, these pills can cause other problems and make the bulimia worse. People who use them may become anxious and irritable. They often suffer from depression, constipation, blurred vision and many other side effects.

Other symptoms suffered by bulimics

- Mouth ulcers are common, as are sore throats.
- Eyes become red and bloodshot. Eyelids are swollen and broken blood vessels can be seen around the eyes.
- Epileptic fits can happen.
- Bulimics can suffer from **irritable bowel syndrome**. This is where the sufferer often has both constipation and diarrhoea. Their stomach hurts and they feel very 'windy' and bloated.
- Muscle cramps, which are caused by an electrolyte imbalance.

- Some bulimics suffer from **oedema**. This is when the body holds onto fluid and it gathers at the ankles and wrists. Although it is not real weight gain since it is only water, many bulimics are afraid they are getting bigger and vomit even more.
- Bulimics may feel sudden changes in temperature - hot and sweaty during binges but cold and tired after vomiting.
- Chest pain is quite common. This is often caused by stomach problems. Our stomach extends behind the ribs and pain in the stomach can feel like chest pain.
- The sex hormones are affected by bulimia and mood swings can occur.
- Bulimics can suffer from low blood sugar, which is known as **hypoglycaemia**. Our bodies need the right amount of sugar to function properly and many organs are affected by low blood sugar, including the brain. As a result, bulimics may suffer from sweating, double vision, weakness, hunger, palpitations, dizziness and feelings of panic or confusion.
- Monthly periods for women become irregular. Women's bodies need to contain about 20% fat for periods to be regular and healthy.
- Constipation is common, as the amount of food a bulimic eats is so varied and irregular.
- Constant dieting, followed by bingeing and vomiting, upsets the metabolic rate. The **metabolic rate** is the speed at which the body burns up food. If you are often on a diet, your body starts to slow down to conserve as much energy as possible and so the metabolic rate becomes very slow.

Most bulimics feel very unhappy with their behaviour and this can sometimes lead them to find other ways of shutting out the pain they are feeling. Drinking and drugs can become part of a bulimic's life, as a way of hiding from reality.

Depression is very common amongst bulimics. Frequent mood swings can make it difficult for them to maintain good long-term relationships. They are trying to hide their illness, which means they often have to lie, cheat and deceive the people around them. They may choose to end relationships just so that they have more freedom and time to spend on their illness. Bulimics can be very lonely people.

Compulsive Eating

Many people who have compulsive eating disorders are overweight or obese. **Obesity** is when a person is at least 20% above the normal weight for their height. A person suffering from a compulsive eating disorder can become obese because they are taking in more calories than their body needs. By bingeing on food, they slowly put on weight.

Feelings of depression about their weight can then often lead to another binge, in an attempt to shut out the pain they are feeling.

There are a number of specific health problems associated with obesity. They are also likely to have feelings of hatred for themselves and their bodies. Many people who are severely overweight may start hiding at home because they feel too ashamed to even go food shopping or to let other people see them eat.

Some of the health problems of obesity

- **Diabetes** (when the body can no longer produce the hormone **insulin**, which regulates the body's blood sugar level) is five times more common in people who are obese.
- People who are obese are twice as likely to develop rectal or bowel cancer.
- Gall-bladder disease.
- Arthritis is common in the knees, hips and back. Although weight loss does not cure the problem, it does help ease the pain.
- Shortness of breath.
- Heart disease.
- High blood pressure.
- Strokes are twice as common for people who are obese.
- Obese women are more likely to be **infertile** (unable to have children) than women of a normal weight. When a woman is obese, her ovaries may not be producing eggs.
- Women may have heavier and irregular monthly periods.
- People who are obese are also more likely to suffer from depression and anxiety.

Chapter 6

Why Do Eating Disorders Start?

Summary

There are many misunderstandings about the causes of eating disorders and a lot of people still believe that they are just illnesses about dieting. This chapter describes many of the real reasons why these disorders develop.

Unfortunately, there isn't a simple answer to this question because there are many different reasons why eating disorders develop. It is not just dieting that has gone out of control. As you read this chapter, you will see that there are lots of triggers that can cause a person to turn to an eating disorder. However, eating disorders do not usually start because of just one trigger - if this was the case, almost everybody could suffer from one. It is how we react to these triggers that decides whether or not we develop an eating disorder. It has been shown that people with eating disorders feel unable to talk about their problems and feelings. This means that all the pain and hurt they feel stays locked up inside. This is not healthy and instead of expressing anger, frustration or hurt, they **internalise** (keep inside) these feelings and punish themselves. Food becomes a weapon that they can use against themselves and sometimes others.

The following are some of the roles that eating disorders play in people's lives:

A Way Of "Coping" With Problems

When you have an eating disorder, you think about food and weight all of the time. For most people the eating disorder is a way of blocking out their problems. Usually when people have problems in their life, they turn to activities that will make them feel better. Some people escape into drink or drugs, even though these cause illness and pain in the long-term. People with eating disorders often don't believe that they deserve to feel better. They don't feel that they should have nice things and this is because they have very low self-esteem.

Self-esteem is the way we feel about ourselves. If you have high self-esteem, then you feel good about yourself. However, if you have low self-esteem, you think badly about yourself - you believe that everything you do is wrong, that no one likes you and that you are ugly. Eating disorders and low self-esteem seem to go hand in hand.

When a person has used their eating disorder to hide from problems and feelings, getting better can seem frightening. As they recover, they realise they will once again experience the feelings that led them into the disorder. This is why help is often needed for people who want recovery. These difficult feelings need to be accepted and the sufferer has to learn healthy ways of dealing with them. Eating disorders are not a solution to problems - they just create new and very dangerous problems of their own.

An Illness About Control

Eating disorders are also illnesses about control. When a person feels out of control in their life and unable to solve a problem, an eating disorder can seem like the answer. This is often the case for people who are being abused. They cannot stop the abuse from happening because they have NO control over the person who is abusing them. They feel frightened and powerless. The only thing they can really control in their lives is how much food they eat.

Control becomes central to a sufferer's life and they are frightened of losing it. They feel that if they allow themselves to eat, they are losing control and have failed. This leads them to feel guilty and they become convinced that they are a bad person. It is this guilt and fear of failure that leads to their frightening control over food.

Through their eating disorder, a sufferer can also control their feelings. Some people feel unable to deal with certain emotions. Anger, frustration and jealousy are just three emotions that many people would say were 'not nice'. Anger is never directed at anyone else but is turned back onto themselves instead through starvation, binge/vomit sessions or self-harming. Many sufferers tell me that they never get angry and I used to say this as well. However, we ALL get angry - it as a healthy emotion that we need to feel. What is important is learning how to express that anger properly because otherwise it can damage us.

An Example Of Why An Eating Disorder Develops

To explain some of these ideas more clearly, let's take my story as an example. The TRIGGER for my anorexia was the abuse that I received from my Grandmother. The REASON the anorexia developed was because I was unable to talk about this abuse. I didn't share the fear, hurt and anger I was feeling about the way I was treated but internalised my pain instead. As a result, I turned to my eating disorder as a way of coping with the abuse. My self-esteem was so low that I didn't feel I even deserved food and I began to starve myself. Even though I couldn't speak about my pain, losing weight was my body's way of showing the world how scared and alone I felt. For me, anorexia nervosa was an escape route. Every time I couldn't deal with a problem, I stopped eating or self-harmed. Instead of facing my problems, I was burying them beneath the eating disorder. It wasn't until I finally talked about the abuse and all my feelings of fear, anger and loneliness that I slowly started to get better.

My diary shows how I hid my feelings and problems beneath the eating disorder:

Monday January 22nd 1996
I've been feeling so down today and I just want to disappear totally. I want to stop eating completely and this was always my way of escaping from my problems in the past. I can't do that anymore because I am supposed to follow a diet plan and I do know that if I break my plan then I will feel so guilty. I will feel that I have let everyone down yet again. So really today I am trying to cope with eating food and dealing with all of my problems. HELP! I just want something to block out my thoughts, the way my eating disorder always did in the past.

Possible Triggers For Eating Disorders

Frequently the triggers for an eating disorder will have occurred in childhood. What we experience and how we are treated as children can affect us throughout our teenage years and adult life. Children are like pieces of clay and as they grow up, parents, relatives, friends and teachers help to mould and shape them. If a child feels safe and is given the right amount of love, support, discipline and understanding, they have a good chance of growing up to be a happy, healthy adult with high self-esteem. A child needs to be shown **unconditional love**. This is a love which never changes, no matter how the child behaves. It is not conditional or dependent on 'perfect behaviour'. However, if a child is shown conditional love, is treated too harshly or given no discipline at all, problems can occur as they grow up.

Abuse

I have already mentioned abuse a number of times as a cause of eating disorders. Abuse can be a huge stress in a person's life and will often lead to further problems, such as eating disorders or other mental health illnesses. Some studies say that at least 90% of all cases of anorexia involve some form of abuse. Abuse can take many different forms. Neglect, bullying, racism, mental torment and physical or sexual acts of violence can all be classed as abuse. Mental torment is spoken abuse and it takes the form of criticism, name-calling, shouting insults and cruel comments that make the victim feel as if they are a bad person.

A child who is abused may grow up feeling that they deserved the treatment they were given. They may feel that they are not worthy of love because they are ugly and often try to lose weight in the hope that people might love them. This was certainly true in my case. When I was a child, my Grandmother constantly told me that no one loved me, not even my parents.

At the age of 17, I remember thinking that if I could just lose weight maybe people would finally start to love me.

Identity

As children develop and grow into teenagers and adults, they need to develop their own identity. Our identity is 'who we are' in the world - who we are in our family, amongst our friends, at school and later at work. Often, a problem arises if a person lives in a family where they are expected to 'fit in' all of the time. Children need to build up their own ideas about life as they grow. If children are not allowed to express their opinions but are simply expected to take on their parents ideas, they do not find their own identity. Let me give an example of how parents can affect the way a child develops.

When a child is upset, they will start to cry. Often parents give standard responses such as *"Don't cry. It's alright. Never mind."* This makes the child feel that it is wrong to cry or show emotion and that they always have to be happy. When a child is told this often enough, they can learn to hide their feelings. Instead of telling the child to stop crying, parents need to be sympathetic and say that it is okay to cry. They then need to talk with the child and find out what the problem really is, rather than just dismissing the problem.

When I was a child, my parents found it difficult to deal with seeing me in pain and I learned to cover up any sad feelings that I had. Sometimes I did cry in front of them but I always pretended to cheer up very quickly when they said those words *"Don't cry"*. I felt that by crying, I was letting my parents down and I soon began to shut down on my emotions. The following diary entry shows how I would always try to put on a brave face for my parents:

Wednesday February 14th 1996
I've been feeling so low today but I haven't told anyone about my feelings because that would be a wrong thing to do. I feel so guilty if I look upset and always try to be a really 'happy cheerful person' instead. I am certain that they will hate me if I show them I am feeling sad. I am trying not to focus on my feelings though. I mustn't be that selfish but I just can't help feeling so sad.

Most teenagers go through a stage when they rebel against their parents, choosing clothes, music and friends their parents do not like. People with eating disorders often never go through this phase. I certainly didn't because I was always trying to please my parents. Although it may be uncomfortable for parents, rebelling is healthy because it is the time when a child begins forming an identity. If a child is not allowed to build their own identity, they may use an eating disorder as their identity instead. Being thin becomes the way they define themselves. Starving their body is something no one else told them to do and this is their way of 'rebelling'. They are trying to show that they are an individual. However, once an eating disorder becomes a person's identity they then feel afraid to give it up and become 'no one' again.

Fear Of Becoming An Adult

Some young girls turn to anorexia because they feel too afraid of growing up. Adulthood brings many new and quite frightening changes. Parents that often talk about the 'dangers of the outside world' can make their children feel scared to leave home. Starting university/college or a new job can be too much for some teenagers and eating disorders seem to offer security.

Girls who have been sexually abused as children may feel unhappy growing into women. They may believe that if they keep a child's body, men will not be attracted to them. They feel safer if they do not have feminine curves.

Others feel too afraid of the responsibility of being an adult. Girls can feel confused about their adult role. Should they be a wife and mother - a caring person who looks after her children, husband and the home? OR should they have a career and become a financially independent woman? Anorexia seems to offer a solution, since the sufferer is often too ill to choose either option. Instead, they need to be looked after and many still live with their parents even though they may be in their late twenties or thirties. Anorexics at a low weight become child-like again and usually lose their independence. People begin to make decisions for them and soon food becomes the only part of their lives they have any control over.

This was true for me, since I lived with my parents until I was 30 years old. At the time I thought I was an adult, running my own business making cross-stitch pictures for people. However, I was using my work as an excuse to stay at home and avoid meeting anybody because I found that too frightening. The only people I saw each week were doctors and counsellors. I went everywhere with my parents and believed that because I was buying my own food and cooking my own meals, I was somehow in control of my life. Food was the only way I could show my independence.

When I started to recover and began meeting other people, I realised just how small my world had become. At the time, I felt safe in my eating disorder and pretended not to notice how much I was missing. This diary entry shows how desperately I wanted to continue hiding at home and how terrified I felt at the thought of joining a group of other eating disorder sufferers:

Wednesday January 31st 1996
I have been worrying for days now about whether I should join the workshop. My therapist Clive is keen that I should mix with the other people there but I feel so afraid. What if they all hate me? I am so sure that I have nothing to offer people. I think Clive only wants me to join because he is being kind to me. Why would anyone want me to be part of their group? I am scared. I want to hide away. I really don't think I can do this but at the same time I am afraid of letting Clive down too, as it is his project. Help! I am so frightened.

A Need For Attention

Another reason why an eating disorder can develop is the need for attention. This applies mostly to anorexics because bulimia is a more hidden illness. People with anorexia may have never received enough love or attention in their lives. This can result in them feeling a strong need to gain attention in another way. I was in hospital with a young girl who desperately wanted her Father's attention. He had never given her the love and care she needed. She was sent to boarding school at an early age and always felt "in the way" when she was around her Father. At 13, she developed an eating disorder. She told me that she wanted him to see how thin she was and unlike most anorexics, who hide in baggy clothes, she would wear tiny shorts and tight T-shirts. She needed her Father to care. She wanted him to say that he loved her and that she did not need to hurt herself with the eating disorder. Instead, he paid for treatment in a private hospital and left her there while he and the rest of his family travelled to Hong Kong. This showed her just how little he really did care and sadly she decided not to try to get better.

Some children will deny themselves food in an attempt to hurt their parents. It could be that the child has never been able to talk about the pain they feel and saying "no" to food is one way of rejecting their parents.

Other Possible Triggers

- The death of a close relative, especially a parent, brother, sister or grandparent can trigger an eating disorder. Some children are especially close to their grandparents and this may be the first time they see someone special to them die. I remember the first funeral that I went to as a child and it was a very painful experience.

- Parents divorcing or separating. Often children can wrongly believe it is their fault that their parents are splitting up.

- A major trauma such as a car crash, a fire or an accident.

- Family behaviour. How parents treat their children affects them throughout their lives. The relationship between parents and children is very important. (This is a big subject and has its own chapter later in the book).
- A serious illness in the family.
- Important examinations or other tests at school, college/university or work.
- The death of a close friend or the ending of a close friendship.
- Loneliness. Some young people feel very alone at school or college for many different reasons. A transfer from another school in the middle of a year can be difficult for example. Loneliness at school can lead to an eating disorder developing, simply because the illness has become the sufferer's only 'friend'.

Some people cannot identify one specific incident as the cause of their eating disorder developing. This may be because they simply can't believe that just one incident could have affected them so badly. I have talked to many anorexics who tell me that they do not know the reasons why their eating disorder started. When we begin to talk at greater length though, they often tell me of a childhood filled with abuse and yet they never thought this could have triggered their present illness.

Are Eating Disorders Genetic?

Genetics is the study of which characteristics we inherit from our parents. Have you ever heard someone say *"Oh look - he's got his Father's eyes"*? They don't mean that you actually have some of your parents' features but that your eyes look just like your Father's. We receive genes from both our parents, so some of our features and characteristics will be like our Mother and some like our Father.

Doctors are now trying to find out if you can inherit eating disorders in the way that you can inherit eye colour. Some illnesses are passed down in families but they are still not sure whether this is true for eating disorders. Some families do have more than one member with an eating disorder. However, this might be due to family behaviour rather than genetics.

When a child grows up with a parent who does not eat normal meals, it can affect them. I grew up in a family where both my Mother and my Grandmother did not eat normally. They had what is known as **dysfunctional** eating habits. In other words, they never ate a healthy diet of three meals a day with snacks in between. I never saw my Grandmother eat a full meal - she lived on cakes, cookies and occasional sandwiches. My Mother suffered from **migraines** (serious headaches) and had cut many foods out of her diet so that she didn't eat anything that could trigger one. She avoided chocolate, cheese, fruits, butter and many other foods. As a child, I saw my Mother live on a strange diet of nothing but currant buns and salad.

Both my Mother's and my Grandmother's eating habits strongly affected me. As I was growing up, I never learned how much food a healthy person was supposed to eat. We only ever had one meal together at home as a family, which was in the evening and for the rest of the day we only ate snacks. When I became anorexic, it was very easy for me cut down on food without anyone noticing that anything had changed.

Is There A 'Type' Of Person Who Develops An Eating Disorder?

There do seem to be some characteristics that people with eating disorders share. However, anorexics and bulimics are often described differently and so the following nine points will not necessarily apply to all people with eating disorders. Many of the characteristics below apply more to anorexics, although any eating disorder sufferers may recognise themselves.

Bulimics are often described as being impulsive, untidy, chaotic and weak people, whilst anorexics are said to be needy, clever, childish and shy. It is very dangerous to make sweeping statements about an entire group of people. There will always be some who do not fit into any of the descriptions. I myself had many, but not all of the characteristics of anorexia. I also know bulimics who are quiet, shy, high achievers and who don't fit in with any of the textbook descriptions. What follows is a general description of some attitudes that eating disorder sufferers often seem to have in common:

1. **Perfectionism**. This is when someone feels that they HAVE to do everything perfectly. It can apply to their work, playing games or even how tidy they keep their room. People with eating disorders are often high achievers but are still very critical of themselves. They feel inadequate and as if they do nothing right. They believe that if they can do things perfectly, they will be loved and accepted. Unfortunately, no one can be totally 'perfect' which means that eating disorder sufferers can never reach their goals. This can lead them to feel more of a failure, so they try even harder to be perfect and the cycle continues.

2. **People Pleasing**. Many people with eating disorders feel a strong need to please everyone else. I tried to become a mind reader and work out what other people wanted all the time. If someone asked me what I'd like to watch on television, I would try to think what it was that they wanted to see. I would then suggest the programme they would like best. I was always putting my needs last. I didn't consider what I needed but just wanted to please others. I also found it hard to deal with arguments. This is often true for eating disorder sufferers. They feel unable to deal with conflict and prefer to try and calm everybody down. They try to make everyone else feel happy all of the time - a situation that is impossible to always maintain. It is important for sufferers to consider their own needs and feelings as well.

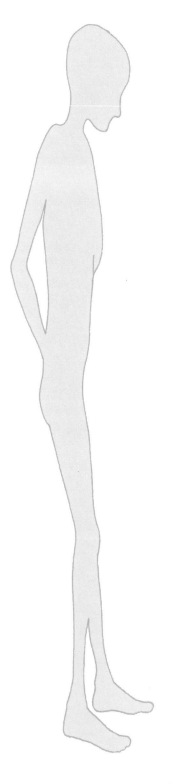

3. **Shyness**. Many people who suffer from eating disorders have little self-confidence. They are often quiet and withdrawn, and are scared of making new friendships. A lot of the girls that I speak with have difficulty talking to boys and feel ashamed that they don't have boyfriends the way that their friends do.

4. **Stubbornness**. It takes a lot of strength and control to have an eating disorder such as anorexia nervosa. People who suffer from this illness can be extremely focused. They set themselves a goal and they will be determined to reach that target. However, this stubbornness can be used positively because if you have the willpower to starve yourself, then you also have the strength to recover from your eating disorder.

5. **Responsible**. Often, people who develop eating disorders have taken on adult responsibilities as children. This happened in my case, since I tried to protect my Mother from my Grandmother by taking all the abuse myself instead. Children who are very responsible often do not have 'fun' or enjoy themselves. They take life very seriously and feel responsible for the whole world. Issues like the environment, poverty in the third world and wars frighten and worry them, while many teenagers are thinking about fashion, shopping, music and dating.

6. **Black And White Thinking**. People with eating disorders often suffer from 'black and white' thinking. By this I mean that if one thing goes wrong, they feel as if the world has ended. They will make huge statements like *"I can NEVER do anything right"* or *"I am ALWAYS wrong"*. No one can ALWAYS be wrong but this is typical of black and white thinking.

7. **Controlled**. People with eating disorders often feel unable to act on impulse. Sudden unexpected changes to their routine can be frightening and they feel a need to plan ahead most of the time. When they start their eating disorder they quickly make up strict rules about food, which keep them even more under control.

8. **Self-hatred**. Eating disorder sufferers all seem to hate themselves and their bodies. They are constantly trying to change so that they can feel happy. They often believe they are bad people and are certain that others hate them. They also usually feel that they are a nuisance and because of this, try not to share their problems. They may feel that they are selfish people although this is usually completely untrue. Many eating disorder sufferers are totally selfless and think only of others.

9. **Self-blame**. Most sufferers blame themselves for their eating disorders. I have spoken with many young girls who tell me that no one should ever feel sorry for them or try to help because they have brought it all on themselves. I remember thinking that my anorexia was simply all my own fault. Some people do not understand eating disorders and often tell sufferers that if

they just ate, they would be okay. It is important to remember that this kind of ignorance about the real causes can affect sufferers very badly.

Food is NOT the problem - it is just a symptom of a much bigger problem. This means that for people with eating disorders, there are other problems in their life that they cannot handle and they are turning to their eating disorders as the 'solution'.

Even though there is a lot of information in this chapter, you may still not have learned why your eating disorder started. Sometimes we need other people to help us look at our past and work out why our eating disorders began. It is not always easy to work it out yourself because you can sometimes be too close to the problem. This is why counselling is usually so important for sufferers.

Eating disorders are different for everyone. Even if the conditions are the same for two people, one may become anorexic and the other bulimic. There are many different reasons for this but it can often be as simple as strength of will. Many bulimics say that they would like to be anorexic but they start to binge and vomit because they cannot resist food the way anorexics can.

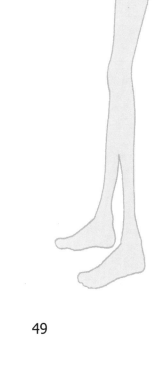

Chapter 7

Do Thin Women in the Media Influence Me?

Summary

Thin models and actresses are often blamed for the rise in eating disorders. This chapter examines this widely held belief and looks at the reality of the situation.

Many people believe that eating disorders start because young women want to look like models. As we saw in the previous chapter, there are many reasons why an eating disorder develops - it is not simply a person's desire to be as thin as a model. However, the way that our society portrays the perfect woman does affect young people when they are growing up. You only have to turn on the television to see the images that our society puts forward as 'the way to be'. Flick through a magazine and you will see pictures of extremely thin models. Diet advice, food and exercise plans are everywhere. If you sit down in a restaurant, you will often hear people discussing their diet and weight. We are all trained to think constantly about our weight. We are told that thin is good and fat is bad. A thin body is seen as a sign of success, beauty and popularity.

This media pressure to be thin affects some people more than others. In the previous chapter, we looked at how self-esteem affects the way people treat us, especially when we are growing up. If a young person has low self-esteem, they feel a failure and often want to do anything they can to 'fit in'. Many people with low self-esteem believe that if they become thin, they will be loved. I know I thought that if I was thin, people might love me. Many teenagers think they are more likely to get a good job and find a partner if they are thin. By trying to control their bodies, they are once again becoming 'people pleasers'. I often wonder if our society said that being large was the ideal, whether people with low self-esteem would desperately try to be larger. When you measure your self-worth by how your body looks, it is very hard to reach a point where you are happy. Guilt becomes a part of everyday life since you constantly try to control the amount of food you eat.

In this chapter, I want to look more closely at how society and culture can encourage young people towards an eating disorder. In recent years, more and more people are showing signs of eating disorders. Both girls and boys are developing these illnesses at an earlier age. A friend of mine has a little girl who, at the age of just five, is already saying that she has a fat tummy and must diet.

Throughout history, we have seen women change their behaviour and go through terrible pain just to try to 'fit in' and be accepted. In China, small feet were once believed to be attractive and feminine. This meant that at birth, the feet of female babies were tightly bound. This caused their feet to become deformed and as they grew up, young girls were unable to walk properly and felt great pain. They went through this pain though because they wanted to be considered beautiful. Another example of this behaviour was when women in the 1920s bound their breasts to give themselves a fashionably boyish figure. There were also the tight corsets of the 1800s that pulled in women's waists. These were often so tight that a woman's internal organs were damaged. In recent years, plastic surgery has become very common. Breast implants, lip enlargements and face-lifts are all painful and potentially dangerous operations. Even ordinary fashions can often be uncomfortable - many young women have damaged their feet and lower backs from wearing stiletto heeled shoes. All these examples show how women feel a strong pressure to 'fit in' and they are often willing to go through great pain to achieve this.

The last fifty years have seen a lot of changes in the way women look and dress. In the 1950s, women were on average a whole dress size larger than they are today. In the 1960s, a model called Twiggy helped to make a new look popular and her long, leggy, boyish figure become fashionable. Twiggy was naturally very skinny but the women who tried to copy her were not and magazines soon began to fill with diet plans. If 'normal' women were to look like Twiggy, they had to starve themselves down many dress sizes to an unhealthy weight. This fashion was not just a phase though, and diets and weight loss continued to be a key topic in women's magazines throughout the '60s, '70s and '80s. In the '90s, there was a slight change in emphasis as fitness became a major feature too, with pop singer Madonna becoming headline news. As the 90s continued, female film stars also began to be affected. The women in films and TV shows were starting to lose weight to seriously dangerous levels. Glamour magazines contained 'Hollywood diets', which stated that you too could be like your favourite star if you just followed the plans. These included all sorts of unhealthy ideas, such as a grapefruit only diet.

Many studies have been carried out on women over the years. In the 1950s, approximately 40% of women believed they were overweight. By the 1970s, this figure had risen to about 55% and by the 1980s, it had risen even higher to around 70%. Finally by the 1990s, nearly 80% of women believed they were overweight. In studies, whenever groups of women are asked to choose what size they would like to be, almost everyone says they would like to be smaller. When asked to describe their own size, they usually point at pictures of women who are bigger than they are. This shows that even among women without eating disorders, there are still many body image problems. It is obviously difficult for women to see their body size clearly. Most women say that they realise men prefer them to be larger. However, fitting into our society may feel more important than being attractive to men because increasing numbers of women continue to diet.

Women are often worried about other people's opinions of them. If you go into a fitting room of a clothes shop, you will probably hear the words *"Do you think I look large in this?"* Women frequently have no confidence in their own thoughts about their image and ask for other people's comments and advice. Very few women feel happy about their own bodies and often hate the way they look in clothes. A whole series of comedy sketches and books developed from the one catchphrase "Does my bum look big in this?" because so many women could relate to this remark.

A growing number of women want to look like models but for most, this means they would have to starve themselves down to a very unhealthy size. Many models say they practically exist on just coffee and cigarettes, in an attempt to hold their weight low enough for their jobs. Not only are models unhealthily thin but magazine photos are also often altered to make them look even thinner. The women that are presented to us in photos are of a size that only a very few people will ever be able to match. The fashion industry is therefore presenting an image that leave many women feeling like failures. A recent study showed that nearly 50% of women are a size 16 or above, yet most models are size 8 or below. When they looked at shop mannequins (the plastic models that are dressed up in clothes) the survey team noticed that if a woman was the same weight and size as these dummies, she would not even be heavy enough to have periods. She would actually be at a weight that is classed as anorexic.

Children under the age of 10 are now beginning to have problems with body image and many are on diets, even though they are not in any way overweight. Some children are refusing to wear swimming costumes on the beach because they feel too large. Children were not born with this level of self-consciousness, so some of this could have been picked up from the media. Even the toys that girls play with give the wrong impression. Dolls are often out of proportion - Barbie for example has a tiny waist, very long legs that never rub together at any point, large breasts and a long neck. This is an almost impossible combination, yet children grow up believing that this is normal.

Many children grow up with the idea that being thin is much healthier. However, this is not accurate and in fact people who constantly diet are as much at risk from serious health problems as those who are obese. It is very important that children grow up eating a healthy well balanced diet. If foods are limited at an early age then a child's body cannot develop properly and their growth may be stunted. Children as young as six already know about the fat content of food and many already understand about calories. Their obsession grows as they get older.

The diet industry has grown dramatically in the last few decades. We are now constantly shown television adverts which promote diet products. Very low calorie diets that offer liquid replacements for meals can be seen daily on TV. In one advert, a thin model shows an earlier picture of herself when she was 'fat' and then promotes the diet product, saying that in just a few short weeks it had changed her life. This sends out the message to very unhappy young people, who are struggling with distressing problems, that weight loss is the solution to everything. "Lose weight and be happy." "Lose weight and your problems will simply vanish."

Another growth area is the fitness industry. A whole series of videos and books have recently been produced to promote fitness. Many of the famous names in Hollywood have their own fitness video. Once again, many people try to copy their favourite stars and this behaviour is thought to be linked to the increasing number of people suffering from eating disorders.

It is very important to remember that everyone is different. We all have a different genetic make-up, which means we all have different bone sizes, body structures and weights. Some people have large frames and however much they try to diet or exercise, they cannot change themselves into a smaller frame. This is why our culture is particularly cruel. It does not allow us to be individuals. It wants us all to look and act the same. Think about that for a moment. Wouldn't it be a boring world if we were all the same size and shape and behaved in exactly the same way?

Of the two main eating disorders, it is believed that bulimia is more closely linked to media images than anorexia. This may be because magazines and television also promote a second image that can be confusing for women. In total contrast to the idea that thin is beautiful and dieting is good, glossy magazines also print tempting pictures of food and high calorie recipes. Food programmes on television show us how to make these delicious rich foods. When a person sees images of tempting food every day, they often want to try them. These foods seem even more appealing if you are on a diet and only allow yourself low calorie foods, which may seem tasteless or boring in comparison. This can lead to the start of binges, where a person eats large quantities of all the high calorie foods they usually avoid.

I have talked here about how the media can affect people. However, as I discussed in the previous chapter, eating disorders are rarely the result of just one cause. The media alone is unlikely to drive people into anorexia or bulimia - if this was the case, everyone could develop an eating disorder. There have to be various elements such as personality, low-self esteem, family influences and other triggers that can cause a person to develop an eating disorder. If a person is already emotionally vulnerable, the media is far more likely to affect them.

Chapter 8

Am I Happy my Body is Changing?
Puberty and Eating Disorders

Summary
Puberty can be a very confusing and frightening time for young people, which can lead to eating disorders starting. This chapter looks at the natural changes that happen to our bodies during this time.

During the teenage years many changes take place in a young person's body. These can be dramatic and some children find them difficult to cope with. It is often the changes in weight and body shape that can cause some teenagers to develop an eating disorder. Not only are the physical changes often quite traumatic but the emotional changes can be overwhelming too. During their teenage years, young people mature sexually and this can be frightening. With sexual maturity teenagers find they have to take more responsibility for their lives. They can no longer rely on others to make all their decisions for them and they have to choose which direction they want their life to take - Which career do they want to follow? Do they want to leave home yet? Relationships also become more intense and this can be worrying for some teenagers. Turning to an eating disorder is a way of escaping these responsibilities. Anorexia in particular takes a person back into a child-like state, where they are once again looked after by others. Decisions are made for them and they have little control over how their life develops.

There are three key changes that take place during puberty which can affect a young person and possibly lead to an eating disorder:

1. Changes in body size and shape.
2. Emotional and sexual changes - Young people become interested in having a partner and may want to start dating.
3. Teenagers have to make decisions about the future and many go through an intense period of schoolwork. Important exams are taken, which can also be stressful.

When you add in some of the other issues that can affect young people, such as abuse or traumatic events at home, the conditions are often right for an eating disorder to begin. Let's look at the changes that occur both physically and emotionally to girls and boys during puberty. This can help us to understand more clearly how these different changes can trigger eating problems.

Body Changes For Girls

Puberty generally starts earlier for girls than boys - any time between the ages of 8 and 16. Most girls begin the change to adulthood between the ages of 12 and 14. The changes start when two glands in the brain called the **pituitary** and **hypothalamus** first send signals to the **ovaries** (the place where a woman's eggs are produced). When the ovaries receive these signals, they increase production of the female sex hormone **oestrogen**. This is the start of between 2 and 6 years of changes:

- For most girls, the first changes that occur are to their breasts. The area around the nipples develops first and then the breasts begin to fill out. Breasts develop at different rates and young women may be afraid that they will be lop-sided, as one breast can become larger than the other. However, this is normal and in time the breasts will even out.

- Hips and thighs widen and the waist gets smaller. The pelvis also expands to prepare for the possibility of childbirth. A young woman develops a curvy figure as her buttocks, legs and stomach change shape. All these changes are important if a woman is to carry a child during pregnancy. Therefore the extra weight that develops on the hips, thighs, stomach and buttocks is a very important part of an adult woman's body. However, it can scare young girls and may be a trigger for an eating disorder developing.

- Hair begins to grow in different places. Soft hair (known as **pubic hair**) will begin growing in the area between a girl's legs. In time, this will become thick and curly and is sometimes a different colour to head hair. About a year after pubic hair starts to grow, underarm hair also appears. Darker hair will grow on a young woman's legs and sometimes also on the face, especially the upper lip. Some women choose to begin shaving as they get older but this is not for any medical reason - it is purely a matter of personal choice.

- Girls usually have a **growth spurt** during puberty. Instead of growing the usual 2 inches in a year, they grow about 4 inches. This sometimes means that girls grow taller for a while although boys soon catch up. Hands, feet, arms and legs develop first and teenagers can feel awkward and clumsy during puberty. This growth spurt can leave some young girls feeling too large and may lead them to start dieting.

- During puberty, the skin becomes oily and teenagers usually suffer from spots or acne. Acne is often a result of the higher hormone levels and it can be quite severe for some teenagers. There are some good treatments available from doctors though. Cleanliness becomes very important for teenagers at this time.

- The sweat glands become more active and for the first time they may notice some body odour. This is the time when most girls start using deodorants and bathe daily. They are becoming more conscious of their bodies and unfortunately feelings of shame can begin to develop if they do not realise that these changes are all perfectly natural.

- About six months before their periods start, girls may notice a milky white discharge on their underwear. This is called **vaginal discharge** and is also perfectly natural.

- A short time after the breasts and pubic hair start to develop, girls have their first **period** (menstruation). Each month, the ovaries release an egg and if this is not fertilized by a man's **sperm**, it will pass out of the body along with other cells and tissue (which were developing in case the egg was fertilized) as blood. Some girls find this very scary at first, especially if they haven't been prepared for their first period. Periods are natural and girls should not feel embarrassed about them. Sadly though some girls do feel ashamed of their periods and this can lead them to try to lose dramatic amounts of weight so that menstruation stops.

- Throughout puberty, teenagers have an increased appetite and can feel very hungry most of the time. This is because they are growing so much. It is important at this time to eat a good diet that contains enough calories, so that healthy growth can continue. Many teenagers do put on weight during puberty but this is nothing to panic about and it is important not to start dieting. This weight increase is natural and levels off in time but unfortunately it can again lead some girls into eating disorders.

Body Changes For Boys

Like girls, boys also go through many dramatic body changes during their teenage years, although puberty usually starts later than for girls. The changes take place between the ages of 10 and 16 but usually start around the age of 14 or 15. This is when the pituitary gland in the brain causes the production of the male hormone **testosterone** to begin. These are some of the effects that puberty has on a young man's body:

- A boy's voice changes and becomes deeper. For some teenagers this is an overnight change, while others vary between higher and lower tones for a while.

- Boys go through the same growth spurt as girls and will find that their hands, feet, arms and legs grow first, leaving them feeling awkward and clumsy. Boys can find they develop a huge appetite and may begin eating large amounts of food.

- Muscles start to develop and their shoulders become much broader. This is a change that often affects how boys feel about themselves. If a boy doesn't develop as quickly as his friends, he can feel self-conscious. Some boys will begin compulsively exercising in an attempt to build up their muscles. This can lead to a possible eating disorder.

- Sometimes boys find that their breasts develop a small amount. This is called **gynaecomastia** and is a temporary condition, which is nothing to worry about. However, this can make boys feel very self-conscious and some will diet in an attempt to lose the slight swelling in their breasts.

- Hair starts to grow under arms, on the legs, around the **penis** and **testicles** and of course on the face. At first though, teenage boys will find they do not need to shave every day. Some boys may also begin to develop chest and body hair.

- The skin becomes oily due to increased secretion from the glands, and spots and acne often occur.

- The penis and testicles grow larger and boys will start to experience **erections**, when the penis becomes stiff and hard. 'Wet dreams' are also common. This is when a boy has an erection and **ejaculates** (releases semen) when he is asleep, and it is very normal. Erections usually occur when a boy is sexually excited but 'spontaneous' erections can also happen. These are also normal and will go away after a few seconds or minutes at the most.

However these are just the external changes that take place during puberty. Many other emotional changes are also occurring at the same time.

Emotional Changes During Puberty

During puberty, teenagers find their feelings begin to change and they start to care more about what others think of them. It becomes very important that they are liked and accepted. Relationships start to change and parents become a less important part of their life, as they spend more time with people their own age. Most teenagers feel self-conscious about their changing bodies and are worried that they are not attractive enough. They find themselves comparing their body with those of their friends but this is not a good thing to do. We all develop at different rates and comparisons are not helpful.

Puberty is the time when young people first become fully aware of their sexuality. This can be a confusing and embarrassing time, when they start to feel attraction for others and may have their first relationship. Problems occur when a person finds that moving into adulthood feels too frightening and they turn to an eating disorder (often anorexia) instead.

Anorexia and Puberty

Two of the most obvious features of anorexia are the dramatic weight loss and the loss of periods. Both of these symptoms take the sufferer back to a child-like (pre-sexual) state. The weight loss means that all the features of an adult woman's body are lost. The breasts, hips, rounded stomach and thighs all disappear and an anorexic's body often looks more like that of a young boy. As her weight drops, her periods also stop and the female hormone (oestrogen) is no longer produced. This means that sexual feelings often disappear completely. The sufferer is unable to notice any remaining sexual feelings because they spend so much time worrying about food, calories and weight instead.

This fear of sexual feelings can begin if a child is brought up in a family that never discusses the subject of sexuality or considers it an 'unpleasant' topic. Children brought up in open families, where they can talk freely about their worries, seem to have a healthier attitude towards their sexuality.

Some anorexics admit to feeling so disgusted with their adult bodies that they turn to the illness as an 'escape'. Disgust and shame at having monthly periods leads them to starve themselves. There may also be a fear of sexual intercourse and their monthly periods show these girls that they are now women. This means that a sexual relationship is a possibility, which can be terrifying. Some anorexics do marry but then often say they prefer child-like cuddles to any form of sexual contact. As I mentioned earlier in this book, some women who have experienced sexual abuse during childhood can turn to anorexia. This may be for a number of reasons but it is usually for protection.

However, it is not only a problem with sexual feelings that can turn someone towards anorexia. It can also be because a teenager feels unable to separate themselves from their family. They feel unable to make their own decisions and are frightened by the idea of being independent.

Puberty is all about change and loss of control. Teenagers have no control over the changes that are taking place in their bodies and this can lead them into anorexia. I pointed out earlier that anorexia is an illness about control. If a person feels totally out of control in their life, their food and weight may be the only things left that they can control.

Bulimia and Puberty

Some bulimics find that they also use their illness to deal with the sexual feelings that begin during puberty. Frequently they will binge in an attempt to distract themselves from any sexual feelings they may have. They see their bulimia as safer than having a relationship, since they are afraid of feeling vulnerable or being hurt by a partner. However, many bulimics feel a desperate need or hunger for love. If they do not find that love, they may also turn to food as an alternative to fill the emotional void inside.

Compulsive Eating and Puberty

Compulsive eaters can use their illness as a way of avoiding sexual encounters as well. Fear of sexual contact can lead some people to overeat. When they overeat, sufferers deliberately put on weight in the belief that their size protects them from relationships. Their weight becomes their protection and they fear that if they stop overeating and lose weight, they will then be expected to have sexual relationships.

How To Cope With Puberty

Puberty is clearly a very difficult time for young people. Constant changes occur in their body and they can feel very emotional without understanding why. It is important during this time to find someone that you can talk honestly with, especially if you are feeling scared. Remember that it is natural to experience massive changes at this time. However, do not be afraid to visit your doctor if you feel that some of the changes you are experiencing are abnormal. The more open and honest you are able to be, the better. Eating disorders develop because of a wall of silence, so speaking out is very important.

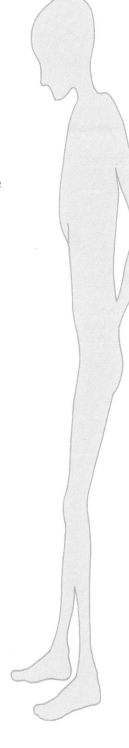

Chapter 9

Why do I Feel I Have to be Perfect?

Summary

A strong need to be "perfect" is one of the most common characteristics of eating disorder sufferers. This chapter looks at how perfectionism can lead to low self esteem developing.

I talked in an earlier chapter about the idea of 'perfectionism' and how people with eating disorders often feel they have to be perfect. Now I want to look at this in more detail and see how this 'need to be perfect' can affect everything we do. It affects the way we behave towards people, controls the way we work and even makes us feel scared to show our emotions.

Children who are 'perfectionists' are usually high-achievers who have unrealistic expectations of themselves. They always feel a need to get good grades at school but even though they often achieve this, they are never satisfied with the results. They believe that their friends or brothers and sisters are more intelligent and much better students.

A need to be perfect is linked to low self-esteem. When you have low self-esteem, you feel very critical of yourself and believe that you do nothing right. Attempting to be perfect is our way of trying to correct this. An extract from my diary shows how a simple mistake could lead me to feel like a complete failure:

Thursday February 29th 1996
I feel so upset with myself today. I am just such a failure. I was one stitch out on my cross-stitch work, so I had to take out a whole section of my sewing. I feel so fed up with myself. All I do is make mistakes all the time. I am stupid and crazy and people must hate me. I spent hours separating baked beans from the sauce ready for my meal this evening and then I tipped the whole plate onto the floor. I am a useless clumsy fool.

It is simply not possible to be perfect all the time. We are human - we make mistakes and do things wrong every day. This is normal and natural. If you constantly try to be perfect, you will end up feeling even more of a failure because you can never reach your goal.

But how is this linked to eating disorders?

Our society says that thin is the 'perfect' way to be and this is one reason why people with low self-esteem can turn to eating disorders. They feel a desperate need to 'fit in' and 'be perfect', and losing weight seems the ideal solution to all their problems. Not only are eating disorder sufferers searching for their 'perfect' body but they are also searching for the 'perfect' love that they have never been given. They desperately hope that one will lead to the other. By losing weight and getting their 'perfect' body, they feel sure that they will then be loved.

Low Self-Esteem

Self-esteem is basically the way we see ourselves. If you ask a person with low self-esteem to describe themselves, they will be very critical. They will use words such as *"ugly, fat, revolting, disgusting, boring, weak, useless or stupid"*. They will also take responsibility for everything that goes wrong, even if it is clearly not their fault. Comments such as *"I can never do anything right, I am just so stupid and useless"* are very common.

Eating disorder sufferers usually had low self-esteem before their illness even began and this is one of the triggers that caused it to develop. The eating disorder reinforces the belief that everything is their fault. Many people think they are to blame for their illness and are certain that they should be able to just 'snap out of it' and start eating normally again. When they find that this is impossible to do, they then feel worse about themselves and their self-esteem drops even lower.

People with low self-esteem cannot even believe that good things might happen to them. If something good does happen, they will explain it away negatively. Let me illustrate this with an example from my own life. When I was suffering from anorexia, I saw a lot of doctors and nurses. Many of these people treated me with special care - they bought me presents and gave me extra time because they thought I was a worthwhile person. However, I couldn't see this and explained away their behaviour by saying: *"They are just being kind. This is their job and they only want to get me better as quickly as possible so that they never have to see me again."*

People who suffer from low self-esteem also find it hard to accept compliments. They cannot understand why anyone would want to praise them. They believe that compliments are just kind remarks or lies. They can see all their 'bad' points very clearly and feel certain everyone else must be able to see them as well.

For anorexics, body size reflects the way they feel about themselves. They believe that they are unimportant and should just disappear. In my case, my speaking voice became quieter as I lost weight and I only managed to whisper to people. I felt I shouldn't be any louder in case I bothered someone. The only way that anorexics think they can make themselves feel good is by the control they have over food and eating. Bulimics and compulsive eaters also usually have damaged self-esteem and try to build it up by controlling their eating. However, the way they feel about themselves varies depending on how 'successful' they are at their diets.

Unfortunately, some children do not receive a good start in life and bad treatment from parents, relatives, teachers or classmates can lead to low self-esteem. Children brought up in a household where the rules are strict and behaviour is very controlled rarely have carefree, happy childhoods. Bullying at school is often a trigger that destroys people's self-esteem. Constant teasing and hurtful comments about weight or appearance can make a young person feel that they are unattractive and horrible. Losing weight seems like the 'solution'.

As I mentioned earlier, abuse is one of the most common causes of low self-esteem and if abusers offer any love at all, it will be conditional love. They only treat the child nicely if they do everything that is expected of them. If a child receives conditional love, they grow up believing that they have to behave perfectly if they want to be loved. I spent my entire childhood frantically trying to please my Grandmother by behaving as perfectly as I could. However, I could never be 'perfect', which meant I wasn't ever able to please her and as a result she always hurt me. Her behaviour led me to draw up a list of rules that I lived by for many years.

Let me share this list with you because it clearly shows how low self-esteem affects behaviour:

Gran's Rules

1) I must always try to please everyone else all the time and keep them happy.

2) I must never think about myself and my needs because that is selfish. Instead, I must always put other people first and myself last because I am not important.

3) I must never buy anything for myself because I do not deserve presents. I must always just give to others.

4) I must never say anything that upsets or angers another person. If I do, they will hate me and it will only prove that I am a horrible person.

5) I must never talk about my feelings because that is selfish. I must always say that I am fine. I am just making a fuss if I say that there is anything wrong.

6) I must never ask for anything because this only makes me a nuisance to other people.

7) I must always cope on my own and never ask for help. Asking for help would mean I was a weak and feeble person.

This list shows how low self-esteem affects the way a person behaves. Let's look at some of these in more detail:

1) A need to please others

   Low self-esteem is connected with a desperate need to please other people. If you look at the above list of rules, most of them (Numbers 1, 2, 3, 4, 6 and 7) are concerned with pleasing others. A need to please others can lead us to keep quiet about our problems and deny many of our needs and emotions. However, we cannot live our lives for other people and trying to do this can actually make us ill. The following is a short paragraph from a letter I wrote to Simon. I was finally beginning to realise that I couldn't live just to please others. I was discovering that I didn't have to behave in that way with him, which made our relationship a healthy one.

   "I try to read people's faces all the time to see if they're okay or if there's something wrong. If they seem upset or angry, I am sure I must be responsible for their bad mood. I am so terrified of displeasing people and that, of course, is because I was always trying to please my Grandmother in the hope that she would be nice to me. Strangely Simon, for the first time ever, I don't spend all my time trying to please you. I'm always totally honest with you. Maybe that's because I feel safe with you and trust you."

   From the time I was a child until the age of 30, I was always seeking the approval of other people. I needed to feel that I had not done or said anything wrong. This is not a healthy way to live and it is one of the reasons why my eating disorder developed. I had to express myself somehow and so my body did this for me physically with the anorexia.

2) Low self-confidence

   Low self-confidence and shyness are also strongly linked to low self-esteem. People who hate both their personality and their appearance often find themselves hiding from social situations. It is very difficult to mix with other people when you feel that you have nothing to offer. When you have low self-esteem, you believe people will dislike you and that no one will want to be your friend. You feel that everyone else is more attractive, intelligent and fun to be with. As a result, you begin to hide yourself away from the world and soon start to become very lonely. This is such a shame because everyone has a great deal to share. The fact that we are all so different makes each of us interesting but it is hard to see this when you have low self-esteem.

3) Difficulty talking about problems

   Many people with eating disorders think that they cannot share their feelings

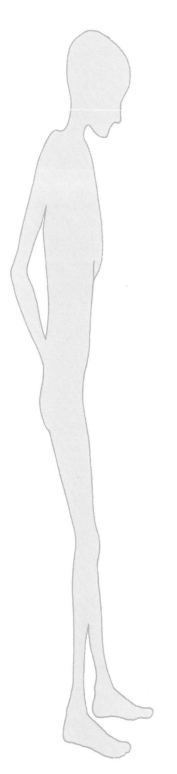

because that would make them a 'nuisance'. Low self-esteem leads to a feeling of being unworthy of help. A need to be perfect also makes some people believe that they are a failure if they ask for help. They feel that they should be able to solve all their problems by themselves. I believed this when I was anorexic and I felt I was a failure if I asked for a doctor's help. I didn't realise until later that asking for help was the bravest step I ever took. Taking that step actually saved my life.

It is also difficult when you have been hurt many times in the past to open up and trust others. I have explained to many sufferers that if they could just share their problems and fears, they would begin to take steps forward. It is a fact that people who are open about their worries suffer fewer psychological problems. However, I have frequently been told: *"But I can't do that. People don't want to know my problems. Whenever I do share them, I always end up getting hurt."* This is obviously a difficult situation but it is important to remember that everyone is different. Even though you were hurt by one person, that won't necessarily happen again. There are other people out there who DO want to help you. Perhaps now is the time to reach out and ask for help again.

Both anorexics and bulimics often have great difficulty talking about their problems because they feel ashamed of their behaviour. Many bulimics have told me that they cannot go to their doctors because he or she might think that they are disgusting. It is very important to remember that bulimia and anorexia are illnesses. Your doctor should understand why you are behaving in this way and can help you to start finding solutions to your problems.

4) Dependency on others

Low self-esteem can lead a person to become very dependent on others. Although sufferers feel they need to be independent and cope alone (because asking for help shows 'weakness') they can also start to rely heavily on others. If you have no self-worth of your own, you need others to tell you that you are a good person. Someone with low self-esteem will constantly put themselves down during conversations, secretly hoping the person they are with will reassure them. They desperately need to hear that they are not a bad person even though they may have difficulty believing this. A child who has not been comforted or loved enough when young, will grow up feeling a great need for affection. This is one of the reasons why they may turn to an eating disorder. Certainly when an anorexic loses a lot of weight, people begin to notice and they receive a lot of attention. Through their thinness, they are saying: "I have a problem. I need love. Help me!"

5) Lacking assertiveness

Low self-esteem can lead to a lack of assertiveness. **Assertiveness** is our ability to say what we want. You 'assert' yourself and say, for example:

"I would like to buy a new shirt" or *"I need some help with a problem."* When you have no feelings of self worth, you believe that you don't deserve anything and so do not assert yourself. Many people with eating disorders will deny themselves any of the pleasures in life. I know that I found it very hard to buy myself even a small gift such as a magazine or a book because I felt I did not deserve it. I was unable to say if I wanted anything. I even found it impossible to choose where we should go for a day out. I wanted other people to say where they wanted to go, so that I wasn't responsible for choosing the wrong place.

We all have needs which have to be fulfilled and feelings that must be expressed. If a child is not allowed to express their needs and feelings, they grow up believing they are bad for even having them. Parents should allow their children to express themselves but some parents find this too difficult. They want their children to have fewer emotions because anger or sadness are just too uncomfortable for them. In truth, they want their children to be something they are not. If the child is to please such parents, they have to deny some of their emotions and sadly this is just what some children do.

Hidden Emotions

Many of the emotions we experience such as anger, sadness, frustration or disappointment are considered 'difficult' or 'negative'. It is these emotions that many people with eating disorders have learned to hide as children. When they get older, they find it even harder to express these feelings and instead turn them on themselves.

The situation for a bulimic is quite similar. A bulimic recognises that they have feelings but believes they should not have them. This confusion over their feelings lead them to think that any negative emotion they have is really a feeling of hunger and this causes them to binge. After bingeing, they feel angry that they have used food as a response to their feelings and will make themselves sick. So the bulimic has two problems:

1) They cannot identify their needs and emotions and turn to food instead, which leaves them feeling angry and dissatisfied.

2) Like the anorexic, they do not think they should have needs, which makes them believe that eating was wrong and so they vomit.

An important part of treatment for both anorexics and bulimics is learning how to recognise and respond to feelings and emotions.

1) Anger

Anger is an emotion that eating disorder sufferers frequently try to deny. This can be a) because of abuse or b) because your family does not handle conflict in a healthy way.

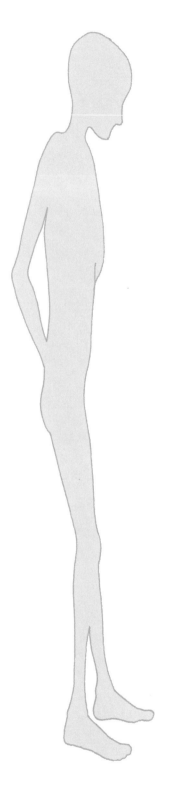

a) When a person is abused, their natural response is to become angry. However, getting angry may have led to more abuse in the past and this is why some people shut down on this emotion. Another possible reason is that as a victim of abuse, they see anger as a destructive emotion. They have become afraid of anger and in response, do not allow themselves to feel that way. If a child has parents who are constantly fighting, they may try to become the peacemaker and only ever show calm, happy emotions.

b) In some families, anger is not expressed at all. Everyone is expected to look happy and remain calm all of the time. In this kind of family, a child never experiences anger and does not learn how to deal with conflict. They feel arguments are frightening and try to cope with negative emotions by denying they exist. They never learn that conflict is a healthy way of expressing feelings, which can lead to greater understanding. Instead, they become people pleasers who avoid conflict at all costs.

Anger is very rarely spoken about by anorexics but sufferers will turn it upon themselves every day when they starve or self-harm. By contrast, bulimics use bingeing and vomiting to express their anger. One bulimic told me that when she vomited, she felt she was getting rid of all the anger in her body. There are much healthier ways of coping with angry feelings though and I will look at these in Chapter 14.

2) Sadness

When some children express sadness, they are told that they are selfish for thinking about themselves. This can make them think that it is wrong to consider their own needs. At other times, a child's feelings can be dismissed as unimportant or silly. Comments such as *"I don't know why you are upset - there really is nothing to be unhappy about"* or *"You really shouldn't be feeling that way"* are dangerous. They leave a child feeling that they have to get rid of these negative feelings of sadness or else the family will not accept them. Many eating disorder sufferers will never cry in front of anyone. They say that this shows they are 'weak'. They feel they are not 'perfect' if they show these emotions. This is a shame because crying is important and it shows other people how much you trust them if you can allow yourself to cry with them.

Children who shut down on their negative feelings seem to be unable to show their happiness either. They grow up thinking they will be rejected if they show their true feelings, so instead they learn to present a false image to the world. They may seem happy but are really just acting out a role in the hope that they will be loved. Underneath, they are sad and lonely and don't feel as if they fit in anywhere. This behaviour does not end in childhood though. Even as an adult, they will still show a happy contented front to their parents rather than talk about their true feelings.

My story as an example

I found that because I did not express certain emotions, I became a very controlled person and could no longer be impulsive. I didn't say or do anything on the spur of the moment because I was too afraid of the consequences. I was a perfectionist and had to know the results of my behaviour before I did anything. I only felt safe if I knew how people would react to me. I planned what I was going to say before I ever opened my mouth because I had to avoid making anyone angry or upset. If I ever did upset someone, I felt very guilty and thought I had failed because it meant that I wasn't 'perfect'. I saw that my parents were upset if I cried and were unable to cope with seeing my pain. So to protect them, I shut down on all these emotions. I did not argue with them because I hated conflict. Whenever I felt angry, I turned it inwards and cut or starved myself instead.

I came from a family where control was very important and I believe that is one of the reasons why I turned to anorexia. Our daily life was very timetabled - we did the same thing at the same time, every day of every week. This meant that to be 'perfect', I had to fit in with this rigid timetable. I grew up learning that being spontaneous was bad and that living by a strict set of rules was good. This led me very easily into my eating disorder, with its own rigid set of rules. I used to spend hours each day deciding how much I was allowed to eat and which exercises I had to do. Once again, my need to be perfect meant I always tried very hard to reach my goals. As time passed, I would set myself even harder targets and punished myself if I felt I was failing.

It wasn't until I met Simon that I learned a new set of rules and started to see that I wasn't a failure after all. I realised that I didn't have to try to please others all the time. I was allowed to have nice possessions and to enjoy myself. I no longer needed to reach the unrealistic targets that I had set myself.

The following were Simon's rules for me, which he listed in one of his early letters. You can see how each one is the exact opposite of the rules that my Grandmother set:

Simon's Rules

1) You are allowed to do what you want and please yourself because you are a worthwhile person.

2) You can think about yourself and your needs because this is both healthy and necessary.

3) You should buy the things that make you happy because you deserve happiness.

4) You need to tell people what you are thinking and feeling, and you don't have to work out their reaction in advance. You have opinions and feelings just like everyone else and you deserve to be heard.

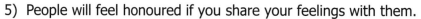

5) People will feel honoured if you share your feelings with them.

6) You should always feel free to ask for things if you either need or want them from someone. You are not a 'nuisance' and like everyone else, you are allowed to have what you want.

7) You don't need to 'cope on your own'. People love you and the more you share, the more you'll get back.

In this chapter, I hope I have managed to show you what Simon showed me - that you do not have to be 'perfect'. Being 'perfect' is not such a wonderful goal to aim for after all. No one could relate to someone who is 'perfect'. It is our mistakes that make us human and allow others to feel comfortable around us. The fact that I am able to tell people about the mistakes I have made in my life with anorexia, allows them to open up and be honest in return. My openness with Simon meant that he could tell me about his life, his true feelings and all the things that he felt ashamed about. You need to learn to accept yourself instead. Building up self-esteem that has been lost is not easy but it is possible, and we will look at ways of doing this later in the book.

Chapter 10

Why Do I Feel That Everything Is My Fault? Abuse and Eating Disorders

Summary

This chapter looks at the link between abuse and eating disorders, and shows how victims often believe that they deserved their ill treatment.

In the last chapter, I showed how people with low self-esteem often feel that they are to blame for anything bad that happens. This not only includes everything that goes wrong in their own lives but also anything bad that happens to the people around them. I remember my doctor saying that I must be a very handy person to have around because I always took the blame. I was the scapegoat and no one else had to admit to being in the wrong.

As I mentioned before, many eating disorder sufferers experience abuse and sadly they often believe that it was their fault. This leads them to feel a lot of guilt and I know that I certainly felt this way. My Grandmother treated both my brother and my cousin very well and only abused me, so I grew up thinking that I was the bad child. I felt certain that I deserved the abuse. Many of the people who write to me each day also feel responsible for their abusive treatment.

These are just two of the many comments I hear from abuse victims:

"Anna what am I doing wrong? I know I must be a very bad person to deserve this abuse. Please tell me how I can be a better person so that it stops."

"My Dad told me I am a bad and dirty person. Please help me to improve so that he won't hurt me anymore."

These comments are very sad but they are not unusual. This is why I want to look more closely at both abuse in general and my own personal experiences. I want to hand responsibility back to the abusers. They are the ones who have behaved wrongly. Victims of abuse are precisely that. VICTIMS.

I thought carefully about whether I should include a chapter on abuse in this book but realised if I ignored the subject, I would be saying that abuse is something we should feel ashamed about. It is sad that so many abused children and adults do feel ashamed to talk about their experiences though. I want to share my story later in this chapter to show that you don't have to feel shame about what has happened to you.

Abusers often rely on threats to keep their victims quiet. If you can find the courage to talk about the abuse you have received, then you take the power away from the abuser. My Grandmother used to tell me that she would kill my parents if I told anyone what she was doing to me. As a child, I believed her and kept quiet about the abuse for over 25 years. My Grandmother was not the only person who abused me though - I was also bullied by a 'friend' at college, sexually harassed and mentally tormented by my first boss and sexually abused by a driving instructor. In each case, I felt that the abuse was somehow my fault. I felt scared and ashamed to talk about their behaviour because I was certain that people would say: *"What did you expect? You asked for that abuse and you deserved it. I can't understand why you are making such a fuss."* It wasn't until I met Simon and saw the look of horror on his face when I described my experiences, that I realised something was seriously wrong. I was so used to being abused that I believed it was normal behaviour. This is why it is VERY important to tell someone if you are being abused or have been abused in the past. I hope that by being honest myself, I can allow a few more people to speak out about the abuse they have received.

What is Abuse?

Abuse is defined as any deliberate act that results in a child, teenager or adult being hurt in a physical, mental or sexual way. This can then cause that person to suffer physical, mental or emotional problems.

Neglect is when a parent or guardian does not provide a child with the care, supervision and environment needed to maintain their physical and mental health. However, this is not just about providing a child with food, clothing, a home, supervision and medical care. If a parent or guardian fails to protect a child from harm then this is neglect. This can be the result of just one incident or repeated behaviour, which leads to serious physical or mental damage.

The following are some facts and statistics about abuse. I always like to give a brief warning before I talk about statistics because you cannot always know how accurate they are. Also, with a subject such as abuse, people often feel afraid to come forward and talk about what happened to them. However, even taking this into account these figures are still very disturbing.

In the United States, between 2,000 and 5,000 children die each year from abuse related injuries.

Child abuse is the leading cause of death to children under the age of four.

Both boys and girls are equally as vulnerable to abuse. One in three girls and one in seven boys are sexually abused before they are 18 years old.

In America, the number of reported abuse cases are rising. In 1974, the figure was approximately 600,000 cases but twenty years later, in 1994, nearly 3_ million cases were reported. This does not necessarily mean that the number of abused children is increasing - it may just mean that more people are finding the courage to report the abuse.

There are many signs that a child has been abused. If you have a friend that you are worried about, the following points may help you. Remember though that everyone is different. I was badly abused as a child but could only say that a couple of these points applied to me. Also, some young people may behave in a similar way to the descriptions below but not actually be experiencing abuse. However, if you are still concerned after having read the list below, please talk with someone you trust.

1) Unexplained cuts or bruises on their body.
2) Unusual eating habits – a child could be eating too much or too little.
3) The wearing of clothes that completely cover their body, even in hot weather.
4) Extreme behaviour, such as aggression or total withdrawal. If a child is very loud and angry or quiet and withdrawn, this can be a sign of abuse.
5) Does not seem to respond to either pleasure or pain.
6) Cries frequently, usually for no obvious reason.
7) Seems very uncomfortable with physical contact and appears to be afraid of their parents.
8) Shies away from other children and often stands on the edges of groups, watching rather than taking part.
9) Can be difficult to teachers at school or bully other children.
10) Is in need of frequent medical or dental treatment.
11) Has trouble with schoolwork and may be behind in many classes.
12) Constantly tries to please adults.
13) Uses drugs or alcohol or is very sexually active.
14) Gives strange or unbelievable excuses for injuries.
15) Often seems tired and quiet.
16) May be very destructive or damage other people's property (vandalism).
17) Plays truant frequently.
18) Seems very depressed and has attempted suicide.
19) Has extreme mood swings.
20) Has a sexually transmitted disease or becomes pregnant.

If you are wondering whether you come from an abusive family, have a look at the following seven descriptions and see if you fit into any of the categories. Victims often find it hard to know whether they are suffering abuse because they have become so used to abusive treatment. Never having experienced any other types of behaviour, they may not actually know what 'normal' treatment is like. In the following points, I am referring to parents but abuse can come from many different sources - brothers, sisters, uncles, grandparents, friends of the family or even strangers.

1. Do your parents pay you so little attention that you have to look after yourself? Are they often out of the house? Do they ignore you when they are home? Do you have to act like a parent to younger brothers and sisters?

2. Is the love that you are given conditional? Do you feel that you are only loved if you behave in a certain way?

3. Are you often threatened with violence at home? Do your parents frequently smack or hit you?

4. Are you called names and shouted at? Do your parents or other relatives mentally abuse you with words?

5. Do your parents take out their anger and frustration on you? Do they neglect your emotional or physical needs? Do they use you as a scapegoat and blame you for anything that goes wrong?

6. Do you feel that your parents show a sexual interest in you?

7. Do you feel trapped by your parents' love? Are you so close to your parents that you are not able to have other friendships or relationships? Do they show an excessive interest in everything that you do?

These seven points show physical, mental and sexual abuse. Many people may not see Number 7 as abuse. However, part of a parents' job is to encourage independence in their children. Smothering them and not allowing their child to develop outside interests is actually a form of neglect.

Mental abuse is often just as damaging as physical or sexual abuse. Adults do not realise that the verbal messages they give their children can affect them throughout their lives. Verbal abuse in particular affects a person very badly over time. Gradually, self-esteem is destroyed as a constant stream of cruel comments leave the victim feeling a failure. Unlike sexual and physical abuse where the victim is often left with visible scars, emotional and verbal abuse is not always easy to prove. The scars of mental abuse are hidden.

Some of the scars from physical and sexual abuse are also hidden. The constant threats of further violence can leave a person terrified. Many victims have said that waiting for the next outburst was worse than the violence itself. Whereas mental and physical ill treatment may continue without any other forms of abuse, victims of sexual abuse often experience mental and physical abuse as well and this combination is the most damaging of all.

How is sexual abuse defined?

Sexual abuse is a huge subject in its own right because there are so many different degrees of it. I will try to list some of them here. If you are being treated in this way or you know someone who is, it is VERY important to talk to somebody about the problem. This is not something that anyone should have to cope with alone.

Have you or someone you know:

1. Been subjected to offensive comments or ridiculed about your body?
2. Been made to look at other people's sexual parts or at sexual acts?
3. Been shown 'pornographic' (sexual) films or forced to listen to sexual talk?
4. Been forced to have unnecessary medical treatment involving the examination of sexual parts?
5. Been bathed or washed in a way that made you feel uncomfortable?
6. Been fondled, kissed or touched in a way that made you feel uncomfortable?
7. Been touched on your sexual parts?
8. Been made to pose for photographs that are pornographic?
9. Been hurt physically or sexually in any way?
10. Been forced to perform sexual acts on an adult (male or female) or sibling?
11. Been raped or otherwise penetrated?
12. Been involved in child prostitution (selling a child's body for sex)?

Abuse is not just limited to children or teenagers and many adults are also in abusive relationships. It is not easy for people who have been abused to talk about what has happened to them. Feelings such as guilt, sadness, shame, fear and anger often stop them from reporting the abuse.

Guilt

Guilt is the emotion we feel when we believe that we have done something wrong. Abused people usually feel tremendous guilt about what happened to them and are certain that they are to blame. Frequently, the abuser tells them they deserve the bad treatment. My Grandmother justified her cruel behaviour by telling me that I was a terrible child who everyone hated and I deserved to be punished. Many victims of sexual abuse are told by their abusers: *"It's your fault I do this because you are so pretty I cannot resist you."* Physical abusers often say that their behaviour is justified. They claim they are only 'disciplining' their child for bad behaviour when they punch, kick, burn or slap them.

Another reason why victims feel guilt is the possible effect that talking about the abuse will have on their families. It can lead to divorce, court action and prosecution (if an abusive parent is convicted and sent to prison). Many children don't want to lose either of their parents and so do not report abuse.

The reaction of the rest of the family is also very important. Sadly on some occasions, the victim is not believed when they finally find the courage to speak out. For example, if a child tells their Mother that their Father is abusing them, the Mother may not always accept the truth. Other family members may even side with the abuser against the victim, leaving them feeling even more alone.

I remember feeling terrified of telling my parents about my Grandmother's abuse because I didn't think they would believe me. My Mother was very close to my Grandmother and it was many weeks before she was able to tell her that she realised I was speaking the truth. Fear can stop parents supporting a child who says that they have been abused. However, this only damages the victim further since they then believe it was wrong to have spoken out.

Not all abuse takes place in the home though. Sexual, physical and mental abuse can happen at any time in a person's life. Sexual abuse in the form of rape also leads to strong feelings of guilt, since a victim believes they must have done something wrong - for example travelled home alone late at night, drank too much or dated someone they didn't know well. Victims of 'date rape' (where rape occurs during an early date) often feel certain they must have 'asked for' the abuse. It is very important that victims understand that they didn't cause the rape to happen. No one 'deserves' to be raped.

It is important not to let feelings of guilt stop you from speaking out about what happened to you, because these feelings will only start to fade if you can talk honestly and openly about the past.

Sadness

Often victims feel a deep sadness, which may be connected to the feelings of grief they have for their lost childhood. When there is constant trauma in a person's life (such as experiencing daily abuse) they never have the chance to recover, heal or grieve before the next incident. Even if the abuse stops for a while, the victim is still living in an unstable environment where care is at best conditional.

When a person has been abused, they suffer many losses:

- A loss of innocence and a carefree childhood.
- A loss of freedom as panic attacks, anxiety and flashbacks set in.
- A loss of self-esteem and self-confidence.
- A loss of trust in other people and of ever feeling safe and secure.

- A loss of family and friends.
- A loss of health, both physical and mental.
- A loss of love and care.
- A loss of virginity (for victims of sexual abuse) and possibly the loss of ever being able to have children.

Survivors of abuse often do not accept that they need to grieve and will try to put on a happy front so that no one knows what happened in their past. I know victims of childhood abuse who have not even felt able to tell their partners what happened. They believe they have to instantly 'recover' from the abuse, which is simply not possible. When a person avoids talking about the abuse, their body responds in negative ways, which can result in an eating disorder.

Only when a victim finally reaches an emotional 'place' where they feel safe and secure, can they allow themselves to grieve. I know this was true in my case. When I met Simon, I found someone who loved me unconditionally. I felt secure in his love for me and finally felt safe enough to admit to the feelings of grief and pain that I had hidden inside for so many years. Over time, memories that I had previously blocked from my mind slowly started to return. With Simon's help, I was able to cope with them. Bad memories are like splinters slowly working their way to the surface - they are extremely painful but once they have been expressed and dealt with, the pain slowly starts to fade.

There are certain triggers which can cause memories to return. If a victim has no help, these returning memories may cause real trauma. The kind of triggers that can bring back memories are anniversary dates of abuse incidents, revisiting places where the abuse happened and seeing people who were involved with the abuser or even who look like the abuser. Flashbacks can happen at any time and it can be frightening and confusing when they begin many years after the events. Eating disorders are often used as a way to block out these returning memories. Some people overeat to bury the memories while others starve themselves, concentrating all their time and energy on how they can avoid eating.

For survivors of sexual abuse, relationships can be very difficult. They can have problems with intimacy and feel unable to have a loving sexual relationship. For them, sexual contact has always equalled pain. Some victims may actually damage their sexual parts so that they never have to experience sexual feelings again. Others may only feel able to have violent sexual contact, even when they are in a caring relationship. Some victims even end up working in the sex industry because they feel unable to have loving sexual relationships. However, there is real hope for victims of sexual abuse. It is still very possible for them to develop healthy sexual relationships, although therapy is often needed to help the victim work through many issues and feelings.

During abuse, a victim is usually threatened with loss of love if they do not do what their abuser wants. This means that victims often later feel unable to refuse sexual contact during a relationship. The ability to say "No" to unwanted sex is vital if a victim is to begin healing - it is strongly connected with learning how to stop being a people pleaser.

Shame

Shame is a very common feeling for abuse victims. Abuse leaves a person with the belief that they are worthless. They have been humiliated, hurt, and controlled. A victim feels unable to blame the abuser for these feelings and starts to believe that they must have somehow 'asked' for the abuse. They feel 'dirty' and 'disgusting' and take on the feelings and responsibilities that the abuser should rightfully accept.

Victims of sexual abuse often feel ashamed of their bodies. They feel unable to speak out about the abuse because they may have been told they are 'dirty' and 'asked for' the abuse. Many victims also feel ashamed that they accepted presents after the abuse. By accepting a gift, they feel they are siding with their abuser and are letting themselves down even further.

If a victim does recognise that they are not to blame for the abuse then they have to accept that someone, who should love them unconditionally, is choosing to hurt them. Many victims are particularly ashamed that they felt a need for love and affection, and as a result did not fight off any sexual advances. It is natural for children to feel a need to be loved and cared for. If this is not shown in a healthy way then they will accept it in any form that it is offered. The greatest shame of all is felt when a victim experiences any sexual pleasure during the abuse. They feel disgusted that their body responded in a pleasurable way to such treatment. However, this is again natural - our bodies are meant to respond in a pleasurable way to sexual contact and this can happen during abuse as well.

Most victims keep quiet and this allows the abuse to continue. The only way of breaking this cycle is to speak out. When a victim speaks out for the first time, they may find it one of the hardest things they have ever done. However, the more you talk, the easier it becomes. In time, you will no longer stare at the floor when you tell someone about the abuse but will find that you can look them straight in the eyes instead.

Fear

Fear is an emotion that abuse victims can feel throughout their lives. While the abuse is taking place, they feel terror about what will happen to them next. They are very scared of their abuser but at the same time are afraid to talk about the abuse. This is for a number of reasons:

a) In the case of abuse within the family, the victim may feel a need to protect the abuser. This irrational family loyalty prevents them from seeking help because they are afraid of what will happen to their parents or other relatives.

b) They are also afraid of the reaction they will receive from the abuser. What are the consequences of speaking out? If the abuser discovers the victim has spoken out then they may punish them even more harshly.

c) Many victims are very afraid that they won't be believed if they do speak out or that they may be judged harshly if they do. How will their family and friends react? This fear often means they continue to keep the abuse a secret.

Anger

Victims of abuse usually feel angry about the way they were treated and this is a natural response. However, since they were never allowed to show this anger to their abuser, it has to go somewhere and instead they often turn it on themselves by starving, bingeing or vomiting. As I mentioned in the previous chapter, many eating disorder sufferers are very afraid of anger because in the past it has led to terrifying situations. It is far more comfortable to turn that anger inwards. They have been taught at an early age to take the blame for everything, so they become extremely self-critical and hateful towards themselves as they grow up.

Others may show an outward anger and start to destroy property or become abusive and rude towards people who have never done them any harm. If you are used to experiencing violent anger, it may be that you begin to show this yourself. If this is the case, you need to get help immediately because you have started to become an abuser yourself. When we feel anger, it needs to be directed in the right place and expressed in the right way. This is not always easy to do, which is why victims of abuse often need help from counsellors so that they can learn to express their emotions in a healthy way.

However, the mental pain of abuse does not end when the abuse stops. There are long-term effects that will often influence a person for life if they do not seek help. Eating disorders are just one of the many possible effects of childhood abuse. Each victim reacts differently to abuse and the level of support and help they receive will affect their future. You do not have to allow abuse to ruin your life. There is a lot of help out there. It is very important to remember that you need to start to let go of the anger and pain you feel. I can understand that desperate sense of wanting a 'normal' family life, just like the ones you see on cosy television programmes. If you do not have a normal family though, however much you wish for one it is not going to happen. Learning to accept this is a vital part of recovery.

Before I share my story with you, let me just sum up why an eating disorder can seem to be a 'solution' for people who have been abused:

1. An eating disorder can block out the feelings linked to abuse and instead cover them with thoughts and feelings about food and weight. When a person is ill with anorexia, bulimia or a binge eating disorder, their main focus is food and this does not allow their memories of abuse to surface. The emotions that they find difficult to deal with such as shame, guilt and anger are denied.

2. An eating disorder can direct people away from the real issues. When a family member has an eating disorder, the whole family only focuses on food as the problem. They do not always see the wider picture and ask why the eating disorder started in the first place. This allows the victim to continue to keep their abuse a secret and to protect the abuser. In the same way, it can also give parents who know about the abuse an excuse to avoid dealing with the real problem.

3. An eating disorder is often used as a 'protection'. For anorexics, when their weight falls too low, they no longer experience sexual desire. They are also attempting to make their body asexual and unattractive. Bulimics will cover their sexual feelings with bingeing and vomiting instead whereas binge eaters may overeat in an attempt to make themselves large, which they see as unattractive. For all eating disorder sufferers, food becomes their closest companion and they are able to isolate themselves from other people and the possibility of new relationships.

4. Eating disorders are an attempt by the victim to recover a sense of control. Children are powerless against adults and have no control in an abusive relationship. The word "No" is rarely heard by an abuser. Through their eating disorder, victims of abuse are trying to regain some control but unfortunately they do not realise that this newfound feeling of control will not last. Before long, it is the eating disorder that is controlling them.

5. For many people, their eating disorder makes them feel 'clean' because the abuse had left them feeling 'dirty'. Anorexics often take dangerous laxatives in an attempt to 'clean out' their bodies and feel comforted when their stomachs are empty. Bulimics also claim that vomiting can leave them feeling clean. Some bulimics have said that they still feel the abuser inside them and by vomiting, they are trying to get that person out of their body.

My Experiences of Abuse

I have already mentioned my Grandmother a number of times but let me now go into a little more detail. When I reached the age of three, my Grandmother started 'picking' on me. Although I did not actually live with her, I saw her every day for many hours. The abuse started slowly as she made the occasional cruel comment and remark, telling me I was a "greedy, fat, ugly child". I was in fact the exact opposite and this is probably why my Grandmother didn't like me. I was a pretty, sweet child and she hated the attention and care that people showed me. Over time, her comments grew more frequent and she began to force me to eat food I didn't like, such as fish with bones or meat covered in fat and gristle. If I said that I didn't want this food, she would get very angry and physically hit me to make me eat.

As I grew older, my Grandmother started to play cruel tricks on me. She would take me shopping and then abandon me in a big department store or busy shopping centre. I was terrified whenever this happened because she had told me never to leave her side. It wasn't until years later that I realised she was deliberately abandoning me. I would wander around looking for her, sometimes for hours, all the while shaking with fear. After a long period of time, my Gran would finally reappear. She would be very angry and tell me off. She said that it was my fault that I got lost and shouted at me for being a bad child.

My Gran would also deliberately damage my toys and other possessions. I once arrived home to find that she had snapped the heads off all my china animals and scratched deep grooves in my wooden furniture. My parents thought I had done both these things and I accepted the blame because I couldn't say it was my Grandmother. She discovered my every weakness and used them to hurt me. She learned from my Mother that I was afraid of the dark, so she would shut me in dark rooms for hours on end. These are just a few of the abusive things that my Gran did to me during my childhood.

I was afraid of my Grandmother but I could not tell my parents about this abuse because my Gran threatened me. She told me that if I said anything, she would kill my parents. As a child I believed this because I thought my Gran could do anything she wanted at any time. As I grew older, I realised that my Grandmother couldn't kill my parents but by then I was too afraid to talk. Gran had convinced me that my parents hated me. I was sure if I told them about the abuse, they would just say I deserved it and ask why I was making such a fuss over nothing. So I kept quiet and, in an effort to protect my Mother who was also afraid of Gran (her Mother), I spent even more time at my Gran's house. I learned quite early on that my Mother needed to be looked after. She often had bad migraine headaches and these started if she was upset. I could see how often Gran upset my Mother, so I tried to prevent this from happening. I realised that I needed to take as much of the abuse as I could. If my Grandmother had me to hurt then she seemed to leave my Mother alone. I became a shield, protecting my Mother from any pain.

The abuse I received from my Grandmother left me with very low self-esteem. By the time I was 17, I didn't even feel I deserved to eat food any more and the anorexia began. At 18, I felt sure I was a horrible person who deserved bad treatment so when a girl at college starting bullying me, I just laughed off the abuse even though it hurt. What began as a good friendship slowly changed. Emma had many worries and problems of her own and like many bullies, made herself feel better by hurting someone else. Emma was overweight and her Mother was always telling her to diet. She had problems with binge eating and I sometimes found her surrounded by chocolate wrappers. Emma seemed jealous of the fact that I was thin and she constantly made cruel and hurtful remarks to me. She also told lies about me behind my back to my other friends.

If my self-esteem had been higher, I would have stood up for myself. I shouldn't have just accepted her insults but I did and instead of completing my degree, I left college instead. I was giving up my dream and my future because of someone else's cruel behaviour. I felt too alone and scared to fight Emma, and once again believed that I deserved to be hurt in this way.

After leaving college, I started work in a solicitor's office as an office junior. I loved this job - it was easy work, there were few pressures and I felt happy and relaxed for the first time in years. Within two months though, I was promoted to the position of legal secretary and that was when the problems began. I had never worked as a legal secretary before and was learning a lot of different tasks in a very short period of time. My boss was quite an elderly man and although he treated all the other secretaries very well, he was abusive towards me.

I was a perfectionist and tried to do the best I could at work. I would always double-check all the letters and legal documents I typed but this just wasn't good enough. I could type twenty-nine perfect documents but if the thirtieth contained a mistake, my boss would ridicule me. He would stand at the door of the secretaries' office and shout across the room at me. He treated me as if I was only five years old, calling me stupid, careless and useless. I felt humiliated and ashamed but once again I did not stand up for myself. I did not say that I wouldn't accept that kind of behaviour. Instead I just worked harder and faster, checking all my work three or four times. However, it is not possible to be 'perfect' so I did make some mistakes and each time I did, I was humiliated.

This was not the only abuse I received from my boss though. I began to notice that his frequent touches, which I had believed were accidental, did not stop. In fact they continued and became even more intrusive. He would try to hug and touch me any chance that he had. I also realised that he only ever called me into his room to take dictation if I was wearing a short skirt. If I wore a longer one, I was not called into his office.

I allowed this abuse to continue for over two years. I now accepted abuse as normal behaviour and did not believe I deserved anything better. Other people would have talked about their abuse to friends and relatives, or complained to someone higher up in the company. My only response was to turn to anorexia as my escape route again. I lost weight rapidly and eventually had to give up my job because I was too ill. The anorexia had 'rescued' me from the abuse but at the cost of my health. Too afraid to take another job, I then hid in the illness for many years.

For seven years, the only people I saw were doctors, nurses and other healthcare workers. Finally, at the age of 28, a psychiatric nurse convinced me that I should start having driving lessons. This was a frightening thought for me because I had hidden away from the adult world for so long. I asked around and was given the number of a very friendly driving instructor. This is what I wrote in my diary after our first meeting:

Wednesday October 30th 1996
"The driving went okay today. The instructor is really nice. He is very jokey and smiles all of the time, which has really helped. He said that I did very well but I think he was just being kind to help build my confidence. He talked constantly, telling me all about his life. He called me 'Darling' all the time, which I actually found quite comforting because that is what Dad calls me. He asked me about my cross-stitch business and then if I had a boyfriend. I had to say "no" and that made me feel terrible. I felt like such a loser and the world's ugliest person. He was kind about it and said he didn't know how I'd escaped - were all the men around me blind? But I'm sure he was really thinking 'looking at you Anna I'm not surprised you're not dating.'"

I started to have two hour lessons every Wednesday morning. Perhaps because I was very innocent (or more likely because I was so used to being abused) I didn't notice the changes in our relationship. The fact that I had never been able to stand up for myself and say: "No, don't treat me that way," meant I accepted everything that happened to me. I knew that he was a man who flirted with women, but felt sure that it was harmless. I was desperate to be liked and the compliments I received made me feel special for once. I felt uncomfortable with his constant references to how he "loved me because I was gorgeous" but my low self-esteem stopped me from believing him. I told myself that he was just being kind and was sure he said the same things to all the women he taught.

As time went by, his comments became more explicit and I felt increasingly uncomfortable. I didn't want to make a fuss because conflict terrified me, so I just tried to mentally block out his words and carry on with the lessons. I didn't want to change driving instructors - it had taken all my courage to start lessons with this man and the idea of switching to a new person terrified me. I was afraid that the next instructor might shout at me. I applied for a driving test date and hoped that I would pass first time. By this time, my instructor had started to touch me constantly on my arms, legs and face. He would hold one of my hands while I was driving and often put his arm around me. After I had been driving for six weeks, I took my written test. I passed that easily, which just left the practical section of the exam.

Two weeks before my practical test, I finally managed to do a perfect three-point turn in the car. For a brief moment I forgot all my fears and smiled at my instructor. He leaned over and kissed me. I was shocked and immediately put the car in gear and drove off but I could hear him beside me, saying how wonderful my lips felt. He began to tell me about other things that he would like to do to me and, winding the window down, started shouting to people in the street: "She's mine you know! No one else can have her!"

I found the kiss very frightening but at the time did not know that this was actually sexual abuse. As always, I felt responsible and knew I should have told him that I didn't want him to behave in that way. I felt ashamed though and thought that I would be blamed if I spoke out.

I spent the next week trying to convince myself that the kiss was a one-off incident. I was shaking before my next lesson but as the two hours slowly passed, he showed no sign of forcing himself on me again. I began to relax slightly and did the final three-point turn of the lesson. Once again he kissed me. This time he did not let me go but kept kissing me even though I was trying to pull away. He didn't seem bothered by the fact that I was uncomfortable and just laughed, telling me again how much he loved me. By this time I hated him and only wanted to get through the test so that I never had to see him again. So much was riding on the outcome of my test that I became very afraid. I knew how nervous I became when I had to do anything difficult and felt certain I would fail.

As we walked over to the test centre, my instructor put his arm around me and started to cuddle me. Sitting in the waiting room, he would not stop kissing me. I felt terrified that the examiner would enter the room, see what was happening and fail me before I even had a chance to take the test. The examiner didn't see anything but my nerves let me down and I failed the test on just one slip. My diary shows how I felt:

Wednesday February 19th 1997
"I feel so down today. I failed my driving test and I feel so bad. I have let everyone down by failing and now I have to carry on with my lessons. I just want to hide away in a corner. I've tried to put on a brave face and joke about it but inside I feel shattered. I have cried so much today. I phoned for another test date and I have to have more lessons. I am scared about what will happen next."

82

I knew that my doctors would see this diary and so I never explained why I was so scared. They just assumed I was afraid of another test. The pattern was set and during the next four lessons, my instructor kissed and touched me constantly. He told me that I mustn't talk about the way he treated me because my Father wouldn't understand that it was totally innocent. Once again, I was being told not to tell anyone but the warning bells did not sound in my head and I just did what he said.

I failed the second test as well - my nerves were too much for me to deal with. I could not turn my mind away from the abuse that took place before each test. His constant kissing and touching left me feeling dirty and ashamed. For the next two months and two tests, the abuse continued. I didn't tell anyone. My parents thought I was having a good time as I related funny stories about my lessons. I was desperate to give up the lessons and tests but my doctor told me I had to continue - this was too important for my future.

Finally, on the fourth attempt, I passed and the relief I felt was tremendous. I realised I never had to see my instructor again. The drive back from the test centre was horrible though because he kept touching me between my legs but I constantly reminded myself that this was the end. He wanted me to promise to see him again and told me to phone so that we could arrange to meet. I never phoned him, so he started to harass me. He often telephoned and my parents slowly began to become suspicious. I told him that he had to stop calling or else they would realise that something had happened between us. Fear stopped him phoning and I only saw him once more in a shop in our local town. There, in front of everyone, he kissed me. I wanted to turn and run out of the shop but my need to please people kept me rooted to the spot until I was dismissed.

I wanted to share my stories of abuse here to show you that the victim should not feel guilty or ashamed. They also show how low self-esteem and a history of abuse can lead a person to accept anything. Instead of walking away when people treated me badly, I just accepted it as if I was wearing a label around my neck that said: "Abuse me - I will accept anything that is thrown at me." Many of the people who read this book will have experienced some form of abuse in their lives. It is important that you talk to someone about this abuse. You need to find someone that you trust and share with them what is happening to you. It could be a teacher, doctor, parent, friend or confidential helpline (the contact details for some of these organisations are in the back of the book). No one should blame you for the abuse - they should just help you to find ways of dealing with the problem until you feel safe.

Chapter 11

Do I have Problems with my Body Image?

Summary

Poor body image is one of the major factors in the development of an eating disorder. This chapter shows how sufferers have a distorted view of their own bodies.

Body image is the way that a person sees their own body. Our body image is formed by our thoughts and feelings, comments from other people, media images and physical sensations such as the tightness of clothes. If you feel comfortable with the way that your body looks, then you have a good body image. However, if you feel unhappy every time you look at yourself in a mirror and hate the way you look then you have a poor body image. Eating disorders and poor body image are very closely linked. Sufferers are preoccupied with thoughts about their weight and body shape and usually have strong feelings of hatred for their own body. They constantly criticise their body, treating it badly and spend all their time trying to change its size and shape. Some eating disorder sufferers cannot even look at their own body in a mirror and feel unable to allow others to touch them in any way.

Distorted Body Image - What do I see when I look in the mirror?

When people suffer from eating disorders, they often have a distorted body image. This means that they cannot see their real body shape and size but instead see a different (usually larger) image when they look in the mirror. For sufferers, this is probably the most confusing aspect of eating disorders. I remember arguing with many doctors about this idea since I could not believe that I saw a distorted image when I looked in the mirror. I was convinced that what I saw was reality.

Distorted body image is most closely associated with anorexia but people suffering from bulimia and other eating disorders also usually have body image problems. When eating disorder sufferers were asked to estimate their size in a recent survey, they all believed they were heavier than they really were. Anorexics cannot see how thin they actually are and when they look in the mirror, they 'see' a much larger body. This distresses them and leads them to continue dieting. When questioned, anorexia sufferers seem to have a fairly accurate view of their upper body but greatly overestimate the size of their lower body. When I speak to anorexics, I usually find that they focus constantly on the size of their hips, thighs, bottoms and stomachs, rather than on their arms and chests.

Even though anorexics may logically know that they are very underweight, they will still usually say: "I feel fat". Often, when a sufferer is experiencing severe body distortion, doctors will send them to have medical photographs taken. A lot of doctors believe that by showing anorexia sufferers photos of themselves, they will then see the reality of their weight loss and realise the seriousness of their situation. However, it does not always work this way. Many sufferers see the same distortion when looking at photos that they experience when looking in the mirror. They see themselves as fat in pictures too and this can actually make matters worse.

I remember looking at my medical photographs and all I could see was a fat body. I wasn't the only person who struggled with seeing the reality of their image either. Another young woman in the same hospital came into my room one evening in tears. She had been given her medical photographs and was horrified by her size. The young woman was extremely thin and I tried to prove this to her by opening a catalogue that showed women modelling underwear. The women in the catalogue were at least three sizes larger than this girl but because of her distorted body image, she simply could not see this. She kept pointing at the women in the catalogue and repeating: "I want to be as thin as those women".

Photographs are not a good indicator of a person's size. We all look different in every photo taken. Lighting and angle are just two of many factors that affect how we look in pictures. I personally believe that seeing their medical photos can be a damaging experience for some sufferers.

This poem by Nicola shows just how difficult it is for some people to see the reality of their size.

"A Poem About Body Image"
by Nicola

Are my eyes distorted?
Because I don't see
The things that you mention
When you look at me

I just see the fatness
And roundness of arm
The soul that is racing
Expression of calm.

I just see the stomach
And green eyes so sad
With the ugliest face
And the fat that I had.

You say that I'm pretty
And not fat but slim
But I cannot believe you
I can't take it in.

Are my eyes distorted?
Because I don't see
The things that you mention
When you look at me.

Body distortion is very hard to understand and it took me many years to accept this concept. The following passage is from a letter I wrote to Simon in February 1999:

"Right. Okay, we will try it your way then. I've had the following discussion with both Dr Brown and Dr Stewart and I'm still not convinced by their arguments, so now it's your turn. You can have a go.

I said to them that whenever I look in the mirror, all I see is a really ugly person looking back - a horrible person that no one could ever love. To which they say "That's just the anorexia in your brain warping your perceptions and distorting the image". But I just can't accept that. A mirror is an inanimate object that only reflects reality. So what I see has to be the same picture that other people see when they look at me, doesn't it? And when your feelings about yourself (and I feel really unattractive) match the picture you're seeing in the mirror, it must surely be reality?"

Simon's response (below) was extremely helpful to me at the time:

"You say that "the mirror is an inanimate object" but is it really? Haven't you ever seen photos of yourself where you look different every time? Haven't you heard people say that appearing on TV makes you look heavier? Haven't you heard of deceptive "skinny mirrors" being used in expensive clothing stores? Or about how camera lenses or different types of lighting can completely alter a person's appearance?

It's a trust thing again Anna. When I tell you that you look really nice, you're just going to have to trust me. It's not just the anorexia

86

but also low self esteem that's distorting what you see when you look into a mirror. I know the second one very well indeed. The way we interpret images is highly subjective. But then everything's subjective isn't it? You could argue that black is white and no one can actually disprove you. So I can't literally prove that what you see in a mirror is wrong. I can only tell you that from my perspective it's very wrong."

The idea of learning to trust someone else's opinion rather than my own was very helpful and I still encourage sufferers to try and do this today. When you feel sure that your own perception is wrong, you need to ask for help. Trusting someone else to tell you what you look like can be frightening at first but it does become reassuring and comforting in time.

Straight facts will also help you to see the reality of the situation. Weight and dress sizes do not lie. Unfortunately, dress sizes vary in each store you visit. If you are a UK size 8 or 10 (US size 4 or 6) there is no way that you can be 'fat'. At that size, you are small. Equally, if the scales say that you are one stone underweight, however much you try to argue your case, you will not convince a doctor that you are 'fat'. Hard facts can help you to see the truth about your body. At times like these, you need to listen to logic rather than to your distorted feelings.

Many studies have been carried out that ask women how happy they are with their bodies. On average, 8 out of every 10 women seem to feel unhappy and it appears that more than half of these have a distorted image of themselves. Unhappiness with appearance starts early in life, especially for girls. By the age of ten, many young girls have already begun to diet (one American study found that 81% of 10 year olds had dieted).

Boys appear to have fewer problems during their childhood years but can begin to feel unhappy with their shape as they reach puberty. As I showed earlier, puberty can be a very difficult time for girls too. One study showed that by the time they reach 17, 80% of all girls are unhappy with their looks and want to change their shape. It appears that men and women are dissatisfied with different parts of their bodies however. Women tend to focus on their hips, thighs, bottoms and stomachs, whereas men are more concerned with their chests, stomachs, muscular build and height.

There are a number of factors that seem to affect body image:

1. **Mood** - When people are depressed, angry or lonely, they can become unhappy about their bodies. When a woman is feeling low, she is inclined to describe herself as much larger than she actually is.

2. **Food** - After a heavy meal or snack food (such a chocolate), many people feel worse about their body than if they had eaten a salad. This is even

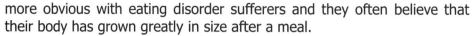

more obvious with eating disorder sufferers and they often believe that their body has grown greatly in size after a meal.

3. **Childhood teasing** - Poor body image can develop because of teasing and bullying during childhood. Once again, we see how abuse may be a part of the problem.

4. **Clothes shopping** - When women try on clothes in shop fitting rooms, they often feel more self-conscious about their bodies and will become very self-critical. This is even more apparent if the changing rooms are shared and a person is trying on more revealing clothes, such as a swimsuit.

5. **Childhood hugs** - If a parent does not cuddle or hold their child often, this can cause problems in later life. It is currently believed that **touch deprivation** strongly affects a person's body image from childhood into adult life.

6. **Periods** - When a woman is **pre-menstrual** (just before her period begins), she is more likely to feel unhappy with her body than at other times during the month.

7. **Relationships** - For adults, relationships can affect their body image. People in long-term relationships often feel happier with their bodies than those who are single. This is probably because they are receiving constant reassurance about their appearance from their partners and are made to feel physically desirable.

Compulsive eaters also have serious problems with their body image, especially if their illness has caused them to become overweight. Poor body image seems to be very strongly linked to our society's idea that 'thin' is beautiful and people often feel ashamed if they are overweight. Studies have shown that many overweight people experience serious depression and are often cruelly teased about their size. This poor body image can then lead them to isolate themselves from the world, for fear of criticism.

Men can also suffer from poor body image and this may lead to compulsive exercise disorder or **body dysmorphia** (which is a condition where people try to change their body shape). They become fixated with one particular part of their body and do everything possible to alter it. Men may focus on building up their chests so that they are more muscular, for example. This kind of focus soon becomes an obsession and an illness. Men may start experimenting with weight gain powders, steroids and other muscle enhancers, and these substances can be extremely dangerous.

On the day I first met Simon, we proved that both men and women can have similar body image problems. We were visiting the Science Museum in London and found ourselves in an exhibit all about the human body. Before we knew where we were, we'd wandered into a display about food and weight. The room was filled with mirrors and weighing scales. Without saying a word to one another, we both turned on our heels at exactly the same moment and quickly walked out. It was only later that we realised what we had instinctively done and although we managed to see the funny side of it, it showed how poor our body images really were.

It is important to remember that we are not identical copies of one another and should not all try to be the same size and shape. There are three distinctly different body types - endomorph, mesomorph and ectomorph. Your body type determines what your size and weight will be. You may find that you do not exactly fit into a body type (you may be a combination of two of them) but you will still find that one type is more dominant.

These are the three different body types:

Endomorph - An endormophic body is quite sturdy and not too tall. Women tend to be curvier with generous figures. People with this body type tend to find that their weight fluctuates quite often. However much they diet though, they will never attain a 'skinny' figure.

Mesomorph - People with a mesomorphic body type tend to keep their weight very level. They are usually quite tall and angular in shape. They are generally more muscular than endormorphs. They can gain or lose weight quickly but usually keep their weight stable. Even at a young age, mesomorphs generally look slightly older.

Ectomorph - People with an ectomorphic body tend to be underweight. This is the typical 'model' build - very petite and slender. They may be flat chested and often seem quite fragile and delicate. They have trouble putting on any weight, however much they seem to eat.

It is important to remember that you cannot change your body type and accepting that fact can help you to learn to like yourself. It is however VERY possible to change our negative feelings about our bodies and I will deal with this in more detail later on in the book. You need to acknowledge that your body is not an enemy that you need to hate and fight all the time. It is important to notice how feelings, events, mood swings and social activities can affect your body image. When you can start to see patterns developing then you can begin to understand that the changes are often nothing to do with physical reality but instead are emotional. I know that when I have a problem and feel down, my body image becomes very negative and I will say to Simon: *"I feel fat today. I know I am not but I feel like I am"*. His response is always to say: *"So what is the problem that's making you feel fat?"* We both realise that my feeling of fatness is nothing to do with reality but is an emotional problem instead.

There are many practical day to day activities that affect our body image:

a) Repeated body weighing and taking body measurements.
b) Focusing on dress size.
c) An obsession with looking in mirrors.
d) A strong interest in the calorie values of food.

Preoccupation with any of these activities can cause a person to focus solely on their body image and negative behaviour patterns can develop.

Why do I feel the need to weigh myself all the time?

Eating disorder sufferers weigh themselves frequently, sometimes many times each day. Bulimics will often weigh themselves before, during and after binges to try to assess if they have vomited all the food they ate. Anorexics tend to weigh themselves every time they eat some food to see if their weight has changed. Once an anorexic has eaten, they are filled with the fear that they have put on huge amounts of weight, and often the only way that they can calm themselves down is by standing on some scales.

For most eating disorder sufferers, their mood for the day is dependent on what they weighed that morning. If their weight is the same as the previous day, they feel relief. If their weight is lower than the previous day, they feel extremely happy but if their weight has risen, depression usually sets in. They begin to set themselves stricter weight loss targets and will cut out more food from their diets and exercise harder.

The reality of the situation is that our weight fluctuates between one and four pounds every day. These changes in weight are perfectly natural - they can be due to water retention (when water collects in parts of the body, which women often experience before their periods) or can even depend on whether or not a person has been to the toilet that day. However, for eating disorder sufferers, these fluctuations can be terrifying and can again lead them to be even stricter with themselves. It is important to remember that you don't need to let the scales decide your mood for the day or tell you whether you are a success or a failure. It is not healthy to weigh yourself frequently - you should weigh yourself once a week at the most. This will give you a much more accurate reading because it will not be affected by daily or even hourly fluctuations.

Also, remember that all weighing scales show different results. I remember finding this very annoying when I was anorexic. I would be asked to step on a different set of scales and find that my weight had risen or fallen by three or four pounds. If you are trying to find an accurate reading of your weight, always weigh yourself once a week on the same set of scales at the same time of day in the same clothes.

Why do I wear baggy clothes all the time?

This is a question that applies mostly to anorexics. As a sufferer loses weight, they try to disguise the changes in their body size and often begin to hide in baggy clothing. This allows them to live in denial for a while longer. The baggy clothes can disguise their problem from friends and family, allowing them to lose more weight before anyone notices.

Anorexics also use baggy clothes to hide the fat they believe they have. I know many anorexics who feel unable to tuck their shirt into their jeans or trousers (I had this problem myself). They buy extra-large sizes (often men's clothes) in an attempt to cover the large bodies they believe they have. Even in the summer, anorexics often wear long-sleeved tops and trousers to cover up their entire body. This is also partly an attempt to keep warm because their own temperature control no longer works correctly.

Baggy clothes are often all that feels comfortable to anorexics. Tight clothes can be very frightening, as they can make an anorexic feel fat. They may also wear the same clothes week after week except for when they need washing. I did this too for many years because I simply did not believe that I deserved to buy myself anything new to wear.

Chapter 12

Why do I think about Food all the Time?

Summary
When a person starves their body, their mind become preoccupied with food. This chapter looks at the reasons behind this.

When you have an eating disorder, food very quickly becomes an obsession. It is no longer just a basic necessity that you need to survive. Instead, it has become a part of your life that you can control and use in many different ways to hurt yourself and possibly others. It becomes a way of denying yourself the basic requirements of life because you do not feel that you deserve them.

When you begin to interfere with your natural eating patterns, your body responds to this. When you start dieting, you are simply not feeding your body enough and you will begin to crave food. Bulimics find that they go from a period of restricting to a period of bingeing and purging. This is because their feelings of hunger grow so strong that they can no longer fight them. Anorexics manage to **restrict** (limit the amount they eat) but their minds will still constantly focus on food. They can think of nothing else and often find themselves watching cookery programmes and even reading recipe books. I can remember flicking through magazines just to look at pictures of food. I would even watch films in the hope that there would be some scenes showing people eating.

The effects of starvation on your mind
When a person decides to stop eating, they are forcing their body into a state of starvation. At first this can actually feel good. Anorexics often feel a tremendous buzz as they see their weight falling and the figures on the bathroom scales dropping lower. As time passes though, the physical effects of starvation begin and along with these come the serious emotional and mental problems. Most people will have felt hungry when they miss a meal. This however does not compare to the intense hunger felt by anorexics. When you do not allow your body any food at all, you will experience constant hunger pains. This intense hunger will slowly affect the mind of the sufferer. They become irritable, moody and are unable to focus on anything but thoughts of food. If they try to do any work, they soon find that their minds will drift.

I experienced this feeling many times but one event in particular sticks in my mind. I was at college taking an exam. I hadn't eaten for 72 hours and felt as though I was almost floating. I sat down with the exam paper in front of me and found that however hard I tried to concentrate, within a few minutes my mind would wander onto thoughts of food. I would look down at the paper and see that I had been writing out calorie information rather than the answers to the questions.

Lack of food affects your memory as well and I know this was also true in my case. I cannot remember much about the early 1990s. When I started talking with Simon, I realised that I didn't know any of the bands from that time. I can watch the television programmes about those years and not know any of the films or music that were popular at the time. I was living in my own tiny anorexic world and was unable to focus on anything except for the food I ate and how much I weighed.

It is not just memory loss and lack of concentration that are serious problems though. Starvation also makes it difficult for a person to think clearly. You find yourself unable to work out the solutions to even simple problems and the answers you finally come up with may be strange or irrational. Your thinking becomes even more black and white and you often start to believe that everyone is against you. If your weight is very low, you will be unable to work properly on any therapy because you will not be able to concentrate or understand the basic ideas. You may find it very hard to accept that you are ill and need help with your problems. The anorexia begins to take over your mind and although you may think you are fine, you are in fact extremely unwell.

Compulsive behaviour is a symptom of starvation and anorexics soon begin to develop strange rules and rituals that are centred around eating. Meals are planned hours or even days in advance. These meals will be of the lowest calorie foods possible and are usually tiny in size. Certain ritual ways of preparing the food can develop and the sufferer may well behave in an unusual way when they eat. Many anorexics cut their food into very small pieces and eat slowly. I would try to take exactly the same time each day to finish my meal, watching the clock to see if I was ahead or behind schedule. I had a certain set time for starting dessert after finishing my main course and I would not allow myself to eat any faster, however hungry I might be. For example, I had to take five minutes to eat every quarter of a sandwich. I was desperate for food and tried to make what little I ate last as long as possible.

Each day my menu plan had to be exactly the same and if the supermarket had sold out of my usual products, I fell to pieces. I was unable to just pick up a similar product - I had to have that exact one. My anorexic rules stated that I must eat only that type of food. Tears and anger often took over at times like these and although therapists would try to help me work through the feelings, I still felt unhappy that a rule had been broken. My doctors would encourage me to try to break the rules that I had set but as my diary shows, I would find this very frightening:

Monday January 20th 1997
The first rule that I have to break concerns what I eat for breakfast. Usually I have just dry toast. Tomorrow my doctor has said that I must have some jam on this as well and not just a thin scraping - it has to be the amount that a non-anorexic person would enjoy eating. I feel very scared and desperately want to back out of our agreement.

When I completed the task, it was always a long time before my mind could settle because I felt such intense guilt over breaking a rule.

Tuesday January 21st 1997
I did manage to add some jam to my toast this morning but it was so difficult, which must sound very stupid. I shook from the moment I woke up this morning. I dropped both my knife and the toast as I was making breakfast because I was so nervous. I didn't feel any satisfaction from completing this task either. I felt I was wrong to eat extra.

I would go to the supermarket with an exact list of the food that I needed to buy and gaze at the higher calorie brands, wishing I was allowed to eat them instead. The rules were set in my head though and breaking them was a crime as far as I was concerned. Sitting in restaurants was very difficult because I would see other people eating cakes and desperately want to have the same. The feelings of being pleased that I could resist were not enough to make me forget the unhappiness I felt at not being 'normal'.

For eating disorder sufferers, the preoccupation with food slowly takes over all aspects of their lives. Their social lives and friendships begin to disappear as meal times become central to their lives. I used to feel unable to go out near meal times and hated it if the phone rang or someone visited when I was about to eat. I would watch the clock and panic as the time when I usually started to eat my meal passed. When I had gone five minutes past my start time, I would then decide that I just couldn't eat. I believed that if I ate later than normal, all my meal times would merge together and I would feel too full. Instead, I would decide to just miss that meal out completely. This diary extract describes some of my feelings about meal times, as well as how I would react to the 'normal' amounts of food other people ate:

Sunday July 13th 1996
Food has been incredibly difficult this week. I haven't been able to have my usual meals at the right time and I've been skipping items from my diet plan here and there. I feel really guilty for not following my plan but I've been struggling to cope

with some very tough things that are going on in my life right now and not eating seems to help. I know that it's the escape route for me when my life becomes difficult. I feel that if I could just stop eating, then everything would be alright. Given time, I'd disappear and then there would be no problems anymore. The hurting would stop and I wouldn't be a nuisance to anyone again. At the moment I feel like an idiot and so stupid for being afraid of food. My brother and his family are staying with us this week and I've been watching everyone else eating. They never seem to worry about food. I constantly see how different I am to 'normal' people. My brother offered a cake round. I couldn't accept any and so he cut the cake into four pieces for himself and Gail, Mum and Dad. I couldn't believe what I'd seen. How can anyone eat a quarter of a cake?

I very rarely went out to eat because I felt too awkward and frightened. If I did go out for a meal, I would only feel comfortable if I was with my parents because I knew they would not force me to try anything new. I had a set meal that I would always have wherever we went - jacket potato and baked beans. I became extremely upset if the restaurant we were in didn't have a jacket potato on the menu and we would have to find somewhere else to eat. Waiting for the meal to arrive was a nightmare. I didn't hear any of the conversations between my parents because I was lost in my own private world of fear. I was shaking and hoping desperately that the meal would not be too large. If the plate was overflowing with potato and beans, I would feel instant horror. Tears would start to flow and I would be unable to manage even a single bite. This terror of eating out led me to isolate myself even more and I became increasingly withdrawn.

As an anorexic builds up more rules and rituals about food, their mind becomes conditioned. Whereas before their eating disorder started, they would have happily eaten food such as chocolate, they now associate chocolate with fat. In their head, fat is 'bad' and so chocolate must be avoided. If an anorexic ever does eat any chocolate, they believe they have broken a rule and will feel intense guilt and panic.

Starvation also causes the loss of sex hormones, which means that the desire to find a partner and have a relationship disappears. This can lead anorexics in particular to isolate themselves even further. They are not experiencing the emotions and feelings of other people their own age, and feel safer and more comfortable on their own.

Starvation and Bulimia

Bingeing often happens because a person is starving their body. When you feel cravings for food, this is your body telling you that it desperately needs to eat. The cravings will grow stronger the more you starve yourself until you can no longer fight them and binges occur. Whenever a binge happens, the sufferer usually responds by cutting down even further on food. This is likely to bring about more cravings and trigger more binges though and a cycle is quickly set.

The cravings are often for sweet foods, which lead bulimics to think that they are addicted to sugar. However, this is not a real addiction but just the body's natural reaction. If you have low blood sugar, you will crave sweet foods. The lower you keep your blood sugar level, the more sweet foods you will crave. When you then eat something sweet during a binge, the hormone **insulin** is released into the blood to allow the cells of the body to absorb the sugar. As these cells absorb all the sugar you have eaten, your blood sugar level falls again and you crave more sweet foods. This is why bulimics feel as though they can never eat enough chocolate or cake during a binge.

I will describe ways that you can stop bingeing in Chapter 17. It is very possible to stop completely. I have worked with many bulimia sufferers, helping them to reach a state where they eat a regular healthy diet again and no longer feel the need to binge.

If you have ever been on a diet, you will understand more clearly how binges can happen. Many dieters will skip breakfast in an attempt to save calories but by mid-morning, they are so hungry they will start eating sugary foods. We are surrounded by tempting food all the time and it can be very hard to resist these temptations when you are on a strict diet. Often a single slip from the diet is all it takes to cause a bulimic to lose control of their eating. If they have eaten just one chocolate cookie, they immediately feel like a failure and may binge in the belief that they have already ruined their diet.

In recent years, the diet industry has grown and every week a new weight loss programme, book or product is launched. Celebrities talk about their new diets and discuss details of weight loss during interviews. Women may be left feeling inadequate if they eat a normal healthy diet. It is very easy to see how food can become an obsession when we are constantly given so many mixed messages telling us how much we should eat.

Other reasons why food can become an obsession

Food can often be used to fill a gap in a person's life. Many bulimics will binge when they feel bored, anxious, angry, stressed or lonely. Food becomes a comfort at these times. Throughout our lives, we associate food with different feelings. As children we may see food as a symbol of love. Parents give us foods that are comforting, such as ice cream in the summer or warm desserts in the winter. These foods are often referred to as **comfort foods**. Often, eating disorder sufferers will turn back to these foods when they are feeling low - they are trying to substitute food for love. It is important to start to separate food from love in our minds because until this happens, eating disorder sufferers will continue to substitute one for the other.

When we are children, our parents often use food as a tool. It may be used as a reward or a punishment and this attitude can then continue into adulthood. Food is often given as a reward for an achievement. Often children are given sweets if they do something difficult or boring. My Mother would always buy me a box of sweets every time I had to go to the hospital. If I had to spend a day with a relative that I didn't want to visit, food would be the reward at the end of the day. We very quickly begin to link achievement with treats and as we grow up, continue to give ourselves food as a reward. If we have suffered a trauma or had a difficult day at school or work, we may treat ourselves to a bar of chocolate. Food becomes a way of easing pain and a 'solution' to all our problems. People often 'comfort eat' sweet and fatty foods in an attempt to cheer themselves up. They may have instant feelings of comfort but as they eat more and begin to worry about their weight, the depression sets in again. That feeling of depression can then lead them to eat even more and once again, a cycle has begun.

The other part of the equation is punishment. Parents often remove food when they are trying to punish a child. Most children will at some time have had sweets taken away from them if they have misbehaved. Some parents will go even further and withdraw food completely if they are angry with their child. They make threats using food, such as: *"You can only have a cookie if you do your homework."* Taken to extremes though, withholding food can actually be cruel and will leave a child hungry, angry and upset. It also teaches them the idea that when you feel a need to punish yourself, you can always deny yourself food. This is what anorexics do when they want to hurt or punish themselves.

Once the idea of using food as a form of punishment has been learned, it can then be taken to extremes in other ways too. If overeaters hate themselves, they may eat food they know will make them feel ill as a punishment. This can be extremely dangerous and may lead to serious stomach problems if it continues.

Parents often worry about children who seem to be 'fussy' eaters and who reject 'healthy' food, eating only 'junk' food instead. A parent may spend hours cooking a meal, only to find that their child will simply not eat it. This can be more than just a matter of taste and may in fact be part of a developing power struggle between the child and their parents. You may remember refusing to eat certain foods, such as vegetables. Parents often respond angrily to this kind of behaviour and say that their child cannot have any dessert until they have finished their vegetables, and so a power struggle begins. However, the parents' anger may be more to do with their own feelings of rejection rather than genuine concern about the child's diet. These power struggles can continue for years and it may become very important who wins each battle. If the child always loses and ends up eating many foods that they hate, they can grow up feeling powerless. These control issues during childhood are important in helping a child to develop their independence and identity.

A feeling of powerlessness may not just stop at meal times for children - it can continue throughout their lives. For example, a person who has learned they must eat everything on their plate can find they always do this, even when they are full. Constantly losing power struggles over food can also leave a person feeling inadequate in any later arguments. They are certain they will always lose and often feel it is much easier to just do everything that is expected of them. If a child has powerful parents then food can become the only way they feel able to assert any control. This can eventually lead people to overeat or to begin starving themselves and an eating disorder may develop.

When parents focus too strongly on when and how much a child should eat, that child is unlikely to learn how to respond properly to feelings of hunger. It is important that a child understands and recognises when they are hungry, and reacts to this by just eating. If meal times are too planned, children may find that they have to eat even though they are not hungry. This can lead to strange eating patterns developing as a child grows up, which can again lead to the development of eating problems.

Food may also be seen as a way of gaining attention and approval. Many anorexics will become so obsessed that they spend hours in the kitchen, just so they can be around food. They believe that cooking elaborate meals can also gain them the love and approval they need. I remember cooking a very special meal for my parents in an attempt to please them. It was my way of apologising to them for being unable to eat and I was trying to gain their approval through food instead. I was using that meal as my gift to them.

'Safe' and 'Unsafe' Foods

When food becomes an obsession and you develop rules about eating, you may also find that you start dividing food into the two groups of 'safe' and 'unsafe' foods. 'Safe' foods are those which contain very few calories and can be eaten without feeling too much guilt. 'Unsafe' (or 'forbidden') foods are higher in calories and fat, and the sufferers feel they are not allowed these because they may lead to weight gain. However, these are also the most tempting foods. They are the foods bulimics usually binge on when they break their diets and which anorexics will dream about. I used to feel strong cravings for sweets myself and this led me to start collecting chocolate bars. I would never allow myself to eat them but would hide them in my room anyway, so that I could look at them occasionally. I felt very ashamed of buying and storing this chocolate, so I hid it from my parents. I didn't feel I deserved this chocolate but the cravings were just too strong and I would continue to buy new bars even though I never ate them. I was torturing myself with this chocolate - unwrapping it, looking at it, smelling it and then hiding it away again.

When foods are forbidden, they become even more desirable and an eating disorder sufferer will find that they simply cannot stop thinking about them. When a sufferer finally allows themselves to eat forbidden foods (usually only during a binge), they may eat larger than normal quantities.

Some sufferers even decide that an entire food group is 'forbidden' (such as carbohydrates or proteins) and will stop eating these completely. The main problem is that although eating disorder sufferers read dieting books and magazines, they don't necessarily learn accurate information about nutrition. Their illness may lead them to cut out foods that are vital for a healthy life. As time passes and a sufferer falls deeper into their eating disorder, they discover they have fewer and fewer 'safe' foods. Even the lowest calorie foods start to feel 'unsafe'. A very important part of recovery is learning how to allow yourself to start eating the 'forbidden' foods again and I will show you how to do this later. It is important to learn that no food is off-limits. All food is allowed - it is just important to eat the right amount of each type for a healthy diet. It is all about taking back the control and not allowing your eating disorder to dictate what you can and cannot eat.

Chapter 13

What Is The 'Voice'?

Summary
Many eating disorder sufferers feel that they are controlled by a negative internal 'voice' which tells them how "wrong" it is to eat. This chapter describes this idea more clearly and shows constructive way to fight this 'voice'.

Many people with eating disorders feel as though they have a 'voice' in their head that controls their thinking. Some people feel it is an actual 'voice' that talks to them continually, telling them that food is bad and eating is wrong but starving is good. This 'voice' tells them that they are fat and should stop eating. Other people see this voice as the negative part of their own thinking. It is much easier to learn how to beat your eating disorder if you can identify this negative thinking as a 'voice'. I spent many years thinking in an anorexic way but it wasn't until I talked in hospital with another girl that I identified this thinking as a 'voice'. Suddenly, I felt more in control because now I had something to fight against. If you can identify all your destructive negative self-talk as a 'voice', you can also start to fight back.

Let me show you some of the statements that the 'voice' told me repeatedly:

"You are a disgusting, fat person. You don't even deserve to be alive."

"You can't eat that food - you are SO fat already."

"You must do more exercise - you are lazy and useless."

"Everyone hates you because you are a terrible person."

"You are selfish and weak. Why don't you just disappear?"

This diary extract shows the voice in action:

Friday April 25th 1997
I was managing all right today until lunchtime. I went on a shopping trip with my parents and we found a restaurant for lunch. Suddenly, everything went wrong. I was completely filled with anorexic feelings. The 'voice' in my head started to shout at me furiously:

'You are disgusting Anna. You're a total pig. Look at all that food on your plate. You know you've got to eat because everybody is watching you but you're going to hate yourself as soon as you take the first mouthful because it is greedy and wrong to eat.'

After the meal, I did hate myself. I felt the voice was right. I was a revolting and greedy person.

You may not be sure that you have a negative 'voice' in your head but the best time to work out if you do is when you are having a really bad day. Does it feel as though there is something talking to you, telling you off for being a failure? Many people are very afraid to admit to this idea of a 'voice', even if they know it is there. They are afraid that other people will say they are mentally ill if they admit to hearing a negative 'voice' in their head.

The 'voice' is all the negative, worrying, destructive thoughts in your life. For me, my 'voice' was my Grandmother. Even when she wasn't a part of my life any longer, I continued to hear her cruel comments in my head. Once I identified the 'voice', with its negative self-talk, I understood that I was a victim. To get better, I needed to fight back and take responsibility for getting rid of the 'voice'.

When an eating disorder sufferer can identify their inner 'voice' they start to realise that they are listening to it, rather than to everyone else around them. People would tell me that I was dangerously thin and yet I still believed my anorexic 'voice', which said I was fat and needed to lose weight. When doctors told me that my health was in serious danger, I didn't even hear them. I only listened to the 'voice', which told me that there was nothing wrong with me. It said that the doctors were just trying to scare me into putting on weight so that I would become fat.

Being AWARE of this negative 'voice' is the first step towards recovery. I can remember a huge feeling of relief when I talked with another sufferer about the 'voice'. We compared the comments our 'voices' made and were amazed to see just how similar they were. When you are aware of having a 'voice' in your head then you can move on to the next step, which is to ANALYSE the voice.

This second step is all about stopping and looking at every statement the 'voice' makes. Each time the 'voice' speaks negatively, it will affect your feelings because thoughts always affect feelings. This is the idea behind **cognitive therapy**. If you are thinking negative thoughts, you will feel negative emotions such as sadness or anger. If you are thinking positive thoughts though, you will feel much happier. As soon as you are aware of the 'voice' in your head, you can start to see how it affects your moods. If a 'voice' in your head is shouting negative statements at you, you will start to feel very low.

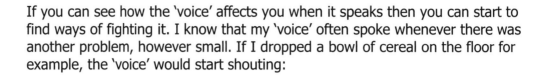

If you can see how the 'voice' affects you when it speaks then you can start to find ways of fighting it. I know that my 'voice' often spoke whenever there was another problem, however small. If I dropped a bowl of cereal on the floor for example, the 'voice' would start shouting:

"You are such a clumsy, careless person. You make such a mess all the time and do everything wrong."

Now, not only was I dealing with the mess on the floor but I also had to fight my own negative feelings. It had gone from being a simple accident to an attack on me as a person.

The third step is to start FIGHTING the 'voice'. There are several different methods of fighting the negative words of the 'voice' by talking to yourself in a positive way instead. One method is to learn how to use cognitive therapy. Every time you hear the 'voice' and its negative comments, you need to argue back. Let's use that example of dropping the bowl of cereal to show how this works:

The negative 'voice' in your head says:

"You are a clumsy careless person. You make such a mess all the time and do everything wrong."

If I had been told that, I would then feel very depressed and start to hate myself for doing everything wrong. To counter these negative feelings and change my mood into a more positive one, I would need to think positive thoughts and talk to myself in a positive way instead:

"You are not a clumsy person. Everyone has accidents and that is all this was. An accident. You don't do everything wrong. You do lots of things right all of the time. Why are you being so cruel to yourself? If someone else had spilled the cereal, would you have called them clumsy and careless?"

When you start to understand the 'voice' in your head, you begin to realise that it uses black and white thinking. If you make one small mistake, it will tell you that you always do everything wrong. People with eating disorders often feel that positive thinking alone cannot rid them of their negative 'voice'. Before you can use the positive thinking though, you often have to shout back at the voice first to take away some of its power. Then you need to use your positive thinking to REPLACE the negative thoughts in your head and this is the fourth step.

These four steps are VERY important for your recovery, so I am going to list them here again to make it completely clear.

1. Recognise the 'voice' in your head that speaks negatively and criticises to you.
2. Discover how the 'voice' affects your mood so that you can work out ways of fighting it.
3. Fight the 'voice' by shouting at it and telling it that you will not listen to it's negative messages.
4. Replace the negative words of the 'voice' with positive self-talk.

There are many ways that the 'voice' hurts you with its negative self-talk. These are some of the tricks that it uses:

a) Black and white thinking - As I mentioned above, the 'voice' uses black and white thinking all of the time. The 'voice' says that if you are not perfect then that means you are a failure.

b) 'Mind reading' - The 'voice' tries to tell you that other people are thinking badly about you all the time. It will encourage you to try to work out what people are feeling and it will always tell you that they hate you.

c) Blame - The 'voice' encourages you to blame yourself for everything that goes wrong. It will tell you that you are always at fault.

d) Magnification - The voice takes every situation and magnifies the negative aspects. Any positive views are removed so that only the negative aspects remain.

e) Jumping to conclusions - The 'voice' can take one small piece of information and use it to exaggerate a situation, making it seem far worse than it really is. If something negative happens once, the 'voice' tells you that this will happen every time.

f) Lying - The voice will constantly lie to you. It will tell you things that are not true and then repeat them many times. For anorexics, the most obvious example of this is the 'voice' telling them they are fat when in fact they are thin.

g) Labels - The 'voice' will always be cruel and label you on the basis of one tiny piece of evidence. For example if you get a 'B' grade instead of an 'A' grade on a test, it will tell you that you are the most stupid person alive.

h) Fills you with fear - The 'voice' constantly tries to frighten you. It tells you that if you eat, you will never be able to stop. It says that you will go out of control and become fat.

i) Gives you responsibility - The voice will keep telling you that you are responsible for other people's happiness. It says you have to behave in a certain way to keep people happy and if they look sad then it is your fault.

j) Rules - The 'voice' sets you rules in all aspects of your life but especially about food. It will tell you how many calories you are allowed to eat, how much exercise you should do, etc.

k) Denial is good - The 'voice' will try to convince you that not eating is right. It will say that you do not deserve anything good in your life. It tells you that it's selfish and wrong to think of yourself and that you must never do anything nice.

l) The 'voice' will tell you that it is right - The 'voice' constantly says that it is right and that even if other people tell you that it lies, they are the ones who are wrong. It tells you that doctors are lying to you about your weight just so that they can make you fat. It will also tell you that it is your only friend.

The following are some very common 'voice' statements and I want to show you just how wrong they all are. You can always find an answer for any comment from the 'voice' because it lies all the time and you can use the truth to defeat it. It is very important to remember that you often need to shout at the 'voice' to be quiet first, before replacing it's negative words with positive ones.

"You made a mistake and that means you are a terrible, useless person."

Look at the way the voice immediately uses sweeping statements. You make a small mistake and it instantly tells you that you are a terrible, useless person. This is a huge exaggeration and it makes you feel like an instant failure. STOP and THINK. What if someone else had made a small mistake - would you call them 'terrible' or 'useless'? Everybody makes mistakes each and every day. This is just human nature. You have to learn to be gentler on yourself. Forgive yourself rather than always pointing the finger of blame and saying that you are at fault.

"You are a horrible person and everyone hates you."

This is another black and white statement that is completely untrue. The 'voice' likes to use words like 'everyone' or 'everything'. This is just the 'voice' trying to torment you. It is hard to believe that every single person you know hates you. Even someone who has done a great many things wrong is not hated by everyone around them. Try and gather evidence to fight the voice rather than just instantly believing it.

"You must never ask for help because that just proves what a failure you are."

The 'voice' doesn't ever want you to ask for help. It needs to isolate you because if you talk about your problem, someone might help you to fight it. Asking for help does not mean that you are failing - it actually means that you are succeeding. You are admitting that you cannot cope alone and need some help to get better. The truth is that strong people ask for help and others usually feel honoured when you share your problems with them. Once again, you need to turn the situation around. How would you feel if a friend of yours was in trouble but did not want to ask you for help because they were being a 'nuisance'?

"If you go for treatment, you will just end up fat."

The 'voice' does not want you to accept treatment because that would mean you were gaining control back from it. It is trying to frighten you with these words and you must fight back. By now you should understand that when you have an eating disorder, you cannot see the reality of your size. You think that you are fat when in fact you are thin. Remember that doctors only want you to reach a healthy weight. They do not want you to be 'fat'. Every time the voice shouts 'fat' at you, try to substitute the word 'healthy' instead.

"If you eat that bite of food, you will grow huge instantly."

Remember how the 'voice' constantly lies and exaggerates? You have to hit back at it with facts. A person has to eat an extra 3,500 calories on top of their healthy daily intake to put on just one pound. How can the 'voice' be right when it says that one bite of food will make you grow huge? It can be very reassuring for eating disorder sufferers to learn that it is not easy to put on weight. You have to eat a lot of extra food to gain even a single pound.

Let me share a diary extract of mine with you, to show how the voice always lies to you about food.

Sunday January 19th 1997
I feel a failure today. I just cannot make food decisions. Whenever I try to eat something, I always end up choosing the lower calorie option because of the 'voice' in my head. I tried to eat something that was a little higher in calories and it just started shouting at me:

"No, no, no, no! You cannot eat that food! It contains calories and will make you fat overnight. If you eat that food, it will just prove that you are a terrible person." I understand that I cannot let the voice win but I don't feel I deserve to eat nice food like other people. The 'voice' tells me that I am a bad person and I believe it.

I know that I have set myself so many rules about food and exercise but I don't know how to break them.

"You must never get upset and cry because that shows weakness."

Many people with eating disorders do not think they are allowed to cry because that would make them look weak. It is the 'voice' that puts this idea into their heads. It tells them that to be a "success" they must always be calm and never get upset or show any emotions. This is wrong because it is actually very healthy to express ourselves. If we bottle them up inside, they can only damage us. I know I feel very pleased when someone is able to cry in front of me. They are showing me trust and allowing themselves to be open and honest.

"You must never say anything that hurts anyone."

Once again, the 'voice' is telling you how to behave and trying to frighten you by saying that you are behaving wrongly. It is not possible for us to please other people all of the time. The 'voice' tries to convince you that you must never say anything that upsets others because if you did that, you would be a terrible person. Yet again, you are being given very strict rules. There will be times when we say things that upset someone else. You cannot go through life never upsetting others - sometimes you have to stand up for yourself and this may well hurt somebody else's feelings. It does not mean this behaviour is wrong though. Standing up to someone who is treating you badly may not always be popular but it is the right thing to do.

When I had to talk to my Mother about a problem with food, I ended up feeling like a horrible person because I upset her. The 'voice' backed up these feelings and shouted at me constantly. The truth was that it actually took courage for me to confront my Mother and I needed to do that for my own health, something she understood in time. This diary extract explains more fully:

Monday July 7th 1997
My doctor told me that I had to talk to my Mum today about her behaviour around food. I am very worried that she has serious food issues and these are really affecting me at the moment. I was shaking when I said the words: "I'm feeling hurt because I think you are playing 'food games' with me." Mum immediately tried to hurt me in return with some comments that made me feel terrible. I now feel like the world's most difficult and evil person. She then said: "Let's tell your Father what you have just said so that he can see how difficult you are to live with." I started to cry and the 'voice' in my head started to yell:

"You are such a stupid, useless, weak person. All you do is upset other people all of the time. You don't even deserve to live on this planet. Why don't you just starve yourself so that you are no longer a problem for everyone?"
I wish I could die just like the 'voice' wants.

"Change is terrible - you must always eat the same food and do the same things all the time."

The 'voice' wants us to follow a strict set of rules and never stray from these. This way we are kept totally under control and the 'voice' is always in charge. Once again, the 'voice' is wrong because change can actually be very good. I remained stuck in my anorexic life for many years, terrified of changing and becoming an adult. I felt that the responsibility of being an adult was just too scary. It wasn't until I started to make changes that I saw how they could actually be positive steps forward. Change gives you new opportunities. You are given the chance to grow and develop in many different ways. Life can be exciting if you allow yourself to try new opportunities. If you reject change, your life will remain static.

I want to finish this chapter by giving you some further tools to help fight the voice. The following is a list of positive statements that you can shout back at the 'voice' when it starts repeating cruel comments in your head:

"I am my own person and I can make my own decisions. I do not need to listen to your cruel words."

"I have facts and evidence to back up my statements. You are just lying to me."

"Feelings and thoughts cannot destroy me unless I let them - I won't let you win."

"You are the one that makes me feel bad all the time 'voice'. I am taking away your power. I am NOT going to listen to you any more."

"I am stronger than you 'voice'. I am going to win and you are going to lose."

"I am human and I am allowed to make mistakes. I don't have to be perfect."

"Nothing bad will happen to me if I stop listening to you. In fact, good things will start to happen and I will begin to feel well again."
"I am no longer going to hate myself 'voice' but I am going to hate YOU instead. I will get rid of you for good."

"Anger can help me if I use it properly and I am going to use it against you 'voice'. I am very angry because you are ruining my life and I will not let that happen to me any longer."

"I am not weak because I ask for help. I am brave to do this and I will succeed."

"I realise that it is you 'voice' that fills me with bad feelings. I am going to stop listening to you - you cannot pass your guilt and fear onto me."
"No matter what mistakes I make, I am still a valuable worthwhile person."

"I am not a failure. I am a success because I am fighting you 'voice'."

"Your cruel words keep me a prisoner in my eating disorder. I will not let you do that to me any longer. I can set myself free."

"I am strong and I can cope in any situation. I may not feel very confident but I can cope if I go in alone without my negative 'voice'."

"I am not ever going to agree with you 'voice' because that just takes away my power. I will not allow you to make me powerless."

"I refuse to let you make me into a helpless victim."

All of these statements are true and will help you fight the negative 'voice' in your head. Perhaps you can think of some more of your own to add to this list. Use them as often as you need to and gradually the 'voice' will lose its power and start to fade. This doesn't happen overnight and I will show you lots of other ways to help beat your eating disorder but fighting the voice is the first step towards getting your life back.

Chapter 14

Why do I feel the need to Hurt Myself? Self-Harming and Eating Disorders

Summary
Often self-harming is closely linked to eating disorders. This chapter looks at the reasons why sufferers feel a "need" to punish themselves.

This chapter about self-harming will be quite personal. By sharing my experiences, I hope I can explain more clearly why self-harming happens. Self-harming is very closely linked to eating disorders because sufferers often feel a need to punish themselves and will do this in many different ways. Instead, I WANT to focus on why people self-harm. For myself, there were two reasons.

Firstly, I believed I was such a 'bad' person that I deserved pain and needed to be punished. The way I did this was by cutting my body in places where no one would see. Once I had punished myself and could see the blood flowing and feel the pain, I felt better. I believed that I had paid the price for being a 'bad' person. However, this instant feeling of relief soon passed when I realised what I had done. I would then begin to worry that people would be angry with me if they knew I had damaged myself.

Secondly, I self-harmed in an attempt to shut out feelings and emotions. I thought that if I hurt myself physically, perhaps I could block out all the mental pain I was feeling. This never worked though and I just ended up hurting both mentally and physically. Although at the time I was cutting myself I could not feel any of the pain, when the angry 'red mist' in my head started to clear, the physical pain from the cuts began.

I started self-harming at the age of 12, when the emotional pain I felt inside became too much for me to bear. I started off by hitting myself hard in the chest. I felt that was where the pain was locked away and if I hit myself hard enough, perhaps it would disappear. Of course the hitting didn't help and I just ended up very bruised. This didn't stop me though and I switched to cutting instead. I started to hurt my hands and if anyone asked about the cuts, I just said I'd had an accident. I realised that I couldn't make excuses forever though, so I started to cut myself in areas where no one would notice. However, I had forgotten about school sports lessons and soon realised that I had to change my clothes in the toilets or else people would notice my cuts.

Throughout my 14 years as an anorexic, I used cutting as a release. I turned to it whenever I couldn't cope with my feelings of being a 'bad' person or was struggling with increases in my food intake or weight. I was actually making the situation much worse by self-harming but I couldn't see that and did not feel able to stop. It is very important to remember that what you do to your body now may well affect you for the rest of your life. I have been left with many scars from my years of self-harming. I hate these scars and feel self-conscious about wearing short sleeves, in case people notice them. Scars are with you for life so STOP and THINK before you start self-harming. This is not a solution to your problems and is just creating more problems for you in the future.

Although it is not always easy for people to understand self-harming, please do not let this stop you from asking for help. Telling my parents about the cutting was very difficult but I knew that I needed to explain to them exactly why I hurt myself. My Mother did focus more on the physical cuts rather than the emotional pain which had led me to self-harm. However, my Father understood the reasons why I self-harmed more clearly since he had tried to hurt himself as a child when he felt unloved.

There were many different feelings that led me to turn to self-harming. Using some entries from my diaries, I want to show you a few of the incidents that led me to hurt myself. All of these situations could have been dealt with better and further on in this chapter, I will show you healthy ways of coping with these negative feelings.

For me, guilt was a very strong trigger. If I felt I had hurt or upset someone I would punish myself. For example, when I started to tell my parents about the abuse I received from my Grandmother, I felt terrible as his diary entry explains:

Friday October 16th 1998
I'm having a really bad time with my feelings at the moment. Since I've started talking about Gran's abuse I have felt so guilty. I feel as though I am betraying her and I feel horrible for telling Mum and Dad. I don't think they should have to hear this stuff. They'll just get hurt and upset and will end up hating me. I hated myself so much today that I started self-harming again. The emotional pain inside is so bad right now that I want to die but I just can't tell anyone about these feelings.

I often felt that I shouldn't share my feelings with anyone else and would harm myself instead as I tried to cope alone. I did not realise that if I shared my thoughts and feelings, people might have been able to help me more.

Monday November 23rd 1998
I was supposed to phone my doctor whenever I felt like cutting myself but I just

couldn't. I felt that was too selfish of me. After all, she deserves her time off without me calling on her all the time. I just feel like I am a bad person through and through. I cannot tell other people my problems because I would only be burdening them. I know how horrified my parents would be if they saw the self-harming, so I have to keep that a secret. I promised my doctor that I wouldn't cut again because the last ones became infected under their stitches but I feel I deserve to hurt. I feel I HAVE to cut myself because I deserve pain. I cannot see any light at the moment. It's as though I am trapped in a dark pit.

The following diary extract shows how feelings from my childhood still affected me as an adult:

Tuesday December 8th 1998
I have not done very well today. I felt physically ill and also a complete failure. My parents went out and I was left alone in the house. My Gran rang and I just froze. I couldn't pick up the phone but instead let her message run onto the answerphone. Her voice triggered so many memories and I just started crying as if I would never be able to stop. I felt so bad about myself and was certain that the abuse only happened because I deserved bad treatment. I was crying from all the pain and at the same time started wishing so much that I was a nice person. I felt I deserved to hurt and grabbed a knife so that I could cut myself. The crying and the cutting went on for hours, until I realised that Mum and Dad were due home. I cleaned myself up so quickly. I couldn't let them know what I had done.

If I felt I had eaten some food that I didn't deserve to have I would also cut myself, as this diary extract shows:

Sunday December 27th 1998
I felt so hopeless today. I've reached the point where I'm finding it so difficult to cope. I hurt so much inside. I don't know what to do with myself. Today I did something that tipped me over the edge. I ate some chocolate. I felt the most unbelievable guilt after I did this and had to punish myself. My head was filled with the loudest 'voice', shouting at me for being such a terrible person and I started to cut myself. It was dark, I couldn't see what I was doing and I just lashed out at myself. When I saw how bad the cuts were, I started to cry. I'm losing control and I just don't know how to cope. I felt I had to punish myself for eating chocolate. Chocolate is enjoyable and only good people deserve to eat it. I am not allowed to have any because I am not allowed to ever enjoy myself.

Feelings of sadness were another trigger for me to self-harm and when I felt the need to block out the pain I was feeling inside, I would start cutting.

Tuesday November 17th 1998
Today has been so horrible. I tried to keep a "smiley" face on for Mum and Dad because I didn't want them to worry about me but inside I was crying with pain. I cut myself again to try and block out some of the emotional pain with physical pain. I cut myself many times, very deeply and they poured blood. As I hurt myself, I didn't even feel any pain. I finally allowed myself to cry and sat on the bathroom floor with blood running down my arms. I am finally remembering all the nightmares of my childhood that I had locked up inside my head for so long. It feels as if I am reliving the events and I am just so frightened.

Tension is another common trigger that causes eating disorder sufferers to hurt themselves. Bulimics often binge to try to relieve the stress in their lives and if this does not work then they can also turn to self-harming. They may also have such strong feelings of guilt after a bingeing and vomiting session that they feel a 'need' to hurt themselves.

Feelings of anger could also trigger a self-harming episode. I would never allow myself to show any anger to my family, so whenever I felt annoyed, frustrated or angry, I would turn on myself instead. When Simon and I were first together, this was still the way that I dealt with any problems. I was unable to express my anger or frustration healthily and instead would run from him and try to hurt myself. This obviously terrified him and during any difficult times, he would often physically hold onto me so that I couldn't run into the bathroom and cut myself. After we had been together for a few months, I could see the intense pain I caused Simon if I ever hurt myself. I realised that the cutting wasn't just about me and my feelings any longer. I had to take his feelings into account as well. Since I couldn't bear to hurt him, I finally promised to never self-harm again. This hasn't been an easy promise to keep but I have now gone for a very long time without self-harming and the instant urge to cut myself when I am upset is starting to fade.

When I made this promise to Simon, I realised that I had to find healthier ways of dealing with the emotions that triggered the self-harming. The following are some alternative ways of expressing 'negative' feelings:

How to cope with anger and tension without self-harming

All eating disorder sufferers experience anger but as we have already seen, it is an emotion that they usually find frightening and try to deny. It is important to allow these feelings to surface rather than to constantly block them out. When you do start to allow yourself to express anger, you soon realise that it isn't such a monster after all but is simply another emotion.

It is important to learn that we are allowed to show anger. I once threw a plate of mushy peas at the wall when I felt very frustrated. I knew that I wanted to self-harm but instead I expressed all my rage by throwing the plate. The relief was instant and although I did have to spend a while clearing up the mess, it was a healthier option for me. I am not suggesting that you start throwing around the family china BUT it is possible to express anger in a healthy way.

How about throwing a stuffed toy against the wall instead? Many people choose to punch a pillow for a few minutes to allow themselves to express their strong feelings of anger. Others choose to rip or scrunch up paper.

If you are in a place where you cannot be overheard, how about shouting loudly or screaming? I have done this and it can feel a great relief. Simon and I have even howled in harmony together when we were driving and it cheered us both up. One simple therapy exercise is to concentrate on a spot on the ceiling and focus all your anger on it. Get the feelings out of yourself by firing them at this spot instead.

Another idea is to write a letter to the person that you are feeling angry with. This may be a letter that you never post but by writing down your thoughts, you are removing them from your head. In this letter say exactly what you are feeling, even if you think that the words might sound harsh or cruel. These feelings need to be expressed because as long as they remain in your head, they are causing you pain. Once the thoughts are down on paper, you will realise that you can finally stop thinking about them. You know that they won't ever be forgotten because they are safely in the letter but you can now allow yourself some freedom from them. Some people suggest that when you have finished writing your letter, you should read it aloud to yourself so that you experience all those feelings one last time before finally throwing the letter away. I leave this choice to you. I have kept many of my therapy letters and although I have never felt a need to read them again, they have helped other people understand my feelings more clearly.

Relaxation exercises can also help you to learn how to deal with anger. There are many different relaxation exercises that you can use. These may ask you to imagine that you are in a place where you feel happy and comfortable - walking along an empty beach on a sunny day for example. You have to try and experience all the wonderful, calming emotions that you would be feeling if you were actually there.

It is important to work out if you are using your anger correctly though. Anger is sometimes used as a cover for other emotions such as fear or shame. This is a way of trying to protect yourself from being vulnerable. Instead of showing people that you are afraid or feel ashamed, you are showing them anger as a defence. When you next feel 'angry', try to work out if it is really anger that you are feeling or if you are actually just trying to cover another emotion. If you are covering up another emotion it is important to deal with that feeling instead and in time, you will find that your anger fades.

Talking to the person that you are feeling angry with also often helps. If you can never express your anger, then the only person you are really hurting is yourself. It is very important to hand back your anger to the person who upset you. However, it is not always easy to get angry with the right person, at the right time, in the right way. Often when people try to express anger, it comes out too strongly and they make comments that hurt the other person. If you can take a break and work out exactly how you need to express your anger, you can help both yourself and the other person. Let me give you an example of this. I felt hurt and upset when I was once wrongly accused of breaking a mug. I felt very angry but I did not try and express this anger correctly. Instead, I turned it upon myself and started to self-harm. What I should have done was said: *"I feel hurt and upset that you are saying I broke this mug. It wasn't actually me who did this and I feel angry that you are accusing me."* If I had done this, I would probably have received an apology, my anger would have faded and I wouldn't have self-harmed.

If you cannot talk directly to the person you feel angry with, why not have a conversation on paper instead? Write down what you want to say and fill in the other person's part too. Talk openly and say exactly what you feel you want from the other person. Try and do this without pointing the finger of blame and do your best to see the problem from both sides. This is often harder than just writing a letter expressing your feelings because you will also be looking at the other person's feelings and the reasons for their behaviour too.

Another idea is to talk aloud to the person that you are angry with when you are alone. Pretend that they are sitting in a chair beside you and tell them exactly how you are feeling. Venting your anger can leave you feeling very emotional though, as many other feelings often surface when you express yourself in this way. It is very wise to have someone close who you can turn to for comfort after you have tried this exercise.

Learn to recognise your feelings of anger and see how easily these can snowball. You will see just how quickly your angry feelings can grow. However, if you constantly let them build up without allowing them an outlet, they can become dangerous. When you feel yourself getting increasingly angry at a particular situation, learn how to calm yourself down. Anorexics, for example, may feel intense anger when someone offers them food. Remind yourself that this is an instant anorexic reaction. You are seeing the food as a threat and you need to talk yourself through these feelings of fear. Tell yourself that your body needs food to survive and it is only the anorexic 'voice' that feels angry and threatened. You ARE allowed to eat and you need to use these feelings of anger to help you shout back at the anorexic 'voice' instead.

Anger can be a positive emotion and if you use it in the correct way, you can bring about real change. For example, if you are being abused and are feeling intense anger, DON'T turn this anger on yourself but instead use it to find a solution for your problem. Speaking out could be the solution because abusers rely on their victims staying silent. Sharing your problem with a friend means that there will be two of you working to find an answer. Use your anger properly and allow it to empower you.

If you are seeing a therapist, there are other exercises that you can do together. I was asked to push really hard against my therapist's hand, so that I felt as if I was pushing away all the anger and fear that I had left inside me from my childhood abuse. I found this difficult at first because I was afraid of hurting my therapist and actually found that pushing against a wall helped me even more. I also did a lot of role-playing with my therapists, which helped me to deal with my anger and I will describe this further in Chapter 16.

If you have been abused there are some different ideas you can try, to get rid of the strong anger you are feeling. They are about showing your anger to the abuser so that you take the power back from them. These are some of the different ways of focusing your anger:

- Draw a picture of your abuser. Talk to the picture as if you are telling the abuser how angry you feel and then tear the picture into little pieces.
- Imagine that your abuser is sitting in the chair beside you and then ask people who love you to shout at the abuser for you. This can help you to learn that you did NOT deserve the abuse you received.
- Make a clay model of your abuser and then squash it and hit it.

If you are finding it hard to deal with your anger alone, you could try an anger workshop or anger management course. These are very popular and you should be able to discover more about them from your local family doctor. You may find that your school or college even runs some classes to show you how to deal better with your anger.

Remember that being able to show your anger is a GOOD step forward - you are starting to change your life for the better. Doctors are often very excited when their eating disorder patients begin to show outward signs of anger. You may find that the first time you get angry, you need to do it with someone who makes you feel safe. I was able to become angry with Simon because he was the person I felt safest with. At first, I felt afraid of my anger because it seemed so powerful and I was not sure if I could control it. Many of the different techniques I have listed above helped me to learn how to control my anger and express it in a positive way.

How to cope with sadness, fear and guilt

Allow yourself to cry. You are NOT weak if you cry. We all experience feelings of sadness and you are just releasing emotions that need to be expressed. I believed that if I started crying, I would never be able to stop. I was wrong. When I finally did allow myself to cry, I soon learned that my tears naturally stopped after a while. I also found that releasing my pent up emotions helped me to feel better.

Talk about your feelings. We all need people that we can share our feelings and emotions with at times. If you feel that there is no one in your family or circle of friends that you can open up to, then remember your doctor. Doctors are not just there for physical illnesses. They are also there to help you with the stresses in your life and if they cannot help you personally then they can refer you to a therapist or counsellor, who will be able to help you further.

Write down your feelings. Remember the idea of writing out a letter to help you deal with anger? Well this can also be used when you are feeling guilty or sad. Write down all your feelings in a letter. You don't have to post the letter but you may find that these thoughts no longer hold so much power when they are written down on paper.

'Hand back' the bad feelings to the people who hurt you in the past. This is a therapy exercise that I learned while in hospital. We were all asked to draw a diagram with ourselves at the centre of the paper and all the people who had hurt us in a circle around us. Then individually we had to draw arrows between ourselves and the other people. Along these arrows, we listed all the bad feelings we remembered that each person had left us with. By drawing this diagram, we were 'handing back' those bad feelings. The arrows were going out from us towards the other people.

Keep a "Thoughts and Feelings" diary. This was a therapy exercise I started when I left hospital and I found it very helpful. You will have seen some diary extracts throughout this book - all of these came from my "Thoughts and Feelings" diaries. I found it difficult to express my feelings during therapy sessions and my doctor suggested that I write them down each day instead. Gradually, through writing, I became more able to talk about my feelings. I realised that it was alright to say if I was feeling sad, guilty or ill. The doctor did not think I was complaining but was actually relieved to know how I was feeling. I encourage many people to write down their thoughts and feelings when they are going through a particularly hard time. It isn't easy to re-create these emotions later and doctors often need to know your exact feelings. They can then help you learn how to cope better the next time you are having problems.

116

Cognitive behaviour therapy. This is a very good therapy tool, which can help you to deal with difficult emotions. I will show you how this works in Chapter 16.

Suicide - The Worst Kind of Self-Harming

A large number of the deaths linked to anorexia and bulimia are suicides. It is currently thought that nearly a third of all sufferers attempt to kill themselves at some time during their illness. I also tried to kill myself at the age of 19. Suicide is often seen as an instant cry for help but no one can help you if you die, so it is VERY important to realise that this is not a solution to your problems. A friend of mine once wisely described suicide as: *"A permanent solution to a temporary problem."* In other words, suicide is a final 'solution'. You are giving no one a chance to help. I know a number of people who had friends that committed suicide. They still desperately wish that their friends had turned to them and asked for help instead of killing themselves. There is help available though and at the back of this book, I have listed some different organisations that can offer support if you are having suicidal thoughts. Remember that your family doctor will also be able to help in many different ways. Please accept some help rather than trying to fight on alone.

Many of the suicide related deaths from eating disorders occur when a sufferer's weight has increased or when they feel that they have overeaten. If an anorexic has spent many years at a low weight, they may struggle to cope with healthy weight gain. Living at a healthy weight can be difficult for many anorexics and I will show you different ways of coping with these feelings in Chapter 19.

I do understand the feelings of desperation that can lead a person to take their own life because I have been there many times myself. This diary extract explains more:

Friday October 30th 1998
I haven't got anything positive to write in my diary tonight so I don't think I should write anything at all. I feel that all I ever do is complain in my diary. I am not like that in normal life. I try so hard to always be cheerful. Strangely, the worse the emotional pain is inside of me, the happier I appear to everyone else. It reminds me of a clown. They have this happy face painted on the outside that is so jolly and nobody can see how they are feeling inside. I don't think my parents know how bad I am feeling at the moment. I just can't tell them how scared and alone I feel. I can't burden them with my fears. I hurt so much right now that I don't even want to live. The pain inside is so bad that I want to drive a stake right through the centre of me so that I can just stop hurting.

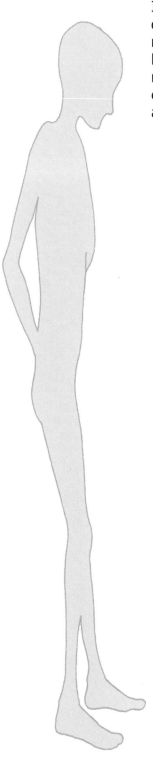

I now look back at these diary extracts and cannot believe quite how far I have come. If you are really struggling, do please remember that things can change. I no longer ever feel this desperate and enjoy my life completely. With Simon, I lead a full and contented adult life and realise that if I had succeeded in killing myself at 19, I would have missed out on so much. Although I have not led an easy life, I am grateful for all that happened to me because my experiences have allowed me to help others who are now struggling as I once did.

Chapter 15

Am I Happy at Home?
A Look at Family Relationships

Summary

Relationships within the family often have a strong influence on the development of an eating disorder. This chapter looks more closely at this issue and the ways in which family members can help sufferers with recovery.

In this chapter I want to look at how eating disorders affect family life and how disruptive they can be. I also want to show how a family's behaviour may cause a person to turn towards an eating disorder.

When you suffer from an eating disorder, it will affect your relationship with family and friends. Some families pretend that the eating disorder does not exist because the parents feel ashamed that their child has such a frightening illness. They may build a wall around themselves as a family and appear to be happy and successful to the outside world. Behind that wall though, they are hiding feelings of shame, confusion and fear. People who know such a family can see that there is a serious problem but are often afraid to speak to them about it. If they try to talk openly with the parents, they are pushed away and told that everything is fine.

Parents are often unsure about how to treat a child who is suffering from an eating disorder. They are watching their child slowly die and don't know the best way to react. Sometimes they can become very angry because meal times always seem to be battlegrounds. They may resent the fact that their child constantly rejects their food and any attempts at care. At other times, they might try very hard to understand and help in any way possible. They may buy special diet foods in the hope that this might persuade their child to eat. These mood swings from feelings of anger to desperately trying to help are natural for parents but they do not help eating disorder sufferers. They can make home life very difficult and traumatic. It is common for sufferers to feel angry and hurt that their parents don't understand their eating disorder. Parents may get frustrated at times and shout comments such as: *"Why don't you just snap out of it?"* Unfortunately, some parents do blame their child for the eating disorder developing and this obviously makes the problem much worse.

It is very easy to judge parents harshly at this point but it is important to remember that however difficult it is to live with an eating disorder, it is also very painful to watch someone you love suffering from one. Rather than just be criticised, parents need to be educated about the best ways they can help their children. I believe that it is very important to involve the whole family in treatment. A lot of eating disorders develop because there are family problems and although for some families the damage is beyond repair, there is hope for others. The parents of eating disorder sufferers are often very caring and do want the best for their children. However, because of problems in their own past, they may have developed negative ways of behaving. These negative behaviour patterns have then affected their children and led to the development of the eating disorder.

I am going to start by suggesting some ways that you may be able to improve your family situation, so that you can feel more comfortable at home. I understand that these ideas will not work in every case but it is important to think very carefully before you reject them. If you are going to try for recovery, it is important that as many people as possible are on your side.

If you haven't told your parents about your eating disorder, think carefully about whether you should. How about writing a list of all the positive reasons for telling your parents about your eating problems and also a list of the reasons why you don't think you should tell them? Look at these two lists and think seriously about whether it would benefit you to talk with them.

If you have told your parents about your eating disorder but actually found that this has made things worse, then you need to re-think the situation. Do they know enough about eating disorders to really help you? How about sharing a book that you found helpful with them? Perhaps they could contact an eating disorder association and ask for more information about the different ways that parents can help their children.

How about asking your doctor to talk with your parents? Most doctors know how important it is for parents to be involved in treatment programmes. It often helps if doctors can explain more about anorexic and bulimic behaviour to parents. Some parents do understand anorexic behaviour but unfortunately cannot cope with their child behaving in a bulimic way. Bulimia is a very hard illness for the sufferer to handle, as they usually feel deep shame. If their parents are constantly watching and criticising them too, it can make the situation even worse. If you confide in your doctor, he or she may be able to help you with these problems.

Explain to your parents the best ways that they can help you to cope with your illness. Tell them about your feelings during meal times and give them some positive ideas about ways that they can help. If you are constantly telling your parents that they are not helping you, this can actually make things worse. It is always better to encourage people to help rather than criticising them for not behaving correctly. By showing them how they can help, you could all begin to make some progress.

Many parents make the mistake of never talking with their children about the eating disorder. It soon becomes a taboo subject in the house, until eventually the sufferer feels betrayed when they discover that their parents have been talking about them behind their back. This often happened in my house. My parents very rarely talked to me about my anorexia because they mistakenly believed that this would upset me. I was too afraid to share my feelings with them and we ended up living in our own separate little worlds. I was frightened because I never knew what they were thinking and felt certain they were planning to have me admitted to hospital again. I often felt that they didn't tell me the complete truth, which left me feeling very alone. I found it particularly difficult to trust my Mother, as the following diary entry shows:

Sunday February 11th 1996
I felt very hurt today. Mum said to me that she was going to do one thing but then in fact did the exact opposite. She does this quite regularly and it makes it very hard for me to trust her. I want to talk with her and discuss my therapy sessions but I don't feel as though she respects my privacy. She tells other people everything that I tell her. This morning when Gran phoned, Mum told her a lot of the private information I had told her about my therapy. After the phone call, she said to me that she didn't want to tell Gran anything but hadn't been able to stop herself when she was questioned. I know that Gran can be demanding but I still felt very betrayed by Mum. Once again, I feel at the bottom of the importance pile. Gran comes first and my feelings really do not matter in comparison.

If you are having similar problems in your family, perhaps it is time to talk with your parents and ask them to be more open and honest with you.

You have to remember that your parents are only human and can get things wrong. If you can see that your parents are really trying to do the best that they can, go easy on them. Remember that you will often feel very uncomfortable when people talk to you about your eating disorder, so try not to be too irritable if someone is offering help. You need to accept that although you want help, you might not always respond in the best possible way. If your parents understand this, your relationship may improve.

Unfortunately, there will be some young people who have parents who are just not willing to help or understand about their eating disorder. Obviously if you are over 18 years old, you can decide to move out if you believe that this will be healthier for you. If you are too young to leave home then discuss the situation with your doctor. There are a number of eating disorder units, re-habilitation hostels and therapeutic community homes where young people can stay if their home life is not helpful for them. These are places that you should not instantly dismiss before you have asked your doctor about them. I know many young people who have been helped a great deal by staying in community hostels.

The Healthy Family

Looking at the ways that a healthy family behaves can give us the first clues to understanding our own family. Look at the following points and see if your family behaves in this way. Try answering true or false to each point.

- All family members are allowed to express anger, sadness and frustration openly without being criticised. The parents do not try to stop their children from crying if they are sad or shouting if they are angry. They show encouragement and warmth if their child is hurt or upset.

- Children are allowed to admit to failing without being made to feel bad. They are told that they are loved regardless of how much they achieve. There is no pressure to reach certain goals.

- Love is unconditional - a child does not have to behave in a certain way to please their parents.

- Conversations are totally open and honest. Children do not feel ashamed to talk with their parents about any problems in their life. They do not try to 'protect' their parents or feel afraid to share their fears and worries.

- The children of the family are encouraged to express their own opinions and to think for themselves. Both parents and children feel able to express their feelings openly.

- Children are encouraged to develop their own identities and learn to become independent as they grow older.

- Parents are willing to admit that they make mistakes too.

- Parents set boundaries and rules that are for the child's benefit. Children are taught to understand that certain types of behaviour are not acceptable for their own good.

- Punishment (if necessary) is fair and children do not feel frightened of their parents. The parents always explain their reasons for punishing their children.

If you have an eating disorder, you will probably find that you answer "False" to many of these points.

Family characteristics that lead a child to develop an eating disorder

Over the years, doctors have studied the families of eating disorder sufferers. They have tried to discover if there are any links between these families. Is there a type of family that causes a child to develop an eating disorder? Certainly there seem to be a number of common characteristics that link many families of eating disorder sufferers. Look at the following headings and see if any of them apply to your family:

- **Conflict Avoidance** - The family avoids conflict at all costs. Children are encouraged to show only happy or 'good' emotions. They soon learn not to show anger or frustration because they are disapproved of. Conflict cannot simply disappear from a family, so instead it is covered up and a false 'happy' front is presented. Underneath the surface though there is often a lot of resentment, anger and bitterness. Many of the family members feel disappointed and hostile but they are not allowed to show these feelings. This leads children to grow up feeling that it is 'bad' to express anger or sadness, and an eating disorder can develop as the child's only way of expressing these feelings.

- **Entangled** - All the members of the family are very closely involved in each other's lives. No privacy is allowed and if a family member wants their own space, this is thought to be suspicious. The children are expected to share their thoughts and feelings, and are discouraged from becoming independent as they grow older. Parents often fill their child's head with their own fears and worries, so that they feel afraid of the outside world and are never ready to leave home. The young person may then turn to an eating disorder to give them a reason to stay at home with their parents.

- **Avoids Change** - The parents do not encourage change in the family. There is often a strict routine that all the family members follow. If the routine is broken at any time, this causes a lot of stress and the family will return to their timetabled life as quickly as possible. Parents will try to keep their children young and never speak to them in an adult way. In some families, if the children do show signs of becoming independent they are punished. Young people experiencing this family situation can turn to an eating disorder as a way of expressing their own identity.

- **Suffocating Behaviour** - Parents control their children by setting them strict rules to follow all of the time. This is done under the cover of love and care, so that the child grows up believing that their parents are concerned about them. This makes it difficult for a child to rebel without feeling very guilty. The parents appear to be denying their own needs but are in fact secretly expressing them. Their children learn that they have to please them all of the time. They feel their parents are kind and understanding and so try to become the 'perfect' child. A child in this situation is very strongly controlled and food becomes the only aspect of their life they feel any control over.

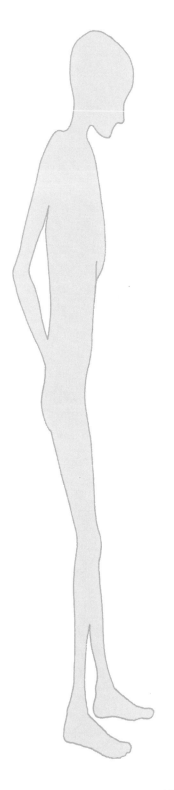

- **Secret Alliances** - The family is seen as a happy group and individual relationships are not encouraged. However, a child secretly forms different relationships with each of their parents. The child then becomes the glue that holds the family together, talking with each parent separately to keep everyone happy and avoid conflict. This allows the family to stay together but it leaves the child feeling responsible for everybody. As we saw earlier, a child that takes on adult responsibilities at a young age is far more likely to develop an eating disorder.

- **Marriage Problems** - Often parents seem to have a very happy marriage. This can just be a cover for the real situation though and there may be many hidden feelings of disappointment and anger, which can affect the children. They may even compete to be the 'best' parent, always trying to prove that they do more for the family than their partner.

- **Perfectionist Parents** - Some parents are perfectionists themselves and may encourage this behaviour in their children, whether they mean to or not. Parents who are high achievers and who are constantly working, show their children that this is the way you are supposed to behave. Children may feel that unless they are always doing homework and achieving 'A' grades at school, they are failures. Parents who often ask to see reports and homework may be putting too much pressure on their child. Some parents even pick out a 'good' job for their children, such as being a lawyer or a doctor. This constant pressure can lead a child to disappear into an eating disorder.

- **Mixed Messages** - Parents may send out mixed messages to their children. For example, if a Mother is cuddling their child one minute and then shouting at them the next, the child never feels safe or secure. These mixed messages can affect all aspects of the child's life. A Mother may comment that the child is 'becoming plump' but then encourage them to eat everything on their plate at meal times. These kinds of mixed messages often leave children feeling confused and guilty much of the time.

- **Focused On Appearance** - If a child grows up in a family where one or more of the parents often talk about dieting, body shape or size, this can lead to problems. Studies have shown that bulimics usually grow up in families where comments are constantly made about their size. It is not just remarks about the child's size that can be a negative influence though. If a child hears their parents making cruel comments about other people's body shapes, this can affect them too. You may have heard your parents make remarks like these: *"Look at that woman - isn't she huge?"* or *"Have you seen how much weight Jane has put on recently?"* This kind of comment can lead a growing teenager to believe that 'thin' is good and 'large' is bad. They may feel that if they do not stay slim, they will also be judged harshly by their parents and this pressure can lead to an eating disorder.

124

- **Parents With Eating Problems** - Children learn behaviour from their parents and this includes their attitudes to food. If a parent does not have a healthy relationship with food then their child is likely to grow up with food problems as well. This was very true in my case, since I grew up with both a Mother and a Grandmother who had unhealthy food habits. My Mother ate very little food during the day. She never had breakfast and lived on a strange diet of currant buns and salad. Although she fed my brother and I in a more normal way, I always watched her behaviour. I remember feeling very shocked when I was invited to a friend's house and saw her Mother eating a normal diet for an adult woman. She had food that I never saw my Mother eat, and she seemed to really enjoy and look forward to her meals.

- **Parents Suffering From Other Addictions** - Alcohol problems are quite common in a family where one member has an eating disorder. This could be because no one in the family can express their emotions. One member turns to an eating disorder, while another turns to drink or drugs. Another possible reason is that depression runs in the family and this has led family members to find different 'escape routes' when they are feeling low.

My own family fits into many of the above categories. I have gradually realised that many aspects of my home life, which I once believed to be very positive, may well have contributed to my eating problems. I had a very 'close' family but this prevented me from developing a healthy level of independence as I grew older. My Mother had many problems because she had a difficult childhood herself and these affected me as I was growing up. My Father had a job that took him away for twelve hours each day and during the week, I would actually spend more time with my Grandmother than with him. My family was very controlled and this may well have led me to develop the idea that control was essential. These are just a few of the many reasons why I developed my eating disorder. Remember though that eating disorders do not start because of just one trigger and are the result of many different factors.

Individual family members and their relationships

There have been many studies examining the character of the individual members in a family where one person suffers from an eating disorder. The following descriptions will not apply in every case because all families are slightly different. However, you may find some similarities between your family and the examples given here. Understanding your parents and the way that you fit into your family can help you to recovery from your eating disorder. It is very important to learn why we behave in certain ways and to do this, we often have to look at our families. We can only start to change our behaviour if we know WHY we act in that way.

Many sufferers think that their disorder is the only thing wrong with their family. They do not realise that the way their family behaves played a very important role in their illness developing. Looking at the ways that your parents and family treat you is not always easy and many sufferers avoid doing this but it is a very important part of recovery. There are reasons why every eating disorder begins and for many people, the family is a very important clue. Our parents influence us throughout our lives and looking at their personalities can help us to understand more about ourselves.

The Father of the Family

There are commonly two 'types' of Father of an eating disorder sufferer. The first is often quite emotionally distant. He may have high expectations of his children, even if he never actually admits this. He may also be very uncomfortable talking about feelings and emotions. The second type is often too close to his children. Although this might not go as far as sexual abuse, he may treat his children in an inappropriate way.

The Mother of the Family

The Mother may be quite controlling and have a history of food problems herself (although she may never have admitted this to anyone). She is likely to be a perfectionist herself and live according to a strict set of rules. Life is very timetabled and her children may grow up feeling that they have to conform all the time. The Mother may have very strict ideas about what her own weight should be and can encourage her children to worry about their weight as well. She may be very anxious and become too concerned with her children's needs, especially if her husband is quite distant and works long hours. She is likely always to do everything her husband says, although secretly she often disagrees with his opinions. Sometimes the Mother did not have a healthy relationship with her own Mother and as a result may be unsure exactly how she should behave towards her children.

Home Life

Children who develop eating disorders often have parents that are high achievers and who are also very controlled people. They are expected to be well behaved and are punished (often physically) if they are naughty. They may be expected to take on adult responsibilities at a young age and always behave in the 'correct manner', which allows them no 'fun' time. They are often asked to look after the younger children in the family and are rarely allowed to just be happy and carefree. Food and body size is important to many members of their family.

I found that I led this kind of life whenever I was with my Grandmother. Although I didn't live with her all the time, I spent many nights and weekends with her. I was always punished if I did not follow her strict rules and was constantly made to feel ashamed and guilty. I also had to be the adult child and look after my younger cousins whenever they came to stay. Food and body size were major issues for the women of my family and I grew up believing that 'thin' was the 'perfect' way to be.

Some exercises to help you understand more about your family

It may now help you to stop and think about your family. Be really honest with yourself here because these exercises are just for you and if you lie about your family situation, you are only lying to yourself. Try and answer the questions accurately and complete the exercises to the best of your ability because only then will the finished results give you a clear picture of what your family is really like. These may be difficult exercises because you may never have admitted the complete truth about your family before. If you have a therapist, you might want to ask them if these are helpful exercises for you to do right now. From my own experience, I found that the more I understood my family and how they affected me, the stronger and healthier I became. We all feel bound to behave in certain ways and understanding our families can help us to break some of our negative behaviour patterns.

1) Try and draw a picture of every member of your family. These don't have to be works of art - you just need to be able to see who it is. Make the faces large enough so that you can draw expressions. Then, for each person, draw the look that you see on their faces most often.

2) If you had to describe your family using just ONE word, what word would you use?

3) Find an object that is very special to you and that reminds you of your early childhood. Look at this object and think really hard. Then try to write down the memories that return to you about your childhood.

4) Try and describe your parents as honestly as you can. Here are some questions that might help you to write a section on your Mother:

   a) How does your Mother behave around food? Does she eat normal meals or does she frequently diet?

   b) What is your Mother's usual mood? Is she easygoing or difficult to talk to? Does she encourage and comfort you or can she be quite sharp at times?

   c) Does your Mother expect a lot from you? Does she spend a lot of time with you or do you usually have to look after yourself?

   d) What is your Mother's weight like? Does this affect you?

5) Do the same for your Father. Write a short section describing him:

   a) What is your Father's job? Does this affect the amount of time you spend with him? Does your Father seem more interested in his working life than in spending time with you?

   b) Do you ever wonder if your Father loves you? Do you feel that he cares and understands you?

   c) Do you feel comfortable around your Father? Can you have easy conversations or do you never really feel able to talk to him?

   d) Is there anything that upsets or angers you about your Father?

6) If you could change something about your parents, what would that be?

7) Do you feel second best in your family? Do you feel that your brothers or sisters are more important and are the successes of the family?

8) If you have brothers or sisters, write a short section about them and how you get on with them.

9) Is there anything that you have always wanted to say to your parents but never felt able to mention? If there is, write this down. There may well be a number of different things that you wish you could have said to your parents but have never felt able to for various reasons. You could be afraid that by speaking out, you might hurt their feelings or upset them in some way. You may just be scared that they will get angry with you or even hit you. Write down all your thoughts on this.

10) Were there any rules in your family that you always felt you had to follow?

Often, as children, we are taught to "keep the family secrets". In other words we are not supposed to talk about the way that our family behaves - that is private information. However, revealing this information, even just to yourself can start to set you free. Recovering from an eating disorder is not just about learning how to eat normally again. It is about learning **WHY** you feel a need to starve yourself or binge and vomit. Often the answers to these questions are revealed when we look at our families and the way that they behave. Many sufferers feel very defensive when they are asked to talk about their families. They immediately say that the eating disorder is their own fault and it has nothing to do with their families, who are all wonderful. It is important to remember that you are not blaming people here - you are just looking at the way they behave. Many doctors and therapists will offer family therapy to eating disorder sufferers and their parents (and often brothers and sisters too) to help them understand more. Although therapy is not always easy, it can help everyone to learn more about each other and find new and healthier ways of behaving.

Family Therapy - How can it help?

Many parents or brothers and sisters feel afraid when they are invited to join in family therapy because they worry that they might be judged. It is important to remember that family therapy is not about blaming someone for the situation. Instead, it is about showing a family how they can help to solve the problems that have caused the eating disorder.

Parents often feel very guilty if their child has an eating disorder and may worry that doctors believe they are 'bad' Mothers and Fathers. I know that my own parents found family therapy extremely threatening. My Mother would become very defensive during therapy meetings because she believed everyone was criticising her. She often spoke first at sessions and would talk about how my brother Mark was such a success, to try and prove that she was a good Mother. This diary entry was written after one such therapy session:

Thursday April 18th 1996
We had family therapy today and I feel so bad tonight. Once again, I feel that everything is my fault because of a comment Mum made. Basically she said: "Anna has had this illness for so long now. When is it going to go? It has affected everyone in the family." This remark left me feeling such a failure. I felt I was responsible for everything bad that has happened in our family. I saw that the anorexia was all my fault. As Mum said, why haven't I managed to get myself better yet? It just proves what a totally stupid and useless person I am.

Then Dad commented on the fact that he thought my anorexia was 'limiting'. This really hurt because I try so hard not to burden them with any of my problems. I try not to affect their lives or be a nuisance. I want them to do what they want all the time. His words just confirmed my feelings that I'm a waste of space and that I ruin people's lives.

Family therapy allows each member of the family to talk about their feelings in a safe environment. There will usually be two different therapists at each session and all the members of the family will be treated in a caring way. If it is done properly, this kind of therapy can help families. The sufferer is encouraged to talk about their problems, both with food and in general. The sessions will often focus on how the child is treated in the family. If there are issues that they feel unable to discuss with their parents at home, these are often discussed during therapy. It may be important to draw up a list of rules when the therapy begins. For example my parents were asked not to discuss the topics that we talked about during therapy after the sessions.

Let me share some of the diary extracts from my family therapy to show a little more about this kind of treatment. Obviously it is not always easy for families to explore conflict but it is healthy. The therapists are there to guide the family and show them different ways of behaving that are healthier.

Thursday March 7th 1996
We had our first family therapy session today. In the morning, Dad walked around the house with this look on his face that said 'I want to be doing anything today except go to a family therapy meeting' and Mum spent her time putting photos of Mark, Gail and Jamie in frames. Her son Mark is the success of the family unlike me, her daughter, who is the failure. Mark certainly never made his parents go to family therapy sessions.

At the meeting, one by one, we had to say what we thought the 'problem' was and what it meant to us. When we had all done this, the psychologist and the psychiatric nurse went away for a while to discuss our answers and choose which therapy would help us most.

They decided that they want to build up my self-esteem. They felt that the way Mum and Dad were helping wasn't really working and they wanted to try a different approach. Mum took this as criticism and I think she felt upset. She had a look on her face that said 'someone has said something to me that I really didn't want to hear'. I wanted to put everything right for her and Dad but I was told that I mustn't try to 'rescue' them during therapy.

Each week we were set tasks to complete by the next therapy session and were told that we needed to work on these tasks alone. Some of these were written tasks and others were practical. The tasks were often quite difficult but they did allow me to start talking more openly with my parents.

Saturday June 22nd 1996
We were set another task as homework from family therapy this week and it's a really tough one for me. We have to deliberately do something to irritate the others in the family. This is hard because I spend all of my time trying to please others and not annoy them, which is of course the reason why the psychologist set us this task. I will be taking a huge risk when I deliberately try to annoy someone because I'm sure I will make them angry and then they will hate me.

Every parent reacts differently to family therapy. My Father seemed to handle it more calmly than my Mother, as he appeared to feel more comfortable and less threatened. As the therapy progressed, my Mother became very unhappy about attending the sessions and after three months, she refused to do any of the homework tasks that we were set. Therapy of any kind is not an easy process. We are closely examining our own personalities and the way we behave, and this is not comfortable for most people. My Mother felt that she was being criticised. She became very defensive and started to verbally attack anyone that talked about her.

Thursday June 27th 1996

Mum is really showing now that she doesn't want to be at family therapy and is being quite difficult. This morning she said that she didn't do the homework because she felt that it was a 'childish game'. At the end of the meeting, she said she was fed up with the sessions. The homework they set us this week was that we are not to discuss anything about today's meeting but must write our thoughts down instead.

We got into the car after the session and Mum immediately started talking about the therapy. Dad told her that we couldn't discuss it but she still tried to speak about it three times. Each time Dad stopped her, finally saying: "You must write down your thoughts", to which Mum said: "I'm not going to write anything down. I don't care what they say. If I want to talk, I will." Dad said: "That's fine but I'll have to tell them about this next week."

I must admit I don't find this 'keeping quiet' task hard because it is what I do all of the time. I always keep my thoughts to myself and when we do discuss sessions, I spend all my time trying to make Mum and Dad feel better about what's been said.

We did start to have frequent upsets like this during the sessions but a psychiatrist explained to me why it was so difficult. Family therapy is **destabilising**, which basically just means that while it is going on, the whole family often feels quite unstable. As the therapy continues though, new and more stable family relationships start to develop which are healthier for everyone.

There are many different ways that parents can help children with their illness. If you are suffering from anorexia or bulimia and you want to ask your parents for help, why don't you share this book with them? I am going to end this chapter by listing just a few of the different ways that parents can help a child who has an eating disorder. Perhaps you can share these with your Mother or Father and discuss them together, so that they can understand a little more about ways they can help you.

Positive ways that parents can help their children

- Give your children time. Recovering from an eating disorder takes a while and it is important to remember that your child will not instantly be able to start eating normally again. Try not to pressure them. It is important that recovery is slow and that the sufferer takes baby steps forward. A slow recovery is far more likely to be a permanent recovery.

- Listen and allow your children to talk. Let them develop their own voice and try not to always influence them. If they need to shout or cry, let them do this. Bottling up their emotions is very unhealthy.

- Try to eat a normal healthy diet yourself. Many parents have issues with food themselves and if this is the case, perhaps now is the time for you to talk this through with a doctor. It is not easy to help your child recover fully if you have problems in this area yourself. Remember that children are strongly influenced by their parents' behaviour and this is true of eating patterns as well.

- Don't feel ashamed. Many parents feel very ashamed of the fact that their child has an eating disorder. They are certain that everyone is judging them and saying that they are bad parents. Eating disorders begin for many different reasons and pointing the finger of blame is not helpful. It is however helpful to understand why your child's eating disorder started, since this will help them with their recovery.

- As a parent, you are likely to be feeling worried and upset yourself. You may feel that you have lost the child you once knew and found that your son or daughter has become withdrawn, depressed and anxious instead. Remember that this is all part of the illness and that becoming angry with your child will not help them to recover. Even when you are feeling very frustrated, try to be patient and understanding.

- As parents, both the Mother and Father need to act as one. If parents disagree on treatment for their child, this can be very damaging. You need to decide together what is best for your child. Remember though to INVOLVE your child in all the decisions. You may not feel that your child is able to make healthy or sensible choices but it is important that they feel their opinions are heard and that their feelings are not simply being ignored.

- Continue to encourage your child to become independent, even though they may be physically ill. Remember that although they have an illness which means they cannot lead a normal life yet, it is important not to 'baby' them. They need to learn to make their own decisions.

- Learn more about eating disorders yourself and encourage your child to learn about healthy eating. Perhaps you can look at the differences in body shapes together and even use a family tree to see what body types the members of your family have.

- Remember that you will all need time away from each other, so allow both yourself and your child to have visitors and other people in your lives.
- Make sure that your child realises that being 'thin' is not the solution to their problems. They need to know that your love for them is unconditional and not dependent on their size or shape.
- Reinforce the fact that you love your children for who they are, not for what they achieve. This is very important because many eating disorder sufferers feel a strong need to be high achievers to please their parents.

These are just a few of the positive ways that parents can help their children to deal with an eating disorder. The more that parents know about eating disorders, the better. If your child has confided in you and shown you this book, perhaps it will help you both to read through different sections together. The more open you can be, the more likely your child is to make a full recovery.

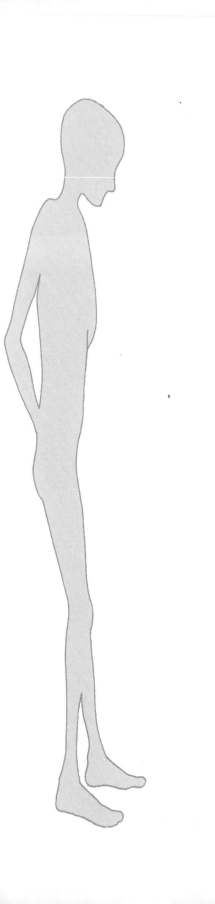

Part Two

Recovering From An Eating Disorder

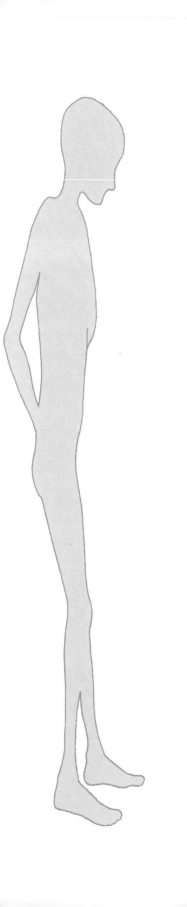

Chapter 16

What Treatments are there for my Eating Disorder?

Summary
There are many different treatments available to help with recovery. This chapter looks at the various options available to sufferers.

There are many different treatments for eating disorders and you may feel unsure which is best for you. In this chapter, I want to explain about the types on offer and try to remove some of the fears that surround the word 'treatment'. Many eating disorder sufferers are too afraid to even consider the idea of recovery because they are frightened by the thought of being treated. They may have heard horror stories about cruel hospital programmes but treatment need not be a frightening experience. As doctors and nurses learn more about eating disorders, it is improving all the time.

If you mention 'treatment' to an eating disorder patient, they immediately think that you are talking about a long hospital stay. However, there are many useful therapies that take place in out-patient clinics. **Out-patient** clinics are usually held in your local hospital and the appointments vary depending on the treatment programme your doctor has arranged. You are likely to find that any kind of treatment is challenging and difficult at times because you are trying to change your behaviour. With the right kind of support and encouragement though, it is very possible to completely recover from an eating disorder without ever being admitted to a hospital.

Eating disorders are physical as well as mental illnesses though and sometimes patients have to be forced to accept treatment. This is ALWAYS a last resort and doctors never **section** patients (legally force them to accept treatment) unless they believe that their life is in danger. If an anorexic is at a life threatening weight, doctors may have to insist on treatment. The problem with this kind of treatment is that it is often only a short-term solution. It is possible to admit a sufferer to hospital and feed them until they are at a healthy weight but this is not solving the real problem. If a sufferer is still deep within their eating disorder, the treatment will not have helped them with their anorexic thinking. As soon as they are released from hospital, they usually start to lose weight until they require emergency treatment again. This shows how important it is for therapy and re-feeding to go hand in hand if treatment is to work.

Accepting that you need help is never easy if you are suffering from an eating disorder. Many sufferers live with their illness for a number of years before they admit to having a problem and often only ask for help when they hit rock bottom. The earlier you are able to ask for help, the better. It is very unlikely that you will be admitted to a hospital if you seek help soon enough though and your recovery can be quite fast.

There are a number of reasons why sufferers decide they need professional help:

1) They may begin to feel afraid about some of the physical problems they can no longer ignore. Girls often write to me frightened because their hair is falling out in large clumps. Others notice that their periods have stopped, and that they feel cold and tired all the time.

2) Many sufferers try to stop their eating disorders by themselves. They try to eat normally but become terrified when they find they cannot manage to do this. They see just how little control they actually have over their behaviour and understand that they need professional help to get well again.

3) Sufferers may feel pressured by the constant remarks about their eating habits and weight from friends and family. I went through many similar situations with my own parents before I agreed to accept treatment and now I often see this happening to other sufferers. Parents and friends can feel afraid when they see a person they care about starving themselves but their fear often leads them to react badly and become frustrated, desparate and angry. Arguments can keep occurring until a sufferer finally accepts that they need help.

4) Many sufferers feel that they are losing much of their young life to the eating disorder and want to stop the illness before they waste any more precious years. They feel that living with an eating disorder is more frightening than asking for help.

For many sufferers, the bravest step they ever take is accepting that they need help to fight their illness. Recovery from an eating disorder **IS** very possible but accepting help is the first major step forward. However, do remember that there are no instant 'miracle' cures for eating disorders. You need to accept that recovery does take time and requires a lot of hard work.

If you have accepted that you do have an eating disorder and you want help, the first person you need to see is your family doctor. I always encourage sufferers who are going to see their doctor for the first time to write down some notes. These don't have to be long or detailed but the more your doctor knows about your illness, the more they can help. You may feel frightened when you enter the surgery and your mind might go blank. You may also feel tempted to lie about your weight or how much you eat. If you have notes explaining just what has been happening to you then you are more likely to speak honestly. If you do avoid talking about your eating disorder when you first see your doctor, don't give up. Many eating disorder sufferers panic during the appointment and stay silent. Just make another appointment and try again.

No matter how long you have been suffering from your disorder, it is always important to have a physical check-up. Your doctor will probably want to run blood tests and, depending on your weight and behaviour (bingeing/vomiting, laxative abuse, etc), checks on your heart and possibly bone and brain scans too. These tests are not painful but they are very important indicators of your physical state of health.

Your doctor may also want to weigh you and measure your height. Many eating disorder sufferers are terrified of this aspect of treatment but unfortunately it is necessary. I have told many doctors that I hated the fact that they weighed me the minute I walked through their door. I felt just like a sack of potatoes and was sure that all they really cared about was my weight. This diary extracts shows exactly how difficult weighing sessions were for me:

Monday June 1st 1998
I didn t want to go to therapy today because I so hate being weighed. I know that my doctor keeps saying that in three months I have hardly put on any weight but I feel so FAT! I look in the mirror and all I see is FAT, FAT, FAT! I feel I am so disgusting. I don t want to be this way. I just want to be thin. I hate myself so much for being a FAT BLOB. I only just managed to stop myself from self-harming today. I wanted to punish myself for being such a bad person for gaining weight but I knew that if I self-harmed, my doctor would tell my parents and I just couldn t worry them any more.

However, I do now understand how important it is for doctors to keep a check on a sufferer's weight. It is an important indicator of how a patient is progressing. Some doctors weigh their patients backwards so that the sufferer does not see any weight changes. I fought against this idea at first and was upset when my doctor suggested it, as the following diary entry shows. In time though, I realised that it was better if I didn't know exactly how much I weighed.

Saturday March 28th 1998
I am really worried about not knowing how much I weigh. How can I learn to deal with weight gain if I don t know how much I have put on? When I was in hospital, we were given counselling every time we put on weight to help us deal with the increases. If my doctor won t tell me how much I weigh, how can I come to terms

with the changes? I am convinced that I am piling on pounds and pounds in weight. I feel so upset about this.

Many eating disorder sufferers constantly weigh themselves and this usually affects their mood for the whole day. However, I know from talking individually to sufferers that they actually feel much better when they don't know their exact weight. Any change in the number on the scales may trigger them into further dieting or binge and vomit sessions. Do remember though that the figure you read on the scale is just a number. It DOES NOT have to rule your life and affect your mood. Don't let the eating disorder 'voice' use it to hurt you. I know that my anorexic 'voice' used to shout loudly at me whenever I was weighed and that I felt more peaceful when I did not know my exact weight.

Monday August 10th 1998
I feel so down tonight that I could just sit in a corner and cry. You would think after all these years I was used to being weighed but I still dread it so much. Whenever I am weighed, the anorexic voice just starts going on at me. It tells me that I must have piled on pounds and pounds and because I feel so huge, I believe the voice. I can hear it shouting constantly at me:

> *"You are such a disgusting person. You are massive now and have piled on so many pounds in weight."*

Unfortunately, not all family doctors completely understand eating disorders. There is a slight chance that the first doctor you see may let you down by not taking your problem seriously. If this is the case, PLEASE don't give up. Most surgeries have more than one doctor and you need to try again, so make an appointment with a different doctor. Some of the new group practices have counsellors and therapists as part of the health team and it may be possible to make an appointment with one of them instead. Alternatively, you can have a complete change of doctor. You are allowed to do this and it is an easy procedure. Ask around your friends and find yourself a doctor who is particularly kind and sympathetic, and make an appointment with them. You may want to choose a female doctor if you feel uncomfortable talking to a man about your problems. The new doctor must be within the boundary area where you live. Go along to the surgery of your new doctor and ask to register with them. It is within your rights to choose a doctor that you feel comfortable with. Remember that this is all part of recovery. You are just saying what it is that YOU need.

Some sufferers feel too afraid to go to their doctors alone but there are other people who can help you with this first step towards recovery. If you feel you really cannot trust your parents to help, find out what support is available at your school or college. Many schools now have nurses on site and they are used to helping people with eating disorders since this is an illness common in younger people. If your school does not have a nurse, perhaps there is a teacher that you particularly like and trust? Share your problems with them and ask for their help. If you are at college, there is likely to be a counsellor available to students. There is always a doctor attached to colleges as well, so it is just a case of finding out how you make an appointment to see them. If you are feeling desperate, you can always go to your local casualty (Accident and Emergency) department where you will be seen by a doctor.

Treatments your doctor may suggest

The treatment that your doctor suggests will depend on your physical state. If you are at a very low weight, the best option for you may be in-patient care. This is not usually the first option offered though, since there are many different out-patient treatments and therapies available for eating disorder sufferers. Before you ask for help though, you may be wondering exactly what treatment hopes to achieve. What do you need to do if you are to recover from your illness?

1) The sufferer needs to change certain negative behaviours, such as starving themselves, bingeing and/or vomiting and purging (taking laxatives).

2) The sufferer needs to reach a healthy weight for their height and maintain this, without returning to their old eating disorder habits.

3) The sufferer needs to look at the attitudes that led them to develop an eating disorder. They may need to learn more about their family and the way they have been treated throughout their life.

4) The sufferer needs to learn how to cope with everyday problems without turning to their eating disorder.

5) The sufferer may need help changing some aspects of their life, if these are what led to the eating disorder beginning.

6) The sufferer will need to learn about nutrition, healthy eating plans and how to eat 'normally' again.

This list may make recovery seem like a lot of hard work but it is important to remember that getting better from an eating disorder does take time. Your doctor will not expect you to complete all these tasks in a week or even a month. Complete recovery from an eating disorder will often take a year or more. There will also be a lot of different people who can help you with these tasks. Dieticians, nutritionists, counsellors, therapists, psychiatrists, eating disorder specialists, psychologists, psychiatric nurses and occupational therapists all work with eating disorder patients. Unfortunately, the treatment available does depend on where you live. Many of the best eating disorder units in Britain are in the South-East of England and I frequently receive letters from people in the North, where there is less help available. It is important to ask your family doctor exactly what help is available.

These are some of the possible options your doctor may discuss with you:

In-Patient Care (Hospital Treatment)

When you start talking to doctors, you will find that treatments are usually referred to as either 'in-patient' or 'out-patient' care. **In-patient** care basically refers to any hospital stay. Anorexics or bulimics may be admitted to hospital as emergency cases. Both of these illnesses can lead to life-threatening problems that need instant treatment. However, you are more likely to be admitted to hospital in a non-emergency situation. This is a voluntary admission, which means that you will have agreed with your doctor that this is the best solution for you. It might be that you tried out-patient care but this did not work or that your weight is so low that it is too dangerous for you to remain at home. If you are being admitted for either of these reasons, it is likely that your doctor will take time to explain the treatment you will receive in the hospital. Being admitted as an in-patient can be a frightening experience for sufferers, although many admit they feel relieved that someone else will finally be responsible for their diet and overrule the 'voice' in their head. I certainly felt this way when I was admitted for both my hospital stays.

The best places for anorexia and bulimia patients to receive treatment are usually specialist units but unfortunately there are not many of these in the UK. Eating disorder sufferers are frequently admitted to psychiatric hospitals or even to the medical wards of general hospitals. For anorexics, treatment involves re-feeding and this can take many different forms. If a sufferer is unwilling to eat or is finding that they cannot keep food down, at first they will either be fed through a drip or a nasogastric tube. **Drip-feeding** is when liquid nutrition is passed through a needle into a sufferer's vein. **Nasogastric feeding** is through a tube that passes up the nose and down the throat into the stomach. Neither of these methods are long term solutions though, because they do not help sufferers to change their eating habits. As soon as the patient is no longer in danger and can eat again, they are encouraged to gain weight in more natural ways.

If the sufferer is willing to co-operate and is able to eat, treatment will usually start with the introduction of small meals, which will gradually increase in size. Many hospitals aim for a weight gain of 2 lbs each week and will increase a patient's diet until it reaches an intake of around 3,000 calories per day. At least 1,000 calories of this daily intake will usually be in the form of liquid supplements. These are high calorie drinks (such as Fortisips or Build-Up) which allow sufferers to receive extra nutrition without having to eat large amounts of food. However, many hospitals feel this level of weight gain is too high for some patients and try to aim for between _ lb and 1 lb per week. This is a more realistic level of weight gain but some hospitals do not have the time or resources to use this gentler approach.

Hospital care is also available for bulimia, although it is not as common as treatment for anorexia. Bulimics may be watched during and after meals (for at least one hour) and in some hospitals, they are not allowed to go to the bathroom without having a nurse present. This is to prevent them from vomiting the food that they have just eaten. On admission, nurses will also usually search patients' bags to make sure they have not brought laxatives, emetics or diuretics into the hospital with them. In-patient care allows doctors to monitor a patient's health more closely, and see how their body reacts to receiving food again. Both bulimics and anorexics may suffer problems when they begin eating a normal diet again. When I was first in an eating disorders unit, a nurse would listen to my stomach through a **stethoscope** (an instrument used to listen to a patient's internal organs) while I was eating, just to make sure that my stomach was working properly.

Hospital treatment will vary in length, depending on how ill the patient has become. The lower a sufferer's weight, the longer they will need to be in hospital. Specialist eating disorder units offer a wide range of therapies to sufferers while they are in-patients. It is important to remember that weight gain alone does not equal recovery. Sufferers need to learn new ways of behaving and understand why they turned to their eating disorder in the first place. Dieticians and nutritionists often visit patients while they are in hospital and continue to see them even after they have been released.

Many anorexics and bulimics begin taking medication while they are in hospital. Anti-depressants can often help a sufferer to deal with their depression. Tranquillizers can be used as well, to help anorexics cope with feelings of anxiety and fear when they eat. Patients may also be given drugs that stimulate their appetites and make them feel hungry again.

You may be afraid of hospital treatment because you have heard some frightening stories. In the 1970s, many hospitals worked on the 'punishment/ reward' system of treatment for anorexics. This meant that patients were given rewards if they gained weight and punished in different ways if they did not. They would not be allowed to have visitors or receive telephone calls. Some patients even had their pillows and blankets taken away, so that they ended up sleeping on just mattresses. This cruel method of treatment seems to have finally disappeared from hospitals. Doctors now understand more clearly why people develop eating disorders and nursing staff are far gentler and more understanding. It is important to remember though that doctors and nurses are not perfect and have probably not experienced an eating disorder themselves. The more that you can talk openly with the medical staff and share your thoughts, the more they will be able to understand and help you.

Hospital treatment does not work for everyone though. Anorexia and bulimia are difficult illnesses to treat and some sufferers become 'revolving door' patients. This means they have more than one hospital stay. When they return home, they lose all the weight they gained as an in-patient and end up being re-admitted.

However, if you want to recover and are willing to work hard with the doctors and nurses, hospital stays can help tremendously. It is very likely that when you leave hospital as an in-patient, you will return as a day patient or even weekly as an out-patient. Some sufferers may leave an in-patient unit and enter a residential hostel for a while. Here they are again living with other sufferers but they are not as closely supervised as in hospital.

Private Eating Disorder Clinics

There are a number of private clinics that specialize in the treatment of eating disorders. Unfortunately, because of the small number of clinics and the high number of sufferers, there are often long waiting lists. If your health is very poor and your condition serious, your family doctor may be able to apply for an emergency admission. If in-patient treatment is not available, the units may be able to offer day patient care. If you have private health insurance, you may be able to arrange admission to a private unit but unfortunately this may only be for a limited period of time.

Out-Patient Care

There are many different types of out-patient care and if you ask for help from your doctor, you are likely to be offered some kind of out-patient treatment. Once again, the number of different kinds of treatment that you will be offered depends on where you live.

You may be referred to a **Child and Adolescent Psychiatric Unit** and it is likely that your parents will attend the first appointment with you. This appointment may take place in your own home, since many doctors want the patient and their family to feel as comfortable as possible. A doctor or therapist will talk to you and your family to discover the best way that you can be helped. As I discussed in the previous chapter, eating disorders are often linked to family problems and you may well be offered family therapy.

Many people are ashamed or embarrassed to see a therapist or a counsellor because they feel that they should be able to deal with their problems alone. There is no reason to feel ashamed if you need to see one. If you had stomach problems you would go to see a medical doctor, so equally if you are having serious emotional problems you may need to see a therapist or a counsellor.

Your first appointment at the hospital may be with a psychiatrist or a psychologist. A **psychiatrist** is a medical doctor who specializes in emotional and mental illnesses. Although they do carry out therapy, they usually concentrate on deciding which medicines may best help you during recovery. A UK psychiatrist will probably refer you to a **CPN** (Community Psychiatric Nurse) or a psychologist. It is the psychologist, nurse or therapist who will work with you on a daily or weekly basis. A **psychologist** is not a medical doctor but is highly trained in human behaviour and emotions. They will suggest the therapy they think can best help you to beat your eating disorder. You may also be referred to a dietician (or nutritionist) to help you with your diet.

It may be that you become a day patient, if your local hospital offers this option. As a day patient, you would go to the hospital every day and have all your meals there, so that the nursing staff can support and help you with your difficult feelings. You will have group and individual therapy, and possibly family therapy as well.

You may also be referred to a **paediatrician**. This is a doctor who specifically looks after the health of children and teenagers. Their job is to give you a physical check up, to see if there are any medical problems caused by your eating disorder.

Different Types Of Therapy

If your doctor has suggested that you start therapy, you may be feeling a little unsure why they think this will help. During the treatment of an eating disorder, therapy aims to:

1) Discover the thoughts and beliefs that led to the eating disorder developing.
2) Help the patient improve their level of self-esteem and self-worth.
3) Help the patient learn to limit their obsession with body shape and size.
4) Help the patient deal with their fears around eating, and establish a healthy eating plan.

It is important to be as honest as possible. Doctors and specialists can only help you if you tell the truth. If you lie to them, you will eventually be caught out and then you will have lost their trust. If you are to beat your eating disorder, you must remember that the doctors and therapists are on your side and the only person you hurt by lying is yourself.

Dieticians (or Nutritionists)

A dietician or nutritionist will offer you very specific help with your diet. They will ask what you are eating now and may also ask you to describe what your eating was like when you were younger. Your dietician will either provide you with diet sheets (where you need to fill in everything you eat each day) or ask you to keep a food diary. They will teach you exactly which foods your body needs every day.

Usually they draw up a special diet plan suited to your particular needs and which takes into account the foods you most like. It is important to remember when you are asked to list the foods you don't like that you are honest. Don't just write down the foods that are high calorie. Your dietician will have worked with eating disorder sufferers before and will know if you are trying to cheat.

You can discuss the diet plan with your dietician. They do not want to frighten you and with your help, will draw up a plan that you find acceptable. You will have regular meetings with your dietician so that they can monitor your weight and progress.

If you are finding the diet too difficult, discuss your problems with the dietician and they will reorganise it so that you feel more comfortable. For example, it may be that you feel unable to eat three normal meals a day. Your dietician could help you by arranging for you to have six smaller snacks instead. As long as you are getting the correct nutrition, meal times can become more flexible.

You need to feel happy with your dietician so that you can ask questions about weight and calories. For both anorexics and bulimics, eating a 'normal' diet is a difficult and painful process, and help from a good dietician can make it easier to cope. Many sufferers are amazed at how much energy they suddenly have when they begin to follow their special diet plans.

Group Therapy

There are many different kinds of group therapy and these are available whether you are an in-patient, a day patient or an out-patient. Studies have showed that the most helpful group therapies are those which focus on problem-solving tasks, teaching skills or dealing with conflict issues. Most eating disorder sufferers have isolated themselves and although group therapy may seem like a frightening idea, it can help in many different ways. Hospitals and eating disorder units often run different courses, including assertiveness training, anxiety management and body image workshops. Specialist units may also offer more unusual courses, such as drama classes, creative writing groups and art therapy.

Individual Therapy

This involves the sufferer seeing a therapist at least once each week. The therapist will listen to the sufferer, ask questions and make suggestions about different ways in which they can change their behaviour and thinking. As the patient, you listen to the therapist and respond to all their questions and suggestions. Together, you reach a deeper understanding of the problem and discover new ways to improve the situation. Therapy is not always a comfortable process. However, it allows you to learn more about yourself and develop a healthier way of behaving.

One of the most common therapies that works well for eating disorder sufferers is **cognitive behaviour therapy.** This helps a sufferer change both their thinking and behaviour. The therapy is based upon the idea that our thoughts affect our feelings, which then affects our behaviour. Let me try and explain this in more detail:

Thought: I **think** that if I eat food I will get fat. (This is a negative thought).

Feeling: I **feel** scared of eating food because I don't want to get fat. (Fear is a negative emotion).

Behaviour: I am not going to eat food today.

In this example, you can see how a negative thought leads to a negative feeling and then to negative behaviour. Cognitive behaviour therapy teaches you ways of stopping those negative thoughts by replacing them with positive ones. Many eating disorder sufferers spend all of their time thinking about their body weight and shape. This thinking then affects their feelings and their eating behaviour. Cognitive therapy helps a sufferer to look at these obsessional thoughts and change them, so that they can regain control of their eating.

Once I had learnt how cognitive therapy worked, I began to use it and my therapist gave me a list of six questions. Whenever my head was filled with negative thoughts, I had to start asking myself these questions:

1. What are the facts? Are my thoughts really true or is there any evidence against them?
2. Are my standards too high? Am I just trying to be perfect?
3. Was the situation really a complete disaster? Am I over-reacting?
4. How much do I want the situation to affect my life? Is it really that important?
5. Was the situation really my fault or am blaming myself for someone else's behaviour?
6. How would someone else view this? What advice would I give someone else in my position now?

I was then given some 'Thoughts and Moods' diary sheets, which I could use to work through my thoughts every time I felt down. This is how they work:

1) You describe the **situation** that upset you.
2) You state what **emotions** you are feeling.
3) You write down all the **negative thoughts** that are in your head.
4) You work out different **positive thoughts** to these negative responses.

For example:

Situation - Coping with increasing the amount of food that I am eating.

Emotions - Feeling scared and miserable.

Negative Automatic Thoughts - I am such a stupid, useless failure and find eating very difficult. Everyone will hate me for behaving so badly around food.

Positive Alternative Thoughts - I need to take it one meal at a time and do as much as I can. I am not stupid for having trouble with food - that is just part of the illness. I am trying for recovery and the people around me can see that and think that I am brave, not useless.

Cognitive therapy can work extremely well and I personally found it very helpful but it does take a lot of practise to use it to fight your eating disorder. At first, you may not believe the positive responses that you are using to replace the negative ones. The more you practise though, the easier it becomes. Soon you will be able to use the therapy without writing anything down because you can change your own thoughts automatically.

Role-Play

Another way to get in touch with your feelings is through role play. This needs to be carried out with a therapist though because it can be very difficult without the right support. Together with your therapist, you will role-play a situation that made you angry or upset in the past. You tell your therapist about the words, gestures and body language that made you really angry or upset. This time though, instead of swallowing your feelings, you are allowed to respond with your real emotions. If you were angry, then you are now allowed to shout your response. If you were upset, then this time you are allowed to cry.

You do need to carry out this kind of therapy with someone you feel safe with, so it is unlikely to be a treatment that your therapist suggests immediately. There needs to be an agreement that no one gets hurt physically during the role-play (if you are feeling extremely angry, this is a possibility). It is also important that you feel able to stop the exercise at any time if you think it is becoming too difficult for you.

My experiences of treatment

Although my eating disorder began when I was 17, I didn't start any treatment until I was 21. The longer you have an eating disorder before you start treatment, the longer it can take to recover. When you have an eating disorder, you have learned negative ways of behaving around food and the longer you behave in this way, the harder it is to stop. I would encourage anyone who is

148

struggling with an eating disorder to ask for help now. When I was finally offered treatment, my psychiatric nurse decided that I had **M.E.** (a condition where the sufferer feels extremely tired and ill) rather than anorexia. I didn't correct her because I didn't want anyone to discover the real problem and try to cure me. This meant that it was another full year before anyone started to help me with the anorexia.

When I was 22, my parents moved to Cornwall. My new doctor was concerned about my low weight and I was admitted to the local psychiatric hospital. Compared to many psychiatric hospitals, it was quite small and I shared a room with another woman. I was very withdrawn and scared by this time and felt afraid of being in hospital. Despite all my fears though, I did feel relieved that someone else had taken control of my diet. After three weeks of bed rest, I was allowed to move around the hospital but I would still hide in my room. I was used to living with my parents and felt too shy to talk with the other patients. When two consultants disagreed over my treatment, I managed to convince them to let me go home. It was too early for me though and within five days of being at home, I had returned to my anorexic ways.

For the next three years, I tried to avoid hospital by maintaining my weight and spent many hours each week with therapists. Although I was making progress with my cognitive therapy, I felt unable to tell anyone why my eating disorder started and I continued to lose weight. At the age of 24, I was again at a seriously dangerous weight and was admitted to a private eating disorder clinic. Just before I entered the clinic, I saw for the first time what I really looked like. Looking in the mirror, I saw a terrifyingly thin person who was dying. My face had disappeared and my head had become just a skull. The doctors later told me that I was only hours away from death and I remained in the next clinic for more than five months.

I had intensive therapy both on a one-to-one basis and in a group situation, and was amazed by how much I actually enjoyed some of the therapy. One day the nurses decided that we needed to learn how to have fun. As eating disorder sufferers, we had never allowed ourselves to just play because we had taken on adult responsibilities as children. The nurses spread a huge sheet of white paper on the floor and we had to take off our shoes and socks and mess around with some paint. We found it very difficult at first because we were not used to just being silly but we soon found ourselves throwing paint everywhere and happily splashing about in it.

I also found the body image groups extremely helpful. One particular exercise showed us all how distorted our views of our bodies really were. Both the patients and nurses all had to lie down on the floor on separate sheets of paper. We were then blindfolded and another nurse drew outlines around our bodies. We removed our blindfolds and had to say which outline we believed was ours.

Every single anorexia patient went and stood next to the larger outlines that belonged to the nurses. We simply could not believe that the really thin outlines were ours.

There were two different groups every day including art therapy, assertiveness courses and drama groups. About halfway through my stay in the hospital, the occupational therapist realised that I understood cognitive therapy but was just repeating my answers without any real feeling. I had learned the therapy but had shut down on my feelings. The therapist sat me down and played me a song by REM called 'Everybody Hurts'. The song's lyrics about "holding on" deeply affected me and I started to cry. I was finally beginning to feel and I gradually started to talk about some of the abuse I'd received during my childhood.

Over the next few months, I began to make good progress and became a more confident and happy person. My weight was rising and, after nearly six months as an in-patient, I thought I was ready to live at home again. Unfortunately, when I did actually return home, I went back into the same situation as before and I slowly began to lose my new found confidence. I started to hide with my parents again and the only other people I saw were therapists. I had one extremely good therapist called Clive, who helped me for many years. I had learned to survive as a **chronic** (long-term) anorexic but I was not happy. Although I was now running my own cross-stitch business and driving my own car, I was very lonely and never went out without my parents because I felt too afraid. One day when I was feeling extremely lonely, I joined a pen friend club and that is how I met Simon.

Simon gave me a reason to get completely well. He loved me unconditionally and I loved him back. Finally I was able to completely trust someone and I told him about all the abuse I had suffered in my life. That was the beginning of the end for my eating disorder. With his help, I really started to fight the anorexia. Using all the therapy I had learned over the years, Simon and I fought my anorexic 'voice' together. His unconditional love showed me that I wasn't the terrible person I believed myself to be, and I realised that I didn't have to punish myself by starvation any longer. I finally learned that talking openly and trusting another person could help me beat my eating disorder. I wished I had felt more able to talk honestly with my therapists over the years but part of me always held back because I was afraid that they would hate me if told them the truth.

Possible problems you may encounter during treatment

The competitive nature of eating disorders - Eating disorder units can work extremely well for many patients but there are still some problems. I found that the competitive nature of eating disorders could make meal times very difficult. In an eating disorder unit, all the patients are at different stages of their recovery. If you sit a sufferer who does not want to recover next to another sufferer who is trying to recover, one patient can upset the other. I remember many mealtimes when all the girls argued about the different amounts of food they had been given. Those who didn't want to recover would just talk about calories and point out how much fat certain foods contained. This was very distressing for those trying to focus on the fact that eating was right, not wrong. Arguments could break out during meals, with some sufferers sending their food back to the kitchen if they thought they had been given too much. Others would just constantly compare their diet plans and complain. I finally asked to sit with other patients in the hospital who did not suffer from eating disorders. This worked very well for me because by watching the other patients, who had a healthy attitude to food, I could see what 'normal' eating was like.

Competitions among patients often take place in eating disorder units without the doctors' knowledge. Patients will compare how much they weigh and many try to become the thinnest in the hospital. They will also discuss tips and other ways of being 'better' anorexics. Sadly, some patients leave hospital knowing new and different ways of losing weight.

Your therapist is moving too fast for you - Remember that it is you who is trying to recover and the therapist is just there to help. If they are setting you too much homework or are scaring you by moving too fast with the treatment, you need to speak out. The speed you recover at is very important and I had to ask a number of different therapists to slow down. If you feel that you are out of your depth and are panicking, you must talk to your therapist. You will have to go through a lot of difficult feelings during therapy and if you try to change too much too quickly, you will become frightened and return to your eating disorder. It is important that you remember to just keep taking baby steps towards recovery. You may not be used to speaking out and standing up for yourself but you need to be brave. Your therapist is there to help you - they do not simply want you to try and please them.

You do not connect with your therapist - I have seen many different therapists during my 14 years of anorexia and naturally I liked some better than others. The therapists that I felt comfortable with were better able to help me progress with my recovery. If you find that you do not like your therapist or just feel that they do not understand you, go back to your doctor and explain the problem. You will not be able to progress in your recovery if you do not connect with your therapist. You need to be able to trust your therapist and share some very personal and private information with them.

You do not understand the therapy - If your therapist is trying to teach you cognitive behaviour therapy, do not feel afraid to ask for help. This is not always an easy therapy to understand and it took me quite a long time before I could use it properly. Eating disorder sufferers often feel they have to be perfect and

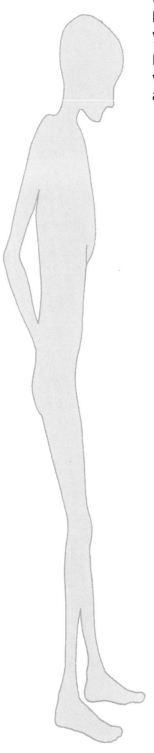

want to understand and use cognitive therapy immediately. Patience is the key here. It will take time, a lot of practice and some help from your therapist before you find it useful.

Do remember that if you are going to recover from your eating disorder, talking is very important. Talk with all your doctors and therapists as openly and honestly as you can and then they will be able to help you fight your eating disorder.

Chapter 17

How Do I Start Recovering?

Summary

There are many practical positive steps that a sufferer can take to beat their eating disorder. This chapter outlines many ideas and approaches that sufferers can use to help them start their recovery.

In the last chapter, I looked at many of the different therapies and treatments that are available to sufferers. There are also a number of practical steps towards recovery that you can take by yourself at home. First of all though, you need to know exactly what recovery involves.

1) You must be willing to stop misusing food. Bulimics may be more willing to give up their negative behaviour because most sufferers hate vomiting and bingeing or taking laxatives. It is often more difficult for anorexics to give up dieting. Even when you do want recovery, you will still have days when moving forward is both frightening and painful. Recovery always has its setbacks but the desire to succeed will keep you moving forward through any difficult times.

2) You must be willing to STOP losing weight and begin your recovery by at least maintaining your present weight. As I mentioned in the previous chapter, if your weight is dangerously low, you will be unable to do this alone and will need help from doctors and perhaps even a hospital stay. However, if your weight is either normal or you are only slightly underweight then you can try to work out your own programme of recovery.

3) You will need a lot of support and encouragement and it is important to decide who can help you the most. It may be that you have very helpful parents who understand and want to support you. If this is the case, then now is the right time to be honest with them. Unfortunately, not everyone has helpful parents so you might need to consider asking a teacher at school or a youth group leader for some extra help. School friends can also be very helpful, especially if you are struggling with your midday meals.

The following is a very good exercise that may help you to organise your thoughts and reasons for giving up your eating disorder. Write out exactly what your eating disorder means to you. Try and think about how it affects your health, relationships and work. Let me share how I responded to this exercise when I was still anorexic:

"What Anorexia means to me and how it makes me feel."

Anorexia feels like a monster that controls me and has taken me over.

I feel that I must be a very bad person and the anorexia is a punishment for something that I did wrong in the past.

It is my fault that I have anorexia. I caused it to happen and I am to blame.

I feel ashamed for having this illness and am sure people think that everything would be okay if I could only eat.

I feel it is impossible for me to eat anything outside the small, 'safe' amounts that I have set for myself.

I feel a coward for being so terrified of food.

I feel so guilty when I let others down and give in to the anorexia.

I am in turmoil and pain inside and I always feel very sad.

I have feelings of dread as meal times approach, total and complete terror when I eat and then afterwards I feel disgusted with myself. I then hurt myself through exercise and cutting myself for being such a bad person.

I feel that I am a nuisance, a problem and a bother to others. Because of this, I find it hard to say how I am really feeling and instead pretend that everything is okay all the time.

I feel physically ill and very tired and weak. It takes a huge effort for me to do anything and I am always very cold.

I have no self-esteem or self-confidence. I don't like myself and think that I am ugly, both inside and out.

I feel a failure and useless. Everything that I do is wrong.

I am scared of other people's anger and want to please everyone all of the time.

I want to be loved but feel that is impossible. I don't believe that anyone could love me because I am such a horrible person.

When you make a list like this, you can see how your eating disorder is robbing you of your life. Giving up your eating disorder is not easy and you may find that looking at your list can help you to keep moving forwards. It is VERY important to remember that if your recovery is to be permanent, you need to take it slowly. Many sufferers try to recover too quickly and end up feeling so frightened that they scurry back to their eating disorder. I always encourage people to take **baby steps** forward in their recovery. You are not in a race to recover and it is important not to put yourself under too much pressure. Here are some tips that might help:

1. Set yourself realistic goals. For example, if you cannot manage to gain one pound in weight every week, aim for just half a pound. Reaching small targets is more sensible and confidence boosting than failing to hit targets that are too high.

2. Don't be too hard on yourself if you do not manage to reach one of your targets. This does not mean that you have failed. It is important to just pick yourself up and start again the next day. You are going to have days when it feels impossible for you to make any progress. On these days, just try to remain stable and not take any steps backwards.

3. Draw up a list of things you will be able to do when you are well. When times are really hard, try to focus on these positive aspects of recovery. I am going to look at this idea in more detail further on in the book.

4. Try to praise yourself for any achievements, even if they are very small, such as eating an extra tablespoon of peas at dinner. Try and focus on these achievements rather than the setbacks you have.

5. When you start to put on some weight, you are likely to feel very panicked and scared. Unfortunately, you need to accept that you are going to feel miserable for a while but if you can ride out these feelings, you WILL come out the other side. Keep reminding yourself how bad the feelings that went with your eating disorder were. When you feel rotten, it is tempting to think that your eating disorder was a safe place to hide but you must keep remembering that it wasn't.

6. As you start to gain weight, you may begin to feel many of the emotions that led you to develop your eating disorder in the first place. As I explained earlier, many people hide from feelings in their eating disorder. You may need extra help identifying and learning how to cope with these difficult feelings, as this is a vital part of recovery. Ask friends, family or your therapist for extra support if you are struggling to cope with new feelings.

7. Try to take control of difficult situations. If meal times are very tough for you, talk to your family about how they can help. Plan exactly what you are going to eat so that you feel prepared before the meal begins. If you cannot make a decision about what you should eat, ask for help. I used to find that I often couldn't even work out what I wanted to eat because my mind was filled with calorie values and I would panic. At times like this, I needed help

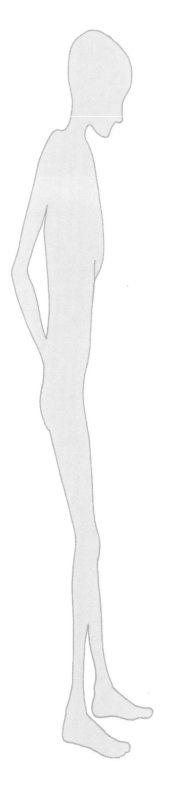

from other people. You may want to ask someone to make all your food decisions for you for a while (which is what would happen if you were in hospital). This is not about losing control but is actually you taking control of your life by asking others to help. This can be a hard step to take and when my parents made food decisions for me, I often had to stop myself from arguing with them. This was my anorexic 'voice' wanting to shout loudly at anyone who tried to feed me.

If you get on well with your Mother, you may find that planning meals together works well. I used to do this with my Mother but sometimes her worries about my health caused problems. She would try to push me into making progress faster than I could manage and this would cause arguments. We would agree on my meal but when I went to wash my hands, she would add extra food to my plate. As an anorexic, I knew exactly how much I was expecting to eat and each time this happened, I would have a panic attack. Both you and your Mother need to be totally honest with each other if you are to make any progress with your meals.

8. You may find yourself constantly focusing on what other people eat because you compare your food intake to theirs. It is time to stop making comparisons and focus instead on exactly what your body needs to recover. There are always going to be people around who are dieting and you may find it very difficult to eat with them. However, it is important that you stick to your own diet plan and learn to ignore what other people are doing.

9. You might find it difficult to know when you are hungry for a while. You are likely to feel full most of the time because you will have become used to eating so little. This will be uncomfortable but the more you stretch your stomach by eating that little bit of extra food, the easier it will feel. Don't allow the feeling of fullness to prevent you from following your diet plan.

10. You may feel afraid that once you start eating, you will not be able to stop. This is a common feeling for anorexics and it starts because your body is starving. You are so hungry all the time that you feel as if you could eat and eat and never stop. This doesn't actually happen though and you will soon discover that you fill up very quickly when you eat. When I was first anorexic, I planned to give myself just one day off from my diet. During this day, I allowed myself to eat anything I wanted. I started the day by eating some cookies and was certain that I could easily eat a whole packet because I craved them so strongly. I'd only had three of these cookies when I found I already felt sick and full. I could not believe what was happening. I had been so certain that I would start eating and never be able to stop.

11. You are likely to have many different fears about recovery. Talk about these with someone who understands. A lot of the fears will be irrational and part of the illness. Many anorexics endlessly plan the different changes they are

going to make to their diets but then feel afraid to even take the first step. Talk about these fears and try to learn that the only way to break out of the eating disorder is to be brave enough to take those first important steps towards recovery.

12. As you put on weight, you may find that people do not worry about your health quite as much. They may seem happier and less concerned, and you might find it hard to adjust to these feelings. It could be that you now feel unimportant and uncared for and cannot understand why everyone else is so happy about your weight gain when it feels so bad to you. You may feel angry with your family for not understanding how difficult it is for you. You may even turn back to your eating disorder as a way of showing everyone how upset you feel. This is why it is always very important to talk about your feelings with the people around you.

I found it very hard to cope with people saying to me that I was looking better. The anorexic 'voice' in my head did not hear the word 'better' but instead heard the word 'fatter'. Keep reminding yourself that the people around you have seen you dangerously ill for a long time. They are not saying you look fat but are just relieved that you no longer look so unwell. Try to see their remarks as positive and don't allow your 'voice' to read anything else into them. It may be wise to ask your family and friends not to make comments about how you look for while, at least until you feel more confident in yourself.

13. Whatever kind of eating disorder you have, you will probably have the occasional binge while you are recovering. This is not a sign that you have failed but is just a natural part of recovery. You have denied yourself food for so long that your body is feeling excited about finally being allowed to have some and this can often lead you to eat more than you feel is 'right'. It is very important to continue to eat properly after you have binged. This may seem impossible because you feel so guilty but if you stop eating your set diet plan, you are more likely to trigger another binge and fall into a negative cycle of eating.

Some tools to help you with your recovery

In Chapter 14, I talked about the idea of a 'Thoughts and Feelings' diary to help you understand your illness more clearly. Writing a diary or journal is one of the most commonly used recovery tools. Your diary is 'safe' because no one else will see it unless you want them to and this means that you will always have somewhere to write down your true feelings. Writing openly about your feelings whenever you feel scared, alone or overwhelmed can help and I would recommend that you write in your diary every day. You do not have to just write about your bad feelings though. Your diary is a place where you can also keep a check on the progress you are making in your recovery. You will start to have some good feelings as well and these may confuse you. I know that when I first started to enjoy the taste of food, I became very scared. I did not feel I was allowed to enjoy food the way that other people did. In my diary, I could explore some of these thoughts to try to understand them.

Honesty is vital in your diary. Even if you are lying to some of the people around you, do not lie in your diary. Record everything about your diet, weight and any negative behaviour such as bingeing, vomiting and purging. If you have avoided meals that you should have eaten, write this down too. Try to take notes throughout the day if you can, rather than only writing in the evening. You need to record your exact feelings at the time an event happens, rather than later in the day when new thoughts may have changed your feelings.

Frequently, therapists set their patients different topics to write about. If you have already been writing in a diary or journal, it will be much easier for you to complete this therapy. While I was in hospital, I was given many different topics and asked to write essays about them. These essays helped me to learn more about myself, my family and the reasons why I became ill.

These are some other possible topics that you may consider writing about in your own journals:

- Describe 10 good events in your life and 10 bad events.
- List 5 good qualities that you have. Simon set me this challenge when we were first writing to each other and it took him six whole months before I finally agreed to list them. Like me, you may find this a very difficult task but remember that this journal is just for you, so be as honest as you can.
- List 10 of the rules that you have drawn up for yourself since you started your eating disorder (such as "I will never eat a meal that contains more than X number of calories"). Put them in order, with the easiest to break at the top and the hardest at the bottom. Then set these as targets for yourself and try to break them one by one.
- Make a list of some of the ways you hurt yourself when you feel guilty for eating.
- Write about some of the comments that have hurt you the most. Describe your feelings when you heard these comments, even if you were told them years ago. I can remember many of the comments my Grandmother made to me as a child and exactly how upset I felt at the time.
- Write about the reasons why you feel a need to be very 'thin'. Describe exactly what your shape means to you.
- Write down some of your dreams or nightmares. I used to do this every night and slept with a pen and paper beside my bed because I was having up to nine nightmares every night. The following are a few examples that

show how my mind was totally obsessed with food and my body shape. I thought about them all day and then dreamed about them all night. My mind was also trying to cope with the abuse I had received from my Grandmother and she was often in my dreams as well.

I am involved in training for summer sports but everybody is laughing at me because of my shape.

I am having dinner with an anorexic girl. She chooses only the smallest meals on the menu and I have to try to explain to her what it is that she has done wrong.

Gran is staying with us for Christmas. I try to ignore her because she is being so cruel but then she trips and hurts herself. I feel very guilty. I am sure that it is my fault because I didn't talk to her.

I open a packet of cookies to see how big they are. As soon as I do this, I am told that because I have opened the packet, I must eat them all.

I am in a restaurant and I have to order a dessert. I start to panic as the sweet trolley gets nearer and I see that all of the desserts are enormous.

Problem Solving

This is another very useful tool to help you with your recovery. Whenever I felt worried or scared by a problem, I always reacted by either eating less food or self-harming. It is important to learn positive new ways of dealing with your problems rather than using negative behaviour. Next time you have a problem, instead of harming yourself, try working through the following points so that you can find a healthy solution:

1) **What exactly is the problem?** You first need to define precisely what your problem is and it helps to write this down, so you are completely clear about what you are trying to solve. *For example: "I want to weigh myself every day."*

2) **Work out some possible solutions.** Do not limit yourself here and write down every single solution you can imagine. Even if the solution seems crazy or selfish, write it down. This is called 'brainstorming' and you can do it alone or with help from friends or relatives. *So in our example, one possible solution is: "How about if I wait a day and weigh myself tomorrow instead?"*

3) **Examine each solution.** Now is the time to look at every solution that you worked out for point number 2. Beside each solution, list the reasons why it could work and the reasons why it might not be a good idea. Do this

for every option and then delete the ones that don't seem realistic. This should leave you with a short list of solutions, all of which could work. *In this case, you might say: "It would be a healthier option if I weighed myself less frequently, so waiting until tomorrow would be a positive step forward".*

4) Consider the consequences of your solutions. This is a very difficult stage because you need to try to think ahead and work out what effect each approach will have on your problem. What you are aiming for is a solution that only has positive consequences for you. *In our example, the solution could have positive consequences as you may actually cut down on your weighing.*

5) Decide on the best solution. Now that you have all the solutions listed, choose the one that seems the most positive to you.

6) Plan the solution. Work out how you can put it into practice. *So in our example you would plan how to stop weighing yourself for a day, perhaps by asking your parents to remove the scales from the bathroom.*

7) Carry out the solution. Do this step by step all the way to your goal.

8) Check out the consequences. Did your solution work? Did it solve the problem and improve anything for you? If it did, then this process worked for you. If the problem has not been solved then you need to return to stage 2 and start all over again, trying a different solution.

You do need to be patient and practise problem solving because although it does not instantly solve every problem, it can work very well. In time, you will learn how to work out solutions to problems very quickly.

Practical help for recovery from your eating disorder

When you have an eating disorder, you need to tackle the physical as well as the mental problems caused by your illness. In other words, not only do you need to change the way that you think but you also need to alter your behaviour. The following are some practical ways that you can deal with your negative patterns of behaviour.

How to stop bingeing

Many eating disorder sufferers feel that if they could just stop bingeing, all of their problems would instantly be solved. Bingeing happens for many different reasons, both mental and physical. Hunger often leads a sufferer to binge, since their mind can focus on nothing but food. When a person has binged, they often skip the next meal and this can then lead them into another binge when they feel very hungry later, and the cycle is set. To help stop the physical cravings that can lead to bingeing, sufferers need to do the following:

- Eat regular meals. Our bodies need the correct amount of food to function properly. If you are starving, most of the time you will have strong cravings for food and these can lead you to binge. Look through Chapter 18 and chose a meal plan that best suits your tastes. If you can stick to this, you are less likely to binge.

- If you do binge, DON'T miss a meal or else you will slip back into a pattern of chaotic eating.

- If you do binge, DON'T vomit afterwards.

- Try to never skip a meal because this is likely to make you become very hungry and lead to a binge.

- Avoid alcohol and/or drugs, as these can affect your appetite and may lead you to binge more.

- In the days before your monthly period you may be more likely to binge. Make sure you follow your diet plan carefully around this time, allowing yourself some extra food at meal times if you are very hungry.

- Learn to deal with the consequences of binges, such as vomiting and laxative abuse.

Bingeing is not just a physical response to hunger though. Sufferers also turn to bingeing because they believe that it solves other problems in their lives. To help yourself deal with this aspect of bingeing, you need to return to your diary. Concentrate on writing down everything you can think of about the binge - the time of day it happened, your feelings before and after you binged, and the reasons why you did it. Write about the foods you binged on and why these made you feel good. After a few days, you should begin to see a pattern forming and this can help you to understand the reasons why you binge.

The next stage is to set yourself some new rules about binges:

1) Try and limit yourself to just one binge a day. If you are bingeing several times each day, this may be too hard so try to cut down slowly - from four times to three to just two binges a day and then finally down to one.

2) Work out your 'danger zones'. For example, some sufferers manage not to binge while they are at school or work but then start again as soon as they get home in the evenings. Draw up a plan for your most dangerous time of day, so that you have other events to occupy your time rather than just bingeing. Perhaps you need to ask your friends or family to stay with you during this time.

3) Write down the situations or events that most frequently trigger your binges, and then use problem solving or cognitive therapy to find healthy solutions to these worries or fears.

4) Try to find ways of distracting yourself from bingeing. Ask for help during

these times and talk with your parents or friends. Focus on a particular activity that keeps your mind occupied and away from thoughts of bingeing.

5) When you are feeling the need to binge, DON'T go food shopping.

6) As time passes and you have managed a number of days without bingeing, try not to panic. Many sufferers feel this way and are certain that one binge will set them right back to the beginning of their recovery. This is not the case though. You must allow yourself to have setbacks without thinking that you have undone all your good work.

7) If you do binge again, try to work out exactly what caused it this time. What changed? Did you stop working through the therapy that helps you to prevent binges? Are you missing a favourite food? No foods should be 'unsafe' and there are ways of slowly introducing all these foods back into your diet (see Chapter 18).

How to stop vomiting

This section will apply mostly to bulimics, although people suffering from bulimarexia and some anorexics also vomit. People who vomit usually fall into one of two groups:

1) Those who only vomit occasionally - usually two to three times a week. They do not vomit straight after a binge but wait a few hours. Sometimes they will even binge without vomiting.

2) Those who vomit many times a day - after snacks and meals as well as following binges.

If you are in the first group then you already have quite a lot of control over your vomiting. You need to record in your diary exactly how many times you vomit every week. Try and do this for three weeks and then look at the results. Are the numbers very similar? Let's say that you vomit four times each week. Now you can set yourself a task. In the week ahead, try to cut down on the number of times you vomit by one, so that you now only vomit three times.

At the end of the week, ask yourself how difficult this task was for you. If it was not too difficult then the following week you can set yourself another task. Cut down even further on the number of times you vomit by one again. This may be a lot harder for you to do and if it is, then stay at this level until you feel more comfortable. As soon as you feel that vomiting only twice a week is manageable, cut down even further so that you are just vomiting once a week. Continue with this exercise until you have stopped altogether.

It is quite likely that you will have weeks when you feel that you have failed because you had an extra binge and vomit. Try not to focus on these slip-ups because they are not the end of the world. We all make mistakes. You need to allow yourself to be human like the rest of us and accept that you don't always have to be perfect. However, it is important to look at why you slipped. Did you try to cut down too quickly on the number of times you vomit? If you did, then go back a week and allow yourself to vomit that extra time until you feel comfortable enough to drop down a level again. It may be that you had a particularly difficult week, with extra problems at school, work or home and these triggered the binge. If this is the case, try and stay level at the same number of vomits for another week and see if you can manage without the extra binge/vomit session.

If you fall into the second group, your diet may have gone completely out of control so that your body is starving, and this is triggering the binge and vomit sessions. It is also very likely that you are using vomiting as a way of dealing with all your fears and worries. What began as a way of losing weight has now become a way of life. Keep a record of exactly how much you eat during a binge. Are you eating large amounts of food? Does food feel like a comfort when you are stressed? Does bingeing and vomiting stop you from thinking about the other problems in your life? If you are going to stop vomiting, you need to learn new ways of dealing with your anxieties. Look at the relaxation exercises and problem solving sections in this chapter, and also at the idea of cognitive behaviour therapy in Chapter 16. These are all good ways of helping you to deal with worries and fears in a healthy way.

It is not easy to stop vomiting when you are used to doing it many times a day. You may have lived for months or even years feeling either very full after a binge or starving hungry after vomiting. You need to adjust to the feelings in between, such as slightly hungry, comfortably full, etc.

The first step towards recovery is looking at your vomiting behaviour. How much time do you leave between eating and vomiting? If there are 5 minutes between the time you have eaten and the time you vomit then you need to set yourself a task. During the next week try and delay your vomiting for double this time period - 10 minutes. If you find that you can manage to do this then during the next week you need to double the time again, waiting 20 minutes between eating and vomiting. As you become more comfortable with the longer time periods between eating and vomiting, keep lengthening the time. Always set yourself realistic targets and remember that this is not a race. If you can only manage to increase the gap between eating and vomiting by one minute at a time, that is fine. It is all progress. Try not to set yourself goals that are too difficult because these can cause you to panic. You could fail to reach your target and may even give up on the idea of recovery.

In the time between eating and vomiting, you are likely to feel very anxious and also very full. Your eating disorder 'voice' may be talking to you about how 'fat' you are becoming. You need to learn how to distract yourself from these thoughts and feelings. Try cognitive therapy or some of the relaxation exercises.

Use your diary to write down all your negative feelings and then answer them with positive thoughts. Ring a friend if you are on your own. Talk with your parents and ask them for their help and encouragement. Go for a gentle walk (no over-exercising though). Take up a new creative hobby such as needlework or painting, which you can work on during the time between eating and vomiting. Try and focus all your anxieties into being creative. You will be able to see that you are progressing with your recovery as your creative project, needlework or painting, takes shape.

Always remember to only make one change at a time. If you make a change that you find too frightening, don't panic - just go back a step. Don't move on and make another change until you feel comfortable and safe again. You also need to reward yourself during this time. Changing your behaviour is very difficult and you need to feel good about your achievements. Buy yourself a present every week. You may have stopped buying yourself gifts because you don't feel you deserve them. Now is the time to learn that you do deserve rewards, especially when you are fighting so hard for recovery. Wouldn't you reward someone else who was working as hard as you?

How to stop taking laxatives and diuretics

If you have been taking laxatives and/or diuretics (water tablets), you are likely to have some side effects if you suddenly stop taking them. Your body may swell slightly as you retain water. This water retention is known as oedema. To avoid this, try to cut down on the number of laxatives you are taking rather than stopping them all at once. Unfortunately, you may still experience some water retention. If you find that certain parts of your body are swelling, try to sleep propped up for a while to prevent fluid collecting around your face and sit with your legs up to allow the oedema to drain from your ankles.

You will also find that when you give up laxatives, you may become constipated. This can leave you feeling uncomfortable and bloated. Many eating disorder sufferers talk of the comforting 'empty' feeling they have after they have taken a large number of laxatives. You need to learn to live without this feeling because it is very unhealthy. You will also need to alter your diet to prevent serious constipation. It is possible to obtain natural fibre supplements from the chemist or your doctor to help at this time but changes to your diet will also make a difference.

As you cut down on laxatives, you will need to eat more fibre. It is important to start slowly though and gradually add cooked fruit and vegetables into your daily diet. Have a hot drink before you eat in the morning, as this will help your bowels to start working properly. Do not eat large amounts of wheat bran though, because this causes wind and stomach bloating and it also affects the calcium levels in your body. As the wheat bran passes out of your body, it takes the calcium with it and this can cause more bone problems. Oat bran is a much healthier alternative to wheat bran. Another idea is to replace each laxative with a dried prune or dried apricot. So every time you cut out one more laxative, simply add another prune or apricot to your diet. As you cut down on the number of laxatives you are taking, try to increase the amount of water that you are drinking. You need to drink at least six glasses of water each day. When you have stopped your laxatives completely, start adding raw fruit and vegetables to your diet again.

If you are going to give up laxatives, you need to realise that this is a permanent change. Don't put some aside for 'use in an emergency' because there is always a danger that you will be tempted to take them again when you are feeling scared by weight gain.

It is important to let your doctor know that you are trying to cut down on laxatives or diuretics. If you are really struggling with bad constipation, they will be able to give you some mild medicine that can help you through this difficult time. It will take you a few months to adjust to life without laxatives but for most people, their bowels do adapt completely.

How to stop over-exercising

Whether you are anorexic or bulimic, you may be over-exercising and you will need to stop this if you are to put on weight. Often, when sufferers start to eat more food they turn to exercise as a way of slowing down their weight gain. Again, honesty is important here and you need to tell your family or friends if you are secretly trying to do more exercise. I used to spend many hours each day exercising to videos or music tapes, which was very dangerous for my health. This diary entry shows how I would use exercise as a way of coping with the guilt I felt after eating:

Monday November 3rd 1997
I had a really bad day today and tried to cover up a lot of the pain I was feeling by over-exercising. I tried a new exercise that I had never done before and did it over and over again until I was shaking and feeling ill. The anorexic voice is telling me that I am good for doing so much. It says that exercise is good and food is bad. I must exercise more and eat less. I know that I shouldn t listen to this voice but it feels like it controls me totally.

Exercising may also be a way of blocking out feelings and emotions that are too painful for you to cope with, so you may find it difficult to give this up. If your weight is dangerously low and your heart is not strong enough to cope, you will need to stop exercising completely for a while. My doctor did tell my parents that

I was over-exercising and I started to spend the time I usually exercised with my Father instead. I needed help at this time to cope with strong feelings of guilt and we tried to keep my mind occupied by working on craft projects together.

The more you exercise, the more food you will need to eat to maintain your weight. So if you are going for recovery, constant exercising will just mean that you have to eat even more food. It is dangerous to exercise if your body has no fuel to use. Professional sports people eat higher calorie diets to ensure that they have enough energy to perform well.

Many sufferers believe that in order to be 'fit', they have to work out for hours every day. This is not true though and too much exercise can be dangerous. Exercise should be something you enjoy in small amounts in order to remain healthy - you should not finish a session and feel totally exhausted. It is recommended that adults exercise for about thirty minutes, three or four times each week. Once people go over these levels, the health benefits decrease and there is a risk of injury. However, it is VERY important that you check with your doctor before you begin any exercise programme. You need to be at a healthy weight before your body is able to cope with **aerobic** exercise (which increases the heart rate). Do remember that you may be doing a lot of aerobic exercise without even realising it, so take this into account when you are planning how much exercise you need to do each week.

Cut down on weighing to only once a week

Eating disorder sufferers often weigh themselves many times each day. Bulimics also usually get on the scales before and after binges, to see the effect this has had on their weight. Sometimes they try to avoid the scales because they are just too afraid of knowing the result but eventually they feel desperate and start weighing themselves again. Everyone's weight varies by between 1 and 4 pounds every day but this can just be due to water retention. For women, their monthly periods can have an effect and even simple events such as going to the toilet can alter body weight. This is why you do not get an accurate reading if you weigh yourself many times a day.

The best way to see how your weight is changing is to weigh yourself just once a week. Make sure you do this at the same time of day each week and that you are wearing the same clothes. Set a time and day that is suitable for you but that doesn't allow you time to binge after the weighing session. Some eating disorder sufferers feel so unhappy with the figure they read on the scale that this can trigger them into a binge. Once you have decided on a time and day, you need to be very strict with yourself. You must accept that this is the ONLY time you can weigh yourself each week.

If you have been weighing yourself very often, you may find that you cannot immediately switch to just once a week. If this is the case, work towards this goal by cutting down slowly on the number of times you weigh yourself each day. For example, in the first week you should weigh yourself only twice a day. For the second week, weigh yourself just once a day. For the third week, try and weigh yourself every other day. Continue to cut down on the number of times you weigh yourself until it is only once a week. You may need to draw up a chart to measure your progress to avoid getting confused. This may take you a while but it is a very important part of recovery.

Eating disorder sufferers will also often measure themselves. By doing this, they are trying to work out how much body fat they have. Again, this is not healthy behaviour and if you are doing this, you need to stop. By constantly measuring yourself, you are encouraging your obsessions about your shape. Cut down on the number of times you measure yourself each week, using the same methods that we looked at for weighing and see if you can stop this behaviour completely.

A solution for panic attacks - relaxation techniques

During meal times, anorexics and bulimics often feel scared and panicked. I used to feel a desperate urge to run away and escape from the situation. Many therapists teach their patients relaxation exercises, which can be used when they are feeling very scared, either before or after meal times. By concentrating on these exercises, it is possible to reduce your stress levels.

Relaxation techniques do not always work for everyone. When you first try to do these exercises, you may find them difficult but don't give up too soon. Try the examples below and see if they work for you. If they do, use them whenever you feel really scared or anxious.

The most common relaxation exercise involves the tensing and relaxing of all the muscles in your body. Start by lying down on a bed or couch in a warm room. Loosen any tight clothing that you are wearing and remove your glasses if you wear them.

Close your eyes and breathe in deeply. Hold your breath and then breathe out again slowly. Concentrate on your breathing until you feel that you are breathing evenly. Don't breathe too quickly or you may start to hyperventilate and feel dizzy or faint.

Tense all the muscles in your right foot. Breathe in as you tense the muscles and out again as you relax. Repeat this and then move onto your left foot and do the same. Tense the muscles as you breathe in and then relax your muscles as you breathe out.

During this exercise work your way up your body, tensing and relaxing each set of muscles, moving through your calves, thighs, buttocks, lower back, stomach, hands, arms and chest. Finish by screwing up your face tightly. Then relax and repeat again. Once you have covered all the muscles in your body, imagine that your body is pressing down hard into your bed and allow your mind to drift away onto pleasant thoughts.

After about five minutes, slowly open your eyes and start to move your body again. You should feel calmer, more relaxed and refreshed. Try to practise this exercise two or three times every day, before or after meals, when you are at your most anxious. As time passes, you will find that you need to tense and relax fewer muscles since you can become relaxed by a mental process rather than a physical one.

Another relaxation technique that is often taught by therapists is quite similar to the first one. Start the exercise by lying on a bed and breathe in deeply. Hold your breath and then breathe out. Repeat this until you have even breathing.

Now imagine that your whole body is filled with sand and that you have little holes in your fingertips and toes. The sand starts to leave your body through these holes and as it does, your body becomes limp. Your head drops and your body presses into the bed. As the sand continues to drain from your body, you become more relaxed as your worries disappear with the sand and your mind drifts into calm and happy thoughts. After five or ten minutes, open your eyes and slowly move off the bed. Again, you should now feel calm and relaxed.

Imagery or 'visualisation' is also a popular way of helping anxious patients to relax. Find a private place where you can be alone for ten to fifteen minutes. Make yourself comfortable, close your eyes and start deep breathing. Allow images to appear in your mind without forcing them or trying to control them. Picture a very relaxing scene, such as a calm lake in the summer time - there is a gentle buzzing of bees in the flowers round the lakeside and crickets can be heard. Or imagine an empty beach in the early evening, or a snowy landscape. Concentrate on all the details - the sounds you might hear, the colours, smells and the temperature, and even imagine touching certain objects there. Allow yourself to really enjoy the place that you are visiting and start to relax.

When you are feeling relaxed, slowly bring the image to a close. Remind yourself that you can return to this relaxing place whenever you want and bring yourself back to the present. If this imagery works for you, then practise doing it at least once a day. You need to allow yourself some time when you can completely relax, undisturbed.

I have covered many different aspects of recovery in this chapter but have specifically avoided mentioning food and diets. This is an important subject, so I have focused on it in the following chapter. Please read on.

Chapter 18

What is a Healthy Diet?

Summary
Most eating disorder sufferers have forgotten what it is like to eat normally. This chapter outlines a number of different healthy eating plans that can be used during recovery.

When many eating disorder sufferers decide on recovery, they do not know what 'normal' eating is any more. In this chapter, I want to describe what a healthy diet is and try to calm many of the fears that sufferers have about weight gain. It is important that eating disorder sufferers reach a healthy weight for their recovery to be complete. When they reach a healthy weight, their minds and bodies will no longer be starving and their preoccupation with food will start to fade. However, it is likely that you will need some help and support to choose a diet plan and organise your meals every day.

Many anorexics feel certain that they want recovery but are scared to gain weight. Others decide not to give up their eating disorders and choose to try and live with long-term anorexia or bulimia. If you do choose this option, you have to accept that you will never lead a normal life because your mind will always be preoccupied with thoughts of food. Your work and personal relationships can never be completely normal because the eating disorder will be such a major part of your life. I lived at a very low weight for many years and was always unhappy. I felt that food ruled my life. It was only when I allowed my weight to reach a healthy level that I began to understand exactly how destructive my eating disorder was.

How do anorexics start to eat normally?

If you have started working with a dietician, it is wise for you to focus on the diet they have planned for you. However, if you have chosen to create your own healthy eating plan then this chapter can help you. Often, books about treatment have very different ideas about which foods you should give to anorexic patients. Some, for example, say that you should never give anorexics diet products. However, I would disagree with this idea because for many sufferers, diet products are the only foods they are willing to try at first. If your weight is low and all you feel able to eat is diet yoghurt, then that is at least a start. I know many sufferers who will eat six slices of diet bread but cannot manage even one slice of normal bread. Gradually though, as you begin to recover, you will want to try different foods when the diet products start to become boring.

I have also often heard it said that you should never prepare special meals to tempt anorexics. I can understand that doctors feel this may encourage anorexic behaviour but I believe it is very important to treat eating disorder sufferers with extra care. By preparing special meals, parents are showing their child that they really do care and feel unconditional love for them. This is a vital part of recovery and can help sufferers a lot.

I also believe it is always important to involve a sufferer in making decisions about their diet. I know that when I started to recover, I had cravings for certain foods. If my Mother cooked these for me, I was more likely to eat them than if she gave me food which she had decided I must eat.

Once you have started to eat then it is important to gradually increase the amount of food in your diet. This is obviously going to be difficult and it is important to work out your diet plan in advance. If you know exactly what you are required to eat each day, this can help. I felt more in control when I planned every diet change myself, with help from my doctors. When I was first anorexic, my parents tried to control my eating by forcing me to have more food than I could manage. This terrified me and so I started to lie about how much I was eating. It is important that you explain to your parents exactly how you need them to help you with your diet, so that you can all work together.

As an anorexic, your mind will be preoccupied with thoughts of food all the time and you may become very interested in cooking. It could help you to start preparing meals with your parents. This will allow you to still feel in control of your eating. You can see just how much food you will receive on your plate at meal times and this helps. Meal times are often the most frightening times of the day and it is important to do everything possible to stay as calm as you can. Discuss the amount you need to eat but try not to argue over every increase your parents suggest. Remember that you need to put on weight in order to get better and fighting your fear of food is a huge part of recovery. You will probably find that your anorexic 'voice' argues about every single increase though. If your parents say two potatoes, your 'voice' will tell you to ask for just one. Compromise is important here so that both you and your parents feel that you are making progress and working towards recovery. Why not agree to have 1_ potatoes for example?

It is very important that the changes you make to your diet are small. Many anorexics will at some time have felt very frightened by a doctor threatening them with a hospital stay and in response may have suddenly tried to eat a normal diet. This is not a good idea. If you have been eating very small amounts for months, you will need to slowly build up your food intake again. It is dangerous to suddenly eat large amounts when your stomach has shrunk. You need to gradually stretch your stomach with small frequent snacks.

Many anorexics do panic when they first start to feel hungry. You may have gone for months without feeling hungry and it can be scary when these feelings return. This is just your body reacting in a natural way though and does not mean that you are losing control of your eating. You may also start to have cravings for certain foods. This is just your body telling you that you need food. Cravings are often a good sign that you are making progress and that your appetite is beginning to return. They will pass if you eat small regular meals throughout the day and allow yourself to enjoy the foods you crave as part of your diet. It is important to eat carbohydrates with every meal, as this helps to maintain your blood sugar level and prevent the possibility of binges.

Some anorexics find it helpful to keep a record of their diets, writing down the increases to show their progress. Others find this too frightening. When they actually see the amount of food they have eaten written down, they often feel it is too much. It is important to work out exactly which method is best for you. If you are seeing a doctor or a dietician, they will usually ask you to keep a food diary so that they can see your progress. Try to remember that for a while you are going to think you are eating a lot, even though your diet is still very limited.

It is important to realise that when you start to eat food, you are not putting on 'fat'. For many months or possibly years, your body has been starving and all your major organs will have suffered. Bone density has been lost and muscles have wasted away including your heart, which is the largest muscle in the human body. Anorexics are also often dehydrated and when they first begin to put on weight, this gain is due to their bodies rehydrating. Try to imagine that your insides have become like dried prunes or raisins. They have shrivelled and shrunk and as you start to eat and drink, they slowly begin to return to their normal size. Try to see food as an important medication. It is a vital part of your recovery and will restore your body to a healthy state.

Exactly how much does an anorexic need to eat to put on weight?

In hospital, anorexics are usually expected to put on between 1 and 2 lbs in weight each week. Naturally, anorexics would rather put on just one pound a week (or even half a pound) and this is often the goal for patients recovering at home. If you need between 1,500 and 2,000 calories to maintain your weight, then you will have to eat an extra 500 calories per day to put on one pound in a week. This is how it works:

500 extra calories per day = 3,500 calories per week = 1 lb in weight.

These extra calories are often eaten as snacks throughout the day. I used to have extra snacks at 11.00 am, 3.00 pm and bedtime. Or you can choose to have some meal replacement drinks instead. These are drinks that are high in calories but not large in volume, so you won't feel too full. You can buy these in chemist shops and there are a variety of brands available (Build-Up and Complan for example). Your doctor can also prescribe different meal replacement drinks (such as Fortisips or Ensure Plus). I personally found that I could only drink Build-Up because I just didn't like the taste of the other medical drinks.

When an anorexic is being treated in hospital, they are usually fed a diet of around 3,000 calories per day. However, it is unlikely that a sufferer recovering at home will eat this number of calories each day. In hospital, doctors and nurses take control of the sufferer's diet and challenge their anorexic 'voice'. At home, the sufferer has to fight their own anorexic 'voice' and it is more realistic to manage a daily intake of around 2,000 calories. If the sufferer is at a very low weight, they will need to build up gently to this number of calories, starting with a very basic diet.

Diet Plans

I talked earlier about the idea of 'safe' and 'unsafe' foods. Most anorexics live on 'safe' foods, eating only low calorie, sugar free diet products and avoiding any higher calorie food. If you do eat just fruit, vegetables and diet foods, you will need to change this pattern to introduce proteins, carbohydrates, dairy products and fats into your diet as well. As you start recovery, it is important to slowly begin to feel comfortable with your 'unsafe' foods again although this does not mean you will have to make major changes. For example, try to start by switching from skimmed milk to semi-skimmed milk or from diet yoghurt to low fat yoghurt. If an anorexic is very underweight and a large amount of their body weight has been lost then it is important for them to avoid high fibre foods. A lot of muscle will have been lost from the wall of their stomach, so it is very difficult for them to digest bulky high fibre foods.

Anorexics frequently skip meals and breakfast is often avoided. This is a very important meal since it kick starts the metabolism and gives us enough energy to begin the day. If you haven't eaten any food first thing in the morning for many months, start with just a glass of milk or orange juice. After a few days, increase this by adding a small bowl of cereal or half a slice of toast, remembering to make your changes slowly and gently.

The following diet contains about 1,800 calories and you will probably need to build up to this diet slowly if your weight is low. Anorexics can put on weight eating 1,800 calories a day if their weight is very low when they start the diet. As soon as you find that your weight has reached a steady level and you are no longer gaining, then you need to increase your intake to around 2,100 calories a day to maintain weight gain.

Start very slowly with a gentle diet, including food such as omelettes, nutritious soups, milky drinks and desserts. When you have adapted to eating this kind of a diet, then gradually start to include solid foods as well. Add cereal at breakfast and a jacket potato at lunch. Try to aim for a diet of 1,200 calories at first and from there, gradually work towards a full diet of 1,800 calories. Depending on your age, weight and height, you will need more than this to maintain healthy growth, so remember that it is just a temporary diet and you will need to add extra food in time.

For anorexics, there are certain parts of their diets that they especially need to focus on. For example, if your periods have stopped then your bones are being damaged and so it is important to make sure that you have enough calcium in your diet. Many anorexics also suffer from anaemia, so try to make sure that your diet contains iron-rich foods.

A Sample Diet Containing Approximately 1,800 calories

Breakfast	A boiled egg and two slices of toast, topped with two teaspoons of low fat spread.
or	2 Weetabix or Shredded Wheat with one small banana and a quarter pint of semi-skimmed milk and one slice of wholemeal toast with one teaspoon of low fat spread.
or	80g (3oz) of muesli with half a pint of milk and a glass of fruit juice.
11am	One piece of fruit and 2 cookies. Coffee or tea with milk.
Lunch	200g (7oz) jacket potato with a small tin of baked beans or a small tub of cottage cheese
or	50g (2 oz) of cheddar cheese
or	a small tin of tuna and one tablespoon of mayonnaise. Add two teaspoons of margarine or butter to the potato.
or	A sandwich made with two medium slices of brown bread, spread with 2 teaspoons of butter or margarine and filled with 50g (2 oz) of cheese
or	two eggs mixed with two teaspoons of mayonnaise or a small can of tuna mixed with two teaspoons of mayonnaise.
Dessert	A 150g pot of yoghurt or a small fruit trifle or two scoops of ice-cream.

3 pm	One small packet of potato crisps (25g). Coffee or tea with milk.
Dinner	An individual meal of 300 calories such as cauliflower cheese, served with 4 tablespoons of peas and 4 tablespoons of sweetcorn.
or	3 fish fingers or 3 vegetable fingers, with 100g (4oz) of oven chips and 2 tablespoons of peas and 2 tablespoons of sweetcorn.
or	100g (4oz) cooked chicken with 200g (7oz) potato and 4 tablespoons of peas.
Dessert	Fruit and one scoop of ice cream.
Bedtime	A milky drink (which completes the daily intake of half a pint) and a cookie.

When you have been eating this diet for a number of weeks, your weight should stabilise and you will need to add extra calories. Try to include extra additions so that your diet increases from 1,800 to 2,100 calories, and then to 2,400 and 2,700 etc. As you start to reach a more normal weight, you will find it harder and harder to gain weight and will need to increase your calorie intake to a higher level. Use the following options to boost your calorie intake.

Dietary Additions

1. One thick slice of bread and butter, to be added to the evening meal. (150 calories)
2. The cookies at 11.00 am should be replaced with a 50g (2oz) bar of chocolate. (250 calories)
3. One cup of milk to be drunk at 3pm, instead of tea or coffee with your crisps. (100 calories)
4. A pudding and custard to replace the individual dessert, e.g. one small fruit pie and 150 ml of custard. (350 calories)
5. Replace the cookie at bedtime with a cereal bar of 150 calories.
6. If you choose the boiled egg option at breakfast, then also add 40g of cereal and half a pint of milk.
7. If you are eating the Shredded Wheat or Weetabix option, then add a second slice of toast spread with two teaspoons of butter or margarine and 2 teaspoons of jam. (200 calories)
8. Add a large banana to lunch. (100 calories)

Again, remember to always take it at your own pace and in time you should slowly try to increase your diet to 3,000 calories a day. It is unwise to go over this limit unless a doctor has specifically recommended that you eat a very high calorie diet. The above diet and the pyramid plan below show you how to eat a normal healthy diet every day. If you continue to follow these plans for the rest of your life, you can maintain a healthy weight.

- An adult woman needs between 1,900 and 2,300 calories per day, depending on weight, height and activity level.
- An adult man needs between 2,400 and 2,900 calories per day, depending on weight, height and activity level.
- The calorie intake a child needs varies depending on age, weight, height and activity level. Please discuss the exact figure needed with your doctor.

If you are eating a very low calorie diet at the moment, this may all seem very frightening to you. This is understandable and you can see from my diary extracts that I often found food increases very tough myself.

Wednesday April 22nd 1998
My doctor decided to give me another food increase today and I feel so bad right now. I feel very scared and alone. I have to increase my protein by 30g and that just feels impossible. My parents keep saying that is nothing but to me it seems such a huge amount. I am certain that I will be elephant size within a day. I hate food increases and I hate myself and I am certain I am getting FAT, FAT, FAT!

However hard food increases are for you, try to understand that they are vital if you are to keep moving forward. Recovery is not easy but it IS worth all the effort. My therapist showed me how to ask myself questions when I was finding food increases difficult. If you are really struggling to make changes, try asking yourself the following questions:

a) Did you try to change too much too soon? *If the answer to this is "Yes", then take a step back and make smaller changes.*

b) Did you decide on the change yourself or was it forced on you? *It is not easy to make changes that you haven't planned yourself. Make sure that you agree with each change before you attempt it.*

c) Did you try to change the most difficult part of your diet? *If the answer is "Yes", then work on something which is easier to change instead and return to the area you are really struggling with later.*

d) Did you make a change at the wrong time for you? *Perhaps you were not in the right frame of mind to make this change. Ask yourself if you were just too tired to make a change. Was your anorexic 'voice' shouting at you?*

Maybe you need to read the chapter about the 'voice' again and arm yourself with more tools to fight it.

e) Have you made too many changes recently and feel in need of a break? *This can happen to everyone when they are trying to recover. You may need to just have a rest for a while. Try to maintain all the changes that you have recently made and avoid slipping back into your anorexic ways. Don't make your break too long though, or else you will find it too hard to get back into the habit of making increases.*

f) Are there enough people helping you to fight your eating disorder? *If you are trying to recover alone, you may be finding it harder to cope with changes. This is a good time to go back to your family doctor and explain what you are trying to do. Ask if they can refer you to a therapist or a dietician who can give you some extra support.*

g) Do you really want to make changes or are you just trying to please others? *Are you ready to let go of your anorexia or are you fighting against recovery every step of the way? Perhaps it is time to reassess whether you really want recovery. Be honest with yourself here.*

Your anorexic voice will shout loudly as you try to increase your diet and you need to fight against it. It will say to you:

"Don't eat that food, it will make you fat!"

Fight back with logic. You know that the voice always lies, so try saying something like: *"I know that my body needs this food. It is starving and it's just the illness that is making me FEEL fat. I understand that I am very thin and because I want recovery, I need to eat this food."*

Pyramid Diet Plan

The above diet plan is one example of a healthy eating plan. You may have been surprised that I included chocolate and crisps, you prpbably believe these are 'junk' foods. Not only is it important to reject the idea of 'forbidden' foods in your diet but you also need to learn that these foods do contain nutritional value as well. Chocolate contains calcium and iron, both of which are vital in our diet, and one packet of crisps has more vitamin C than an apple. Do not just dismiss these foods as 'junk'.

As you recover from your illness, you may find it hard to eat all the different types of food on the plan. Try to aim for the correct number of calories that your body needs right now, even if you cannot manage all the different food types. As you start to recover, you will feel more like experimenting with them.

You may already know about the pyramid food plan for healthy eating, which is currently very popular. I am going to describe it here so that you are able to design your own healthy eating plan. This allows you to take control of your recovery. It is important to learn exactly how much of each food type we need to eat every day to maintain a healthy weight.

The basic idea of the pyramid is to take the five major food groups and arrange them in a pyramid shape, to explain exactly how much of each type you need to eat. You may be worried by the number of servings that you are expected to eat. It helped me to know that if I ate the lowest figure for each set of servings (6 servings of carbohydrates, 5 servings of fruit and vegetables and 4 servings of protein), I was eating just 1,600 calories per day. The higher figure (11 servings of carbohydrates, 9 servings of fruit and vegetables and 6 servings of protein) equals about 2,800 calories per day. Knowing this, you can work out how to increase your intake to a level which allows you to gain weight.

At the bottom of the pyramid are the group of foods you need to eat the most of in your diet. This is the group of carbohydrates, which includes bread, cereals, rice and pasta. You need to eat between 6 and 11 servings from this group each day. An average serving is one slice of bread, 1 oz (28 g) of cereal, one small roll or muffin, or half a cup of cooked rice or pasta.

The next step up is the fruit and vegetable level, from which you need to eat between 5 and 9 servings per day. One serving of fruit is a whole item such as an apple, a pear, half a grapefruit or a wedge of melon. One serving of vegetables is half a cup of beans, peas or cooked vegetables.

The third layer is the protein level. This includes dairy produce such as eggs, cheese and milk as well as meat, fish, beans, nuts and lentils. You need to eat between 4 and 6 servings from this group. One serving is equal to 1 glass of milk, 2 oz of cheese, a pot of yoghurt, 1 egg, half a cup of cooked beans, 5 to 7 oz of meat or fish, or 2 tablespoons of peanut butter.

At the top of the pyramid you find the layer of fats, oils and sweets. These are an important part of your diet. Everyone needs to eat a certain amount of fat for their body to function properly. It is unhealthy to eat too much from this group.

I was surprised when I discovered just how much I needed to eat to maintain my weight and this actually helped me with my recovery. I began to realise that my weight would not balloon if I ate just one cookie.

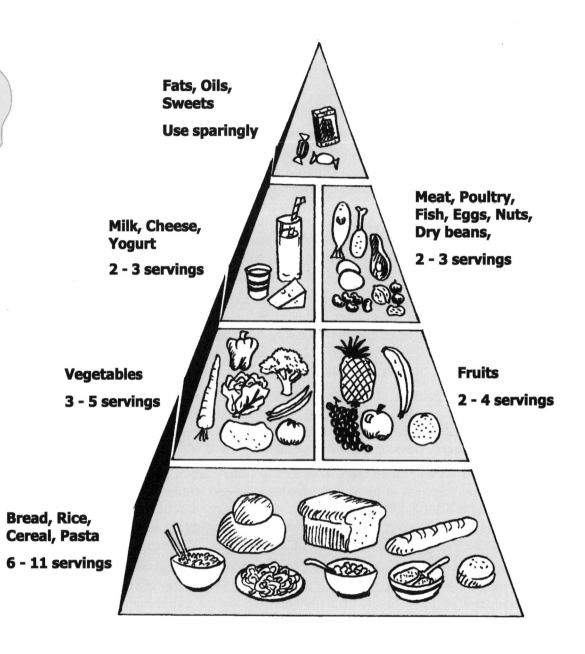

Fats, Oils, Sweets

Use sparingly

Milk, Cheese, Yogurt

2 - 3 servings

Meat, Poultry, Fish, Eggs, Nuts, Dry beans,

2 - 3 servings

Vegetables

3 - 5 servings

Fruits

2 - 4 servings

Bread, Rice, Cereal, Pasta

6 - 11 servings

Vitamins and Minerals

Vitamins and minerals are of vital importance in our diet. Many eating disorder sufferers notice that they are losing their hair, their skin is becoming dry and flaky, and that their nails are brittle and broken. These are all the result of vitamin or mineral deficiencies. If your doctors are concerned about your health, they are likely to recommend multi-vitamins.

Vitamins

The following are some of the major vitamin groups and the symptoms that you will experience if you are lacking them:

Vitamin A - This helps to maintain healthy vision, the health of the eyes, hair, skin and gums and build bones and teeth. A lack of this vitamin can lead to chest infections, flaky skin and poor eyesight and hair quality. Vitamin A is found in carrots, eggs, margarine, dark green vegetables, tuna, mackerel, melons and pumpkins.

Vitamin B1 - This is vital for energy and helps to maintain healthy nerve function, muscle tone and normal appetite. If it is lacking, this can lead to muscle weakness, tiredness, stomach problems, loss of appetite, sickness, depression, poor memory and concentration. Vitamin B1 is found in pork, sunflower seeds, wheatgerm, pasta, watermelons, peanuts, brown rice, oranges and oatmeal.

Vitamin B2 - This is vital for growth and for tissue repair. It is important for the metabolism of carbohydrates, proteins and fats and helps the forming of red blood cells in the bone marrow. A lack of this vitamin causes painful eye problems, hair loss, sleep problems, dizziness, skin flaking, cracked lips and sore mouths. Vitamin B2 is found in skimmed milk, cottage cheese, cereals, tangerines, avocados, prunes, mushrooms, lean beef, chicken, salmon and broccoli.

Vitamin B6 - This is needed for the production of red blood cells and also for the metabolism of carbohydrates, fats and proteins. Of all the B vitamins, it is most vital for maintaining a healthy immune system. A lack of this vitamin can lead to mouth and skin problems, migraines, moodiness, depression, breast soreness and swollen stomachs, fingers and ankles. Vitamin B6 is found in fish, soya beans, avocados, chicken, bananas, cauliflower, spinach and raisins.

Vitamin B12 - This is essential for the forming of red blood cells, maintaining the nervous system and helping carbohydrate, protein and fat metabolism. A lack of this vitamin can lead to anaemia, nervous problems and problems with menstruation. Vitamin B12 is found in cottage cheese, salmon, shellfish, lean beef and pork.

Vitamin C - This protects the cells in the body. It builds and maintains the substance called collagen, which holds cells together. It helps with the healing of wounds and maintains healthy gums, teeth, bones and blood vessels. It also increases the absorption of iron into the body. A lack of this vitamin can lead to dry skin and gum problems, muscle and joint pains and bleeding beneath the skin, the eyes and the nose. Vitamin C is found in fresh fruit and vegetables such as oranges, melons, broccoli and brussel sprouts.

Vitamin D - This helps with calcium absorption in the body and builds strong bones and teeth. A lack of this vitamin causes aching legs, muscle weakness and spasms, and brittle bones. Vitamin D is found in skimmed milk, tuna, salmon, sardines and fortified cereals.

Vitamin E - This vitamin protects the cells in the body from damage. It also protects lung tissue from damage through pollution. If it is lacking, a person suffers from tiredness, muscle weakness and loss of concentration. Vitamin E is found in nuts and vegetable oil, wheatgerm, apples, broccoli, spinach and wholewheat bread.

Vitamin K - This is vital if you are on a very low calorie diet. It controls blood clotting and helps maintain normal bone growth and the healing of bone fractures. If it is lacking, a person is at greater risk from brittle bones and blood problems. Vitamin K is found in green vegetables, lentils, chickpeas, carrots and tomatoes.

Minerals

Calcium - This mineral helps to build healthy bones and teeth. It also aids in muscle functions and blood clotting, and helps maintain a strong immune system. A lack of this mineral leads to bone and muscle problems. Calcium is found in milk, cheese, yoghurt, salmon and sardines, broccoli, green beans and almonds.

Iron - This mineral carries the oxygen in the blood and helps with energy metabolism. A lack of this mineral leads to anaemia. Iron is found in asparagus, chicken, raisins, red meat, prunes, soya beans and tofu.

Magnesium - This mineral is essential for all the major body processes. If you are lacking it, you will suffer from low blood sugar, cramps and tremors, your eyes may twitch, you could have an irregular heartbeat, feel nervous, have problems swallowing, feel weak, dizzy and even have fits. Magnesium is found in seafood, nuts, spinach, cheese, potatoes, broccoli, bananas, wheat germ and seeds.

Potassium - This mineral is involved with muscle functions. It is needed for the release of insulin and helps maintain normal blood pressure. It works with sodium to keep a healthy fluid balance in the body. If it is lacking, this can lead to sleepiness and confusion, thirst, lack of appetite, stomach bloating, vomiting, low blood pressure, muscle weakness, 'pins and needles' and even paralysis. Potassium is found in potatoes, avocados, yoghurt, melons, bananas, mushrooms, milk and tomatoes.

Zinc - This helps the body to fight disease and infection. It maintains healthy hair, bones and skin. It helps with digestion and breathing and is important for the development of the reproductive organs. It is also involved in the healing of wounds and in maintaining a healthy sense of taste. A lack of this mineral leads to nail problems, skin diseases such as eczema, a poor sense of smell and taste, infections, hair loss and tiredness. Zinc is found in lean beef, oysters, milk, nuts, root vegetables and cheese.

These are just a selection of the most common vitamins and minerals that our body requires. Each one is vital and when you have an eating disorder, you are likely to be lacking in many of these vitamins or minerals. Just from reading this list, you may have identified some problems that you currently have yourself. I would strongly advise that until you are eating a full and healthy diet, you take any vitamin or mineral supplements that your doctor prescribes.

Problems you may encounter when you start eating again

It is hard to explain to a person who eats normally just how terrifying it is to eat when you are anorexic. This is why you may find that some of the people around you might get impatient and frustrated with your progress at times. Remember that it is important for you to recover at a pace which works for you. Don't allow others to try and force you to eat more than you can manage before you are ready. This could actually lead you to take steps backwards because you feel very afraid. You DO have the willpower to recover, even though at times this may not feel possible. You have used your strength in the past to starve yourself and now you need to channel this willpower and energy into recovery instead.

It may not always be an easy ride though and the following are some of the problems you may encounter, as well as some tips about how to cope with them:

1) If you have been ill for a while, you will not be used to eating. Your stomach will have shrunk and might react badly to food at first. You may feel bloated and full, even when you eat just a small amount of food. This is a natural reaction because the lining of your stomach has become very thin while you have been starving and you may have some stomach pains for a while. Do not let these put you off eating because your digestive system will return to normal quite quickly if you continue with your diet plan. Be gentle with your stomach at first and eat foods that are easy to digest, such as yoghurt and honey, rather than higher fibre foods. Milky drinks and desserts are a good starting point because they are very neutral foods. Many anorexics do find it easier to begin by eating baby-type foods, such as mashed potato and porridge.

2) You may wake up in the morning feeling very positive but as you go through the day, each meal gets much harder. With every meal, you may find that you feel less and less like eating. By lunchtime you may already feel full before you even start to eat. It is VERY important to keep going with your diet plan though. Don't try to avoid the later meals. You agreed to try this diet plan and now is the time to stand by that agreement. The only way to beat the feelings of fullness is to continue to gently stretch your stomach.

3) Don't try to move food from one meal to another because you will end up with a backlog. You may think that if you cannot manage your yoghurt at lunch, it is wise to have it later in the day but this is really just a way of putting off eating. You are behaving anorexically again by avoiding food that frightens you or that makes you feel full. Be strict with yourself and eat the correct foods at the right time.

4) You will feel very tempted to change the meals on your plan. You may want to switch some of the foods to lower calorie options. Don't allow your anorexic 'voice' to convince you to do this. Once you start to opt for lower calorie foods, you may then find yourself cutting out foods completely and before long, you will be eating a very limited diet again. Take responsibility for your illness and don't allow yourself to slip. It feels horrible if other people have to watch you all the time, just to make sure that you are not cheating on your diet plan. Once trust is lost, it takes a long time to regain it from parents or friends.

5) Understand that you will feel frightened. Eating is likely to make you feel panicked and scared. Use the tools that I have talked about earlier (cognitive therapy, relaxation exercises and problem solving) to help you cope with these feelings. Also, if the people around you want to help, learn to trust them and ask for their comfort and support. In time, your eating will get much easier but it is a slow process. Dealing with the guilt that you feel when you eat can be difficult and there are no quick fix solutions. You need to just fight the voice with logic as much as you can. Reassure yourself that eating is good and that you are RIGHT to do it. It may help you to write this statement on a large piece of paper and stick it on your wall. Every time you are really struggling, read these words and try to remember that they are the truth.

6) Do also remember that you have an illness and it will take you time to recover. Try to see your food as the medicine that you need to help you get well. You HAVE to take this medication. It is not a choice. It is vital for your survival. I know that when I could see food in this light, it helped me to progress in my recovery. You will get many days when you want to give up. At times like these, try to focus on how much better life will be without your eating disorder.

Bulimia and a healthy diet

When you are trying to recover from bulimia, there are several different problems that you are facing. A bulimic may be at a normal weight, so their diet would need to maintain their weight rather than increase it. A healthy eating plan will help you to stop feeling cravings for the foods that lead you into binges. However, there are some difficulties that you may encounter while you are starting a healthy eating plan. I talked earlier about ways to give up vomiting and you will need to work through these too as you start your new plan.

You need to agree that you will not try to lose weight while you are changing to the new plan. If you try to diet while you are reorganising your eating, you are likely to feel too hungry and fall back into the binge/vomit cycle. Eating a normal diet might seem like a frightening idea because you may have been on a weight loss programme for a long time. However, eating regular meals does not mean that you will put on a lot of weight - in fact it could actually cause you to lose some. When you start to eat healthy regular meals, your metabolism will speed up and this means that you can eat more food without putting on weight.

Many bulimics have no structure to their diets at all. If you vomit almost everything you eat then it is important to start re-introducing foods to your diet very slowly. Choose which meal you would find the easiest to eat. Try not to decide on a meal that is too late in the day because you will be very hungry by that time, which could lead you to binge afterwards. If you decide that lunchtime is the best for you then you need to choose a meal. Look at the diet I have described below and read through the pyramid plan. What can you manage to eat? If you have decided on a jacket potato with baked beans for example, choose to have this the next day. Set yourself a time to eat or else you may find that you keep putting off the meal all day.

You may feel afraid that you will binge once you have eaten your meal. If this is likely to happen then make sure that you eat with another person or have the meal in a restaurant or canteen, where you are less able to binge. If you are at home, try to plan activities so that you are busy after the meal and have no time free to binge. Do something that you really enjoy so that it feels like you are rewarding yourself for eating the meal.

Remember that you will have days when you do binge after your meal. Try not to see these as total disasters and don't call yourself a failure. Stop yourself from focusing on the slip and instead plan your meals for the following day and write your thoughts in your diary. Ask yourself questions about why you binged and try to understand the reasons why it happened.

Once you are used to eating a meal at lunchtime and you are feeling less anxious, then it is time to add a second meal to your plan. Start the day with a healthy breakfast as well as eating your lunch. When you have adapted to eating both breakfast and lunch, then you need to add some more food to your diet. It may be that you want to try for a mid-afternoon snack before you can manage a full evening meal.

You may feel that your diet is very repetitive at this time because you are too afraid to experiment. It may be wise to wait until you are eating a full and healthy diet before you start to change your meals and try new foods. If you have a craving for something different, introduce it into your diet on a day when you are feeling less anxious about eating.

Diet Plans

You are aiming to eat three meals and three snacks every day, and you need to balance your food to make sure that it is spread evenly throughout the day. This might be quite a change as you may only be used to eating in the evenings. Each meal needs to contain proteins (e.g. cheese, egg, meat, fish or beans) and carbohydrates (e.g. pasta, bread, potatoes or rice) as well as fresh fruit or vegetables and a small amount of fat. Meals need to be satisfying so that you are less likely to binge. Protein is more satisfying than any other food so it is very important to include this in your diet. Hot food is more comforting than cold food so taking the time to prepare a cooked meal can help prevent bingeing. Solid food is also more satisfying than liquid food so, for example, have beans on toast rather than soup.

The following diet should keep your weight level but it is important to be honest with yourself. If you are underweight, you will need to add extra calories to this diet plan. Also, if you lose weight on this plan, you will need to increase the amounts you eat:

A suggested diet plan for recovery

Breakfast	A glass of fruit juice. 30g of cereal with a third of a pint of milk. One slice of brown toast, with one teaspoon of low fat spreaand one teaspoon of marmalade. Tea and coffee with milk.
11 am	A cup of coffee with semi-skimmed milk. One piece of fruit - e.g. apple or pear.
Lunch	200g (7oz) jacket potato with a protein filling such as bake beans, cottage cheese, tuna or hard cheese. (See 1,800 calorie diet earlier in this chapter for amounts)
or	A sandwich made with two slices of wholemeal bread and two teaspoons of low fat spread, filled with tuna, cottage cheese, chicken, hard cheese or egg.
Dessert	An individual yoghurt, trifle or mixed fruit salad with one scoop of ice cream. A cup of tea or coffee.
3 pm	A cup of tea or coffee with milk. Two cookies or a cereal bar.

Dinner   A piece of meat (such as 150g of chicken) or a vegetarian dish served with 150g of potato (or a cup of rice or pasta) and vegetables.

Dessert   The same as lunch.
                Coffee or tea with milk.

Bedtime   A hot milky drink and a cookie.

You need to drink water throughout the day to keep your body re-hydrated, especially if you are still occasionally vomiting or taking laxatives. It is important to drink at least eight glasses of water per day.

You may be unsure about correct portion sizes, so refer back to the pyramid plan and also try watching other people. See how much they have on their plates at meal times and copy their behaviour. Try not to single yourself out from your friends. If they are all going out for a meal, try to have the same as them (as long as they are not dieting). If you find it difficult to decide on your meal at home, why not try supermarket ready meals for a while and serve them with vegetables?

I have discussed the idea that the end of a meal is an important time and it may be that you choose to end each meal with a specific food. You then know that when you reach this food, you need to stop eating. This can be a specific food item, such as an apple or a yoghurt.

Once you are eating a balanced diet and your body is receiving the correct amount of nutrition, you will find that your cravings will decrease. Remember to make sure that your meals and snacks are no more than four hours apart, so that you will be less likely to feel hungry and want to binge.

Allow yourself to eat 'unsafe' foods

Most eating disorder sufferers will have a list of foods that they consider 'unsafe' or 'bad', such as chocolate or cakes. Bulimics often find that eating an 'unsafe' food can trigger a binge. However, when you place a food 'off limits' you are likely to crave it even more, so it is important that no food should be forbidden.

Write down all the foods that you have cut out of your diet because you feel that they are 'unsafe'. Try to write them down in order, with the most frightening ones at the top and the ones that you can just about manage to eat at the bottom. You need to begin introducing these foods back into your diet and the best way to do this is by starting with the easiest ones first. Look down at the bottom of your list and see which food you fear the least. You need to add this to your diet once in the next week. Work out the exact amount you are going to eat and tell yourself that this will not trigger a binge because it is no longer a forbidden food.

185

Decide exactly when you are going to eat this food and choose a time when you are not too stressed or hungry.

With this exercise, you are teaching yourself that you can eat 'unsafe' foods in normal quantities. In the past, having just one cookie meant that you needed to eat the whole packet. Now you are learning for example that you can eat a cookie after your midday meal and enjoy the taste without feeling the need to binge on the rest of the packet.

Another suggested way of introducing 'unsafe' foods is to swop one 'safe' food for an 'unsafe' food. The only problem with this is that, once again, you are limiting your food intake by stating that you can only try a new food if you drop another one. I know from my own recovery that I found the "Just Go For It!" method to be the best when introducing a new food. Decide on the food you are going to introduce and then enjoy it. However panicked you may feel, try and enjoy the taste and texture of this food that you have denied yourself for so long. You are likely to feel very shaky and guilty when you eat a new food. Keep repeating to yourself: *"This is just food and I need to eat it if I am to recover. It cannot hurt me. It will not make me fat."*

While you are recovering from an eating disorder, you will need to follow a regulated diet. Many diet books encourage you to eat when you are hungry and stop when you are full. However, this doesn't work for people with eating disorders. You no longer have the natural sensations of hunger or fullness because they have been affected by your negative behaviour. It is therefore important to allow these sensations to return naturally and stick with your diet plan until you reach and can maintain your healthy natural weight.

As you start to reach a healthy weight, you may become very frightened and feel a need to start some of your negative behaviour again. This is one of the most difficult parts of recovery and I have dealt with it in the next chapter.

Chapter 19

How do I learn to live at a Healthy Weight?

Summary

One of the most difficult and frequently ignored aspects of recovery is learning how to live at a normal weight. This chapter gives practical advice and suggestions to help accept your new healthy body.

If you have an eating disorder, I am sure that you will be familiar with weight charts. These charts show you the weight that is healthy for your age and height. If you are below the age of 15, you may have found that there are no specific weight charts to tell you your ideal healthy weight. This is because, under the age of 15, your body is still rapidly growing. It is not until we are older that our body size and shape becomes comparable. Charts are often inaccurate though and it is best to follow a doctor's advice on this matter. They will be able to tell you the recommended weight for your height. Many anorexics will argue for hours with their doctors about what a healthy weight range is for them and then try to aim for the lowest possible figure within that range. This is NOT a healthy attitude though and if you set your target weight too low, you will just end up back in the eating disorder.

Recovery is all about recognising that your body needs to find its own healthy level within the weight range for your height. You will only discover exactly what weight is healthy for you when you begin eating a normal diet that contains the correct number of calories. Healthy weights vary for everyone. Some people have a lower than average natural weight, some are average and others are higher than average. When you reach your natural healthy weight, this is the level at which you are least likely to fall back into your eating disorder. Your body will be receiving the correct amount of nutrition, your mind will not be preoccupied with thoughts of food and weight, and you will have plenty of energy and strength.

Some hospitals only focus on getting their patients to reach a target weight, while others are also concerned with helping the sufferers to adjust and feel happy with their new body. Try to remember that your target weight is just a number. Don't focus on this number but instead concentrate on the fact that you are regaining a healthy body. You may have hated your body for many years and if you are to cope with living at a healthy weight, you now need to learn to like your own body.

You may be wondering exactly why you would want to live at a normal weight. I know that this question often crossed my mind. I am going to look at all the positive reasons for beating your eating disorder in the next chapter but I want to focus here on the fact that if you reach a healthy weight, food will no longer hold you back. I spent many years frightened to go out with anyone in case they offered me food. I didn't want to join the adult world because the idea of sharing meals with other people was just too scary. Now at a healthy weight, eating out has become a very enjoyable part of my life.

Unfortunately, many treatment programmes end when the patient reaches a healthy weight but this is in fact the time when sufferers frequently need the most help. Doctors often believe that once a patient is at a normal weight, they are recovered. This is not the case though and it can take a number of months for you to completely heal your mind and accept your new body.

If you are struggling with feelings of being 'fat', now is the time to ask for help from someone you trust. Ask someone who you know never lies to you if they think you look fat. I found that doing this always helped me. When I was struggling with feelings of fatness, I would ask Simon for his opinion. I knew that he would always tell me the truth and I found his words helpful and reassuring.

Do try and use your diary when you are struggling with poor body image. Write down your thoughts and look at possible reasons why you could be feeling this way. I used to find that I would start feeling fat whenever I was trying to cope with another problem. It was as if my brain didn't want to deal with this difficult new problem and started focusing on my weight instead. By concentrating on feeling fat, I was taking my mind off the other problem. I found that if I actually tackled this new problem though, the feelings of fatness would disappear. This shows how problem solving can really help you to feel better about yourself.

Cognitive therapy can also help you to work through feelings of being fat. Look at this example and try to do similar ones for yourself:

Situation - I tried on an old pair of jeans and they don't fit like they used to.

Emotion - I feel angry and sad.

Automatic negative thoughts - I am so fat now. Everyone must hate me because I am so disgusting.

Alternative positive thoughts - I am not fat. I am healthy. Those old jeans were a child's size and no young woman should be wearing children's clothes. People don't hate me because I am now healthy - they just feel relieved that I am no longer ill. I am now a healthy young woman who is in control of her life. I am glad that those jeans don't fit. If they had, that would show me that I was still very ill.

Remember that when you are at a healthy weight, you may still get feelings of being fat but that is all they are - **feelings**. You may **feel** fat but you are **not** fat - you are **healthy**. This is a very important statement to remember. I would encourage you to write it in large letters on a sheet of paper and stick it on your up somewhere on your wall:

"I may feel fat but I am not fat - I am healthy"

As you reach a healthy weight, many of your negative feelings will start to disappear. This is not instant and for a number of months you may still feel drawn back towards your eating disorder. During this time, it is wise to stick very strictly to your diet plans. Once you have reached your healthy weight, you need to learn how to maintain that weight with your diet. You may feel worried that you will continue to gain weight above your target level. Remember that there will be natural fluctuations. While you are adapting to a new size and a new diet, your weight will go up and down a little at times.

You also need to find the right balance between how much you eat and the amount of activity that you do. By 'activity', I am not just talking about physical exercise though. It is important to learn that nearly 75% of our calorie intake is used up just keeping us alive. That only leaves 25% of our calories left for all the activities we do. This is why you must not over-exercise when you reach your healthy weight. If you do, it is actually a clue that you are trying to return to your eating disorder. You need to accept your weight and any slight changes as natural and if you immediately start exercising, you may need some extra help with your recovery.

Even at a healthy weight, it may be a while before you can rely on your feelings of hunger to tell you when to eat. You are also still going to have times when you don't feel like eating and this is likely to be connected with feelings of losing control. Try to remember that you are very much in control while you continue to eat your diet. You are choosing to be healthy and this is the wisest decision you can make. You can only lose control if you return to your eating disorder again.

You will know when you want to try a new food. I found that I introduced new foods very slowly into my diet over a long period of time. I do not remember exactly when my diet started to change - it was just a natural process. One day I suddenly realised that I no longer counted calories. I chose the food that I wanted to eat from the menu in a restaurant without thinking how much fat or how many calories it contained. Allow yourself to take it at your own pace. Stick to your set diet plan for as long as you need before you start to experiment.

Remember that the eating disorder has always been your escape route in the past. As soon as you hit a problem, you may still feel a need to stop eating.

Whenever this happens, you need to ask for help or turn to your 'Thoughts and Feelings' diary. Try to use your cognitive therapy or problem solving as a way around the problem and TALK about the issues that are upsetting you. Don't try to swallow your feelings again because these are important and you need to express them in a healthy way.

Body Image

People with eating disorders usually hate their bodies and constantly fight or punish them. To feel happy with yourself and your eating, you need to stop battling with your body and learn to accept it - not just conditionally when you reach a certain weight but all the time. Your body is a complex machine and you have to treat it with care and understanding if it is to continue working properly. Now that you are recovering from your eating disorder, it is time to fight those negative feelings that you have about your appearance. These are just some of the thoughts you may have about your own body:

"I hate my thighs - they are revolting."

"I am so fat - no one will ever love me."

"People must talk about my disgusting body all the time."

"I hate myself so much because I am fat."

Thoughts such as these might have led you to diet in the past. Now you need to deal with these thoughts in a positive way. Start by understanding that you are not alone in feeling negative about your own body. Many eating disorder sufferers hide at home because they feel fat and are ashamed of showing their bodies in public. The majority of women have problems with body image but it is important to realise that when you go out, people are not all focusing attention on your body.

The next step is to accept yourself. Are you trying to be perfect again? Are you looking at models in magazines and trying to look like them? Remember that you are a unique person and you need to accept yourself for who you are. It is not easy to learn to accept yourself but this is something that you can work at in many ways. You need to take responsibility for your thoughts, feelings and behaviour. You can do this by using cognitive therapy to help fight your own negative self-image.

1) You need to identify your exact negative thoughts about your body (as I did above).

2) You need to challenge these thoughts with positive talk about your body.
3) You need to learn to like your body. You can start by accepting that there are certain parts of your body that you do like.

Let's take one of the above examples and work through it using cognitive therapy:

"People must talk about my disgusting body all the time."

With this statement, not only are you assuming that people are talking about you all the time (something that is very unlikely) but you are also saying that everyone else thinks like you do. You are assuming that everyone believes that you are large and that large is wrong.

Firstly, you need to remember that you are suffering from eating disorder distortion and this will affect the way that you see your body. Everyone else will see the reality, which is a slim person at a healthy weight.

Secondly, not everyone views body shape in the same way that you do. You believe that to be perfect, you need to be very thin. Most men prefer women to be curvy though and do not find very thin bodies attractive. When healthy people watch documentaries about anorexia, they are horrified by the thinness.

Finally, you are also saying that being overweight is wrong and that it proves you are lazy, weak and disgusting. This is a very wrong statement. Just because a person is heavier than average, this does not mean that they are weak, lazy or disgusting. Even if you were overweight, this would still be no reason to be so cruel about yourself.

Can you see how I have challenged every part of the negative statement? Try and do this yourself with some of your own negative statements about your body. Write down the statement and then look at every individual part of it. Try and give yourself a positive alternative to each negative statement. If you are struggling to do this for yourself, pretend that you are helping a friend with her body image problems. What would you tell her if she was feeling fat? Remember that these positive thoughts you are working on are not simply fantasies. They are the truth and they can help you to feel much better about your body, if you only allow yourself to believe them.

Many eating disorder sufferers try to avoid certain situations that make them feel bad, such as looking in mirrors or wearing tighter clothes. It does not help to continue avoiding these situations because that just reinforces the idea that there is something wrong with your body. Fear can stop us from doing too many things in our lives. It stops us from going out in public, from looking in mirrors, from going clothes shopping and from wearing tighter clothing. You need to face your fears and start to confront them. Take each problem one step at a time and ask for help if you need it. Confront your fears when you look in the mirror. Work through them step by step, using cognitive therapy and problem solving to help you accept your body. Each time you confront your fears, they will grow weaker.

It can help to rehearse difficult situations in advance. If you are going into a shop to try on clothes and you are expecting this to be hard, work through your cognitive therapy before you go. Prepare yourself with lots of positive answers to all the negative thoughts that may fill your head when you are in that tough situation. This early preparation can make it much easier for you to work through your problems.

Many of the body image problems people develop are the result of making too many comparisons. We constantly compare ourselves to other people in the street, to models in magazines and to people on television. I know that I always used to consider myself a failure in comparison to other people. However, what we never seem to do is look at our strengths. We pick on our weaknesses (many of which are imagined) and compare ourselves negatively to other people. If you are having a bad day or feeling fat and ugly, it doesn't help to read a magazine filled with glamorous photos of celebrities. You are probably going to end up feeling even worse and think that they have fabulous perfect lives compared to you. This isn't necessarily the truth but when you are feeling low, it can be hard to see the full picture.

The next time you are feeling in a calmer mood, sit down and write a list of all the positive aspects of your life. List everything that you do well, the compliments people pay you and all of your good qualities. Remember that these don't only have to be about your appearance - you are more than just an outer shell. Write down everything that you feel you have achieved (however small) and keep this list to hand because the next time you compare yourself negatively to someone, you need to read about yourself.

Self-Help Groups

Remember that reaching a healthy weight is just the beginning of recovery. You will still feel that you need help and support, so do not be afraid to ask for these when you need them. Now may be the time to join a self-help group. There you can gain extra support and encouragement from people who know exactly how you are feeling. You can build up a support network, so that when you are feeling scared and alone there are people you can phone who will understand and help you through a difficult time.

You also need to continue learning about yourself and your past. You may have discovered a lot of new information about yourself from reading this book. Some of the exercises may have shown you that your family have trouble communicating. Don't stop exploring your past now and continue to learn about the reasons why you turned to your eating disorder. It may help you to talk to different members of your family and find out how they feel about their own bodies. You might, for example, discover that your Mother has a very negative image of herself and that this has affected you.

You may also want to learn more about relaxation exercises or even join a yoga class. Both these will help you to become more in touch with your body. You will learn to understand how feeling calm can help you deal with situations in a more positive way. We all have too much stress in our lives and it is important to learn how to slow down and take some time out for yourself.

Remember that learning to like who you are on the inside will help you to feel more comfortable in your healthy body. It is important to let go of the eating disorder as your defining identity. You will no longer need the illness to define you as a person.

Preventing relapses

If you are a recovering sufferer and feel that you are likely to have a relapse, it is important that you talk with your doctor. You need to know that help will be available if you require it. There are some other tips that can also help a sufferer avoid a relapse:

1) It helps if a sufferer allows their weight to increase a little above their target weight. This means that their body can find its own natural level. If you stop at your exact target, this doesn't allow for fluctuations. there is no reserve. If you lose any weight in a stressful week for example, this would mean that you were immediately underweight again and will need to return to a weight gain diet.

2) Try not to change your routine too much if you are feeling fragile in your recovery. Holidays can be very difficult times for example, because your whole routine changes. Starting a new college or a new job is also a big change and you may need extra support and help to prevent a relapse if you are doing either of these.

3) Many eating disorder sufferers choose a career or part-time job in catering because they feel a need to be around food all the time. This is not always a healthy choice for the future if you are at a fragile stage in your recovery. If you have decided on this as a career, stop and really think. Did you choose this because you felt a need to be around food all day? If the answer is "Yes", it may be wise to think about different career options that might appeal to you.

4) Many doctors advise anorexics not to become pregnant until they have been in recovery for two years or more. The weight gain necessary to have a healthy baby can frighten some ex-sufferers back into their disorder.

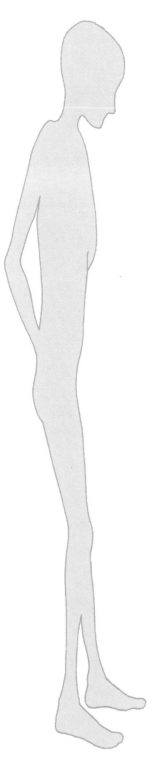

Full recovery can take months or even years and you may well have setbacks and relapses but a good support network can help you with them. Ask for help whenever you are struggling. Try not to side with the eating disorder and allow it to isolate you from people. Remember - if you can work with people to fight your disorder then you will win.

Chapter 20

What are the Benefits of Beating my Eating Disorder?

Summary

Eating disorders are incredibly destructive illnesses that rob the sufferer of much of their life and health. This chapter looks at the advantages of recovery and the freedom that comes with it.

By now, you may be seriously considering the idea of recovery. In this final chapter, I want to show you exactly what the benefits of beating your eating disorder are, and also give you some final tips about how to treat yourself better if you do decide to recover.

Recovery from an eating disorder is a difficult task and it will not happen overnight. However, from my own personal experience I can definitely say that it is well worth the effort. Many times in the past, I took one or two steps along the road towards recovery but then scurried back to the safety of my anorexia. Change felt frightening and even though it was very painful for me to live with an eating disorder, somehow it seemed safer. As time passed though, I realised that my life was just getting worse and worse. I was withdrawing from the world completely and could no longer cope with strangers visiting our house. I couldn't talk to anyone on the telephone and I even struggled to buy goods in shops. I had become an anorexic hermit and was using my illness to hide from the world.

I lived this dead, empty life for many years. I was always in physical pain and had become so thin that I couldn't even sit or lie down without bruising my back. Baths had long since become impossible. I felt alone, frightened and lived in constant fear that I would be admitted to hospital at any time. I knew the disadvantages of my eating disorder but I clung onto the illness because of my fear of change. Eventually the pain and loneliness became too much for me to bear and I started to take tiny steps towards recovery. Those first steps were not easy and I had many setbacks but in time I realised how many advantages there were to leading an adult life.

I cannot tell you that as soon as you decide to give up your eating disorder, you will suddenly be living a wonderfully warm, sun-kissed life. There are likely to be problems, new feelings and hard times that you might encounter. First of all, I am going to look at the disadvantages that there are to getting well. Many of these may already be in your mind if you are trying to decide whether or not you should give up your eating disorder. Some of the following points (such as the fact that you will look healthier) could actually be listed under both advantages and disadvantages. Many people think that looking healthier is a positive aspect of recovery but most anorexics will see this as a drawback. As I mentioned before, for anorexics 'healthy' often means 'fat', so that when people say "you look healthier" this can actually feel upsetting.

These are some of the other disadvantages of recovery:

1) *You may not receive as much attention from those around you.* You might not think that your eating disorder is a cry for attention but be really honest with yourself for a moment. Do people treat you differently because you are ill? Do you think that if you lose your eating disorder, people will pay you less attention? It may be that your parents treat you with special care because you are unwell but would you get the same level of attention from them without the illness? I actually discovered that people were far more interested in my thoughts and opinions when I was in recovery than when I was a very sick young woman. As an anorexic, I was "looked after" and other people always made decisions for me. I wasn't treated like an adult and my opinions were often ignored. This all began to change when I started to recover.

2) *You will have to take some risks and face the unknown.* This is one of the points that could be either an advantage or a disadvantage. When you are deep in an eating disorder, making any changes to your life can be frightening and might not always work out well. Even going out with a friend can be a terrifying experience and it may feel easier to hide in your illness. Taking risks is all part of recovery but it does take courage and strength, and you may need some extra help when you start to take steps outside of your usual routine.

3) *You may have setbacks in your recovery that leave you feeling disappointed.* Recovery is not a smooth ride and you will have days when you feel like giving up. You are likely to feel depressed and disappointed when you are struggling. On these days, try to remember that nothing really worthwhile ever comes easily. Recovery is important and you need to work hard at it but the end results will be worth all the effort.

4) *You will lose your 'eating disorder identity'.* You may have turned to your eating disorder because you felt you had no identity on your own. Your family didn't allow you to have your own opinions and your illness became the only way that you could express yourself. As you recover though, you will no longer need your eating disorder because you will learn to become a more assertive person. Letting go will not be easy since you may feel the eating disorder is part of you and that without it, you are just an empty shell. Hopefully by now, you will understand that it is alright to express your feelings and emotions, and it is not wrong to be assertive and have your

own opinions. You will be able to build your identity if you gradually allow your personality to show, instead of simply agreeing with everybody else all the time.

5) *You will have to go through a lot of pain, guilt and anxiety when you start to eat again.* This is going to be an uncomfortable time and many sufferers are put off trying for recovery because of these feelings. One of the most common questions I am asked is: *"How do you deal with the guilt that you feel after eating?"* There is no simple answer to this question because you have to learn a way of coping that works for you. You may have to accept that you will feel physically uncomfortable when you eat but you do not have to feel this guilt. You ARE allowed to eat food and you are NOT bad if you do. Learn how to do the relaxation exercises, try to keep yourself occupied when the guilt hits and work through the feelings with cognitive therapy. In time, the pain will lessen and you will eventually reach a point when you can eat free from guilt.

6) *You are likely to go through periods of feeling fat.* Remember that it will take a while to adjust to your new body. Keep reminding yourself that you have reached a HEALTHY weight and are NOT 'fat'. I talked earlier about the idea that feelings of fatness often occur when you are struggling with another problem. If you are feeling fat, try to write down all the emotions that you are feeling and see if there is another reason why you could be feeling this way.

7) *You are going to start experiencing some of the emotions (such as anger) which you blocked out when you had your eating disorder.* I have talked a lot in this book about different ways of dealing with the new emotions that you are feeling. It may be frightening at first as you learn to understand a whole range of new feelings but this can be the key to a healthier new you. As you learn to express these emotions correctly, you will no longer feel the need to turn back towards your eating disorder.

8) *You will start experiencing feelings of hunger again, which can be frightening. You may also feel full and bloated at times.* You will experience many new physical feelings when you are recovering. Hunger, fullness and bloated feelings are all very common. I remember telling a nurse when I was in hospital that I felt like "a balloon with legs". This was just a feeling but it was uncomfortable and was due to the fact that I had eaten so little for so many years. These uncomfortable feelings do pass though. Hunger is a feeling that can be frightening but it doesn't need to be. Your body is just starting to tell you what it needs. Listen to it rather than simply trying to ignore your hunger.

9) *You may find that some people are not comfortable with the 'new you'.* This is a very difficult problem that I have experienced a few times myself since

I recovered. Often, eating disorder sufferers are people pleasers. You may have always done everything possible to keep other people happy. Now you are finally starting to consider your own needs though. You may have become more assertive and with your newfound confidence, you will find that you do not always agree with the people you once tried so hard to please. You might show new emotions such as anger, sadness and fear, which some people find hard to handle. Remember however that you are RIGHT to show your emotions and you are RIGHT to be more assertive and consider your own needs. Your opinions are important too and you have a RIGHT to express them. It is vital that you do not allow yourself to slip backwards while people adapt to the new healthy you.

10) *You will start to become sexually mature and if you are a young woman, your breasts and thighs will develop and your periods will restart.* This is a difficult time for many anorexia sufferers. As I said earlier, some people turn to an eating disorder as a form of protection, especially if they have been sexually abused. They believe that it makes them 'unfeminine' and therefore unattractive. If this is the reason you turned to your eating disorder, it is important that you receive a lot of support and help while you are gaining weight. You may need some extra help adjusting to and accepting your new feminine body.

Please notice that there are more advantages than disadvantages to recovering.

Advantages of Recovery

1) *You will be able to live free from guilt and fear.* This will not happen overnight as recovery takes time and a lot of work but gradually you will find that your feelings start to change. As you learn to eat more, the intense fear you felt when faced with food will fade and after eating, the levels of guilt will fall so that you feel more comfortable. The process is slow and some days will be easier than others but you CAN reach a point where you feel happy eating. I have reached that point myself and after 14 years filled with feelings of guilt and fear, it is a wonderful place to be.

2) *You will feel better emotionally, physically and mentally.* On a daily basis, I can see people improving as they recover. Food is essential for our well being. When we starve ourselves, our bodies suffer greatly but a healthy diet can reverse the whole situation. It can help your depression lift and you will find that you have more energy and feel more emotionally stable.

3) *You will be able to make new friends and your existing friendships will also improve because people are able to talk more openly with you.* You may have spent much of your time hiding at home while you had your eating disorder. As you recover, you will probably feel more like spending time with

other people. You may start to feel adventurous and want to go out more, which can lead you to make new friends.

4) *Hospital will not be a constant threat, since your weight is no longer in the 'at risk' category.* I know that this was a huge relief to me when I began to recover. During my anorexic years, I spent many months living on the edge, terrified that if I lost any more weight I would be admitted to hospital. This is a frightening feeling and it is wonderful when that threat no longer hangs over your head.

5) *You will become more aware of how your eating disorder controlled your life.* You will begin to understand how your self-image was distorted and how your feelings were affected. You will finally be able to look at the effect your eating disorder has had on your life. You will see how badly it affected your work, relationships, health and happiness.

6) *You will look and feel healthier.* You will feel less constipated. Your sleep will improve. You will be in less physical pain without the vomiting, laxatives and over-exercising. As your recovery progresses, you will be amazed at how much better you will feel.

7) *You will no longer be starving and will feel less likely to binge eat.* For bulimia sufferers, the urge to binge will slowly disappear as they start to eat a healthy balanced diet, leaving them feeling in control of their lives.

8) *Your mind will not be constantly preoccupied with thoughts of food any longer.* You will have more time to spend on new hobbies, reading books, watching television and your work. Your mind will focus more easily and you will find that your concentration improves. When I suffered from anorexia, my mind would wander most of the time and I would find myself thinking about food or calories. As I started to recover, I was able to watch TV programmes without feeling a need to rewind the videotape to see all the parts that I had missed. You will find that your concentration and memory improve dramatically as your weight becomes healthier.

9) *You will now be able to finish your school work, go to college, get a full or part time job, etc.* New options will begin to open up for you all the time. Suffering from an eating disorder takes up most of your time but as you start to recover, you will want to look to the future and make plans.

10) *You may be better off financially.* You might have spent a lot of your money on diet products, exercise videos, diet magazines and laxatives. If you suffered from bulimia, you may have also spent a lot of money on food for binges. When you start to recover, try to spend this money on treats for yourself - you are working very hard and deserve some rewards.

11) *You will become sexually mature and if you are a young woman, your thighs and breasts will develop and your periods will restart.* Becoming sexually mature shows that you are now an adult. You will find the idea of relationships

exciting (although you may also feel nervous) and being independent will no longer seem so frightening.

12) *Clothes shopping will be easier and more fun.* At a normal weight, you are able to choose clothes from all the popular shops. No longer will you have to hunt around in the children's sections, looking for the tiniest sizes. You will also find that you are no longer an object of curiosity. For many years, I found that people in the street stared at me. They would point and laugh, or look in horror at my frighteningly thin body. When I recovered though, people started to compliment me on my looks and commented on what a lovely figure I had. I often found this very hard to believe, as I still felt fat. I looked at my body and saw a large person, when the reality was that I had a very slim figure that many women actually envied. No one envied my anorexic body, apart from other anorexics and why would I want to be envied by people who were as ill as I was?

13) *You will gradually grow to like yourself as a person.* This is a very important point and you may find that this is something you will have to work at for a while. Remember that you have hated yourself so much that you were once willing to harm yourself, both physically and mentally. Now it is time to learn to be kind and gentle to yourself.

How to learn to like yourself

For the very last section of this book, I want to look at point number 13 in more detail - learning to like yourself as a person. This is a very important part of the book and is all about building up your self-esteem. You will have already learned a lot about this as you have been working through the recovery section. You may find the idea of liking yourself impossible but we all have the ability to care for ourselves. Would you ever treat other people the way you treat yourself? Would you bully and hurt them the way that you hurt yourself every day? Now you need to treat yourself in the same way that you treat others. You need to learn to listen to your body and not fight against its needs all of the time.

As you recover, you will have to watch for any signals that could indicate you may be relapsing at any time. This will require you to be totally honest with yourself and admit if you have started to cut down on food or binge occasionally again. Most sufferers have small relapses and if you can catch them early enough, your recovery can continue. You are able to learn more about yourself and your recovery if you can handle relapses well.

Hopefully you will have tried out some of the relaxation exercises. When you learn to relax, you are treating your body with some respect. You need to understand that too much stress can make you ill. Working through cognitive therapy and problem solving also teaches you that there are healthier ways to treat yourself when you have a problem. You do not need to immediately turn on yourself and punish your body when you have fears and worries.

You are a worthwhile person and are allowed to be seen and heard. Most anorexics for example have very small neat handwriting, almost as if they are saying that they really don't deserve to take up any space in the world. I know that as I began to recover, my handwriting started to become larger and a little more artistic.

Writing in a diary should have helped you start to learn more about yourself. Continue to write notes and explore some of the reasons why you behave in certain ways. For example, many eating disorder sufferers feel a strong need to always be neat and tidy. Set yourself the challenge of leaving your bed unmade for one day. This may not sound too hard but it can be very difficult for some people. It is good to set yourself challenges like this. Try and write down some of the problems that you still have and set yourself tasks that can help you to deal with them.

Allow yourself to develop in all aspects of your life. You may feel like experimenting with a new haircut or hair colour. You are forming your own identity now and are not relying on your eating disorder to show who you are as a person. When you were ill, you may have hidden inside baggy clothes and never worn make-up. As you grow in confidence, try to buy yourself some new clothes. It can help you to put some distance between yourself and the person you were when you were ill. Many of the clothes that fitted you when you were ill may be too tight now. It is time to move on and treat yourself to something new.

As you recover from your eating disorder, you will start to discover who you are as a person. An illness like anorexia or bulimia takes all of your time and energy, and does not allow you to be creative or express yourself in different ways. When I started to recover, I realised that I had many talents which had previously been hidden by my illness. Expect surprises when you begin recovery.

There are many different aspects of your life that you can start to change. As I recovered, I began to develop into an adult woman. The following are some of the aspects of my life I started to change, as well as some other ideas for change that you might want to try. Remember that this is just the start for you. Try to examine your life and look at different aspects that you can change to make yourself feel happier.

- Eat at different times of the day. When I was anorexic, I felt that if I did not eat at my exact meal time then the world had ended. Now I eat a full and healthy diet but I am not limited to set times of the day or night - if my meal is an hour or two early or late then that is fine. Don't allow yourself to skip meals when you experiment with new meal times though. This is about learning to be honest with yourself, as well as becoming less rigid in your thinking.

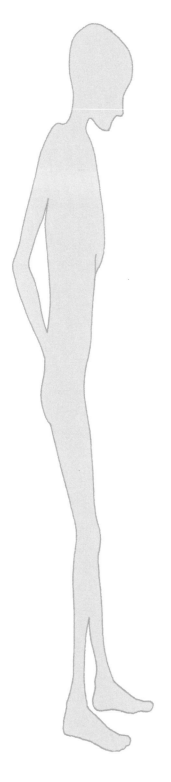

- Travel more. When I was anorexic, I led a very sheltered life and never travelled far. Since I recovered though, I have started to become more adventurous. It can be exciting to stay in different parts of the country and to break your usual routines.

- Pamper yourself. For example, take baths instead of rushing through a shower. Many eating disorder sufferers do not feel they deserve to have a long relaxing bath and only allow themselves quick showers. Buy yourself some special bath products and have a long relaxing soak.

- Be more spontaneous. When you are suffering from an eating disorder (and anorexia in particular) your life often becomes very timetabled and you live by a set of rules. Now is the time to break them. You don't have to plan everything weeks in advance. Allow yourself to do something on the spur of the moment.

- Treat yourself. You may have found it very hard in the past to buy presents for yourself. Now is the time to start to show yourself that you are a good person and do deserve enjoyable times and gifts. The presents you buy yourself do not have to be big - just a new magazine, book, item of make-up or jewellery for example.

- Try new experiences. You may have become locked into an identical pattern of behaviour. Now may be the time to try something new. This can be in any area of your life - a new kind of music, film or book, or even a new hobby.

- Allow yourself some time off. Many eating disorder sufferers work too hard and it is important to allow yourself some time to relax. Your work will not suffer if you have a few evenings off each week. In fact, it is likely to benefit.

- Try different foods. You are likely to have become stuck in a routine of eating very limited foods. As you recovered, you may have introduced your forbidden foods into your diet but did you try any new ones? Go to the supermarket and pick a product you want to try but DON'T look at the calories before you buy it. You are buying food for the taste now, not because it contains a certain number of calories.

- Allow yourself to be photographed. I know that when I was anorexic, I avoided cameras and would not allow people to photograph me. Try not to hide in future if people want to take pictures. Be proud of the healthy person you have become.

- Allow yourself to share problems. It is not always easy when you have been used to living a very private life but the more you can share and be open, the more help people can offer you. I started sharing my problems with Simon and found that this helped me tremendously, and I have gradually learned to trust more and more people.

202

- Let yourself have fun. As an anorexic, I rarely allowed myself to do anything I enjoyed. When I was in hospital, we had a number of therapy sessions when we just played games. Sometimes it can really help to be a child again. This may sound very strange but I have had a lot of fun with modeling clay, colouring pads, badge sets and other children's activity kits in the last few years.

- Get rid of anything that links you to your eating disorder. For myself, this meant that I needed to clear my room of the boxes of chocolates that I had stored away for many years. I used to use them to torture myself - I would look at all the chocolate and even unwrap some of it but I never allowed myself to eat any. I also needed to throw away my diet magazines and books, and even some old laxatives that I had kept just 'in case'. If you are throwing away laxatives, ask a friend to go with you to the chemist and hand them in to the pharmacist, since this is the safest way of disposing of medication.

- Start looking to the future. When I suffered from anorexia, I lived on a day-to-day basis. I wasn't able to plan for the future because I didn't know if I would ever be well enough to work. Now that I am recovered, I enjoy making decisions and planning for the future. You may want to look at ideas for your future career, university plans, part time jobs, etc.

- Are all your friendships healthy? Sometimes when we are not well, we can make unhealthy relationships. We become dependent on people because we are not physically or mentally able to cope alone. As you recover, you need to look at your relationships and see if they are all healthy ones. You may find that you want to end some friendships but you are likely to make many new ones now that you feel less scared and withdrawn.

- You might want to learn more about psychology or eating disorders. Many people who suffer from a serious illness find that when they recover, they want to use their experience to help others. You may now be thinking that you would like to work in the caring professions as a doctor or nurse, or you might want to study psychology to learn more about therapy. People of all ages find that recovery can change the course of their lives, since they now feel they have a new purpose.

These are just a few changes that you can make to your life when you are recovering. When you are ill, they may seem like huge life changes that you cannot even attempt but as a recovering sufferer, they will actually be exciting.

Closing Thoughts

I have tried to show you the reality of what it is like to live with an eating disorder. These are not 'lifestyles' or 'fashionable' illnesses and they cause great pain for a lot of people. There are solutions and I have outlined many of them for you to try. The most important message I want to leave you with is **never give up hope**. Eating disorders CAN be beaten and although it will often be quite a long and difficult fight, it is a fight worth winning. I did not believe that I would ever beat my illness. I thought that I would end up as a long-term anorexic for life. My recovery did take many months and even though I still occasionally have minor problems with my body image, I now know how to deal with these in a healthier way. I have no problems with food any more and love eating a full and healthy diet.

Sadly, many people still do not understand eating disorders. The media often talks about anorexia as "the slimmer's disease" and describes sufferers as just "difficult teenage girls" who refuse to eat. As I have shown in this book, eating disorders are very complex. They are not simply illnesses about weight or food - they run much deeper than that. I believe that it is vital to discover WHY your illness began in the first place and you will need courage, knowledge and support if you are to beat it.

If you are worried about a friend who has recently started to lose weight, try talking with them. Be kind, patient and understanding when you speak. Tell them your fears, ask if they would like help, offer your support and try to encourage them to visit a doctor. Don't shout at sufferers or try to force them to eat though, because this will only cause more problems. If you are at school, how about going to see a teacher together to explain the problem? Eating disorders should not be ignored. Many people feel afraid of discussing the subject because sufferers can sometimes become very defensive when they are confronted. However, if you care about someone then you ARE doing the right thing by seeking help for them. You cannot just sit back and allow them to harm themselves. That is not care but is actually a form of neglect.

If you are a sufferer and decide that you WANT to get better, remember to take recovery at your own pace. Don't allow others to force you into moving faster than you can manage and ask for help every step of the way. There is a list of addresses of different organisations at the back of this book if you need some extra support. Don't be alone with your eating disorder. For further information about eating disorders and recovery, please come and visit me at my website: www.annapaterson.com

I hope that I have been able to help you by sharing my knowledge and experience of these illnesses with you, and have left you with some real hope for the future.

Take care.

Glossary

Abuse - To mistreat a person either mentally, physically or sexually.

Aerobic exercise - Increases oxygen production by raising the heart rate, for example jogging, swimming etc.

Amennorrhea - When a woman's monthly period stops, usually due to dramatic weight loss.

Amphetamines - A drug that is used as a stimulant and which, at first, causes a person to feel very wide awake.

Anaemia - An illness caused by a lack of iron in the blood.

Appetite Suppressants - A medicine that stops a person from feeling hungry.

Assertiveness - An ability to put forward your point of view and opinion.

Atonic Colon - When the bowel stops working completely.

Bingeing - When a person eats large quantities of food in a short space of time.

Body Dysmorphia - An illness where the sufferer believes that parts of their body are extremely ugly.

Bulimarexia - An illness that combines the symptoms of both anorexia and bulimia.

Calorie - A unit of energy.

Chilblains - A dark red itchy swelling that forms on the hands and feet during cold weather. They can also form when a person frequently feels cold due to poor circulation.

Cognitive Therapy - A form of therapy that uses positive thoughts to reverse negative thoughts and feelings.

Comfort Food - Food that people turn to for comfort when they are feeling low, such as chocolate pudding.

Constipation - This is when someone has trouble passing waste products (faeces).

CPN - An abbreviation for Community Psychiatric Nurse.

Dehydration - A lack of water in the tissues of the body, often caused by vomiting or laxative abuse.

Depression - A mental state of great sadness.

Diabetes - A disease where there is too much sugar in the blood due to a lack of insulin.

Dialysis - When a machine does the work of the kidneys, to remove harmful substances from the blood.

Dietician - An expert in diet and nutrition.

Distortion - A misrepresented and warped view.

Diuretics - Otherwise known as water pills, these medicines increase the production of urine.

Drip-feeding - Feeding liquid nutrition directly into a patient's vein.

Dysfunctional - Not working properly.

ED - An abbreviation for 'Eating Disorder'.

ED-NOS - An abbreviation for 'Eating Disorder Not Otherwise Specified'.

Ejaculates - The releasing of semen from an erect penis.

Electrolytes - Otherwise known as 'salts', these are chemicals such as potassium, sodium, magnesium and chloride which are necessary to keep the heart rate constant.

Emetics - A medicine used to make people vomit.

Endorphins - A chemical produced naturally in the brain during exercise, which brings about a feeling of well-being and happiness.

Enemas - When a quantity of liquid (soap or olive oil) is passed into the rectum to have a laxative effect.

Empower - To give strength and power.

Epilepsy - A disorder of the nervous system that leads to convulsions (fits).

Erection - The sexually active state of the penis when it becomes rigid.

Fasting - When a person goes without food for a number of hours or days (otherwise known as 'starving').

Fits - Sudden attacks or seizures (convulsions).

Genetics - The study of which characteristics we inherit from our parents.

Growth Spurt - A sudden burst of growth during puberty.

Gynaecomastia - Affects men and is a slight enlargement of the breasts during puberty.

Hypoglycaemia - A condition of low blood sugar level that leads to dizziness, weakness, mental confusion and sweating.

Hypothalamus - A region of the brain that is responsible for sending signals to the ovaries during puberty.

Infertile - When a person is unable to have children.

In-patient - When a patient is admitted for a stay in hospital.

Insomnia - Sleeplessness and restlessness at night.

Insulin - A hormone produced by the pancreas that controls the amount of sugar in the blood.

Internalise - To turn your feelings inwards.

Irritable Bowel Syndrome - A common condition where the sufferer has stomach pain and bouts of constipation and diarrhoea.

Lanugo - A fine covering of dark hair that grows on the body of an anorexic.

Laxative - A medicine which causes the bowels to empty more often.

Menstruation - The discharge of blood once a month (otherwise known as a 'period') when an egg is unfertilized.

Metabolic Rate - The speed at which the body burns up food.

Metabolism - The way that the body uses food to keep itself functioning.

M.E. - (Myalgic Encephalomyelitis) This is otherwise known as chronic fatigue syndrome and is an illness where the sufferer feels extreme tiredness.

Migraines - Severe headaches, usually on one side of the head.

Neglect - Failure to protect a person from harm.

Nasogastric feeding - Feeding through a tube passed up the nose and into the stomach.

Obesity - A condition when the sufferer is at least 20% above the recommended weight for their height.

Oedema - A condition where fluid collects in the body tissue, especially around the ankles.

Oesophagus - The tube that leads from the mouth to the stomach, down which food is passed. It can be easily damaged by vomiting

Oestrogen - A female hormone.

Osteoporosis - An illness caused by a loss of bone mass, which usually develops in middle age. Bones become brittle and are at risk of breaking.

Out-patient - When a patient has treatment on a daily or weekly basis at a hospital or clinic but does not stay overnight.

Ovaries - The reproductive organ in a woman which produces eggs.

Paediatrician - A medical doctor who specializes in helping children.

Palpitations - When the heart rate is irregular and beats harder or faster.

Penis - The male organ through which urine and semen are released.

Period - The time once a month when a woman bleeds (menstruates).

Pituitary - A gland in the brain which releases hormones and works with the hypothalamus.

Pneumonia - An inflammation of the lungs caused by bacteria.

Pornographic - Sexual in nature.

Pounds - A measurement of weight, which can be written as "lbs".

Pre-menstrual - The time just before a woman's monthly period, when their hormones cause physical problems and mood swings.

Psychiatrist - A medically qualified doctor who specializes in the treatment of mental and emotional problems.

Psychologist - A person who, although not a medical doctor, is specifically trained in the treatment of mental and emotional problems.

Puberty - When a young person's body begins to change in preparation for adulthood.

Pubic Hair - Thick and curly hair that starts to grow in the genital regions during puberty.

Pulse - The movement of the arteries as blood is pumped around the body by the beating of the heart.

Purging - When a person takes laxatives in large quantities to empty the body of all waste products.

Restrict - When a person is limiting their diet and avoiding certain foods.

Rituals - A series of repeated behaviour patterns.

Section - When a doctor has to legally force a patient to accept treatment.

Self-esteem - Your own opinion of yourself.

Sperm - The fluid released from the penis during sexual activity.

Starvation - The condition caused when a person doesn't eat enough food.

Stethoscope - A medical instrument used for listening to the sounds within a person's body.

Stomach Ulcers - A break in the lining of the stomach that is painful.

Testicle - One of a pair of male sex organs where semen is produced.

Testosterone - A male hormone.

Touch Deprivation - A lack of physical affection during childhood.

Unconditional Love - A love that is not dependent on a person's behaviour.

Vagina - The lower part of the female reproductive system.

Vaginal Discharge - A white substance that is released from the vagina approximately six months before a young girl's period begins.

Vegetarian - A person who does not eat meat.

Vomiting - When someone is physically sick and brings up food they have recently eaten.

Weights

28 grammes = 1 oz

454 grammes = 1 lb

600 millilitres = 1 pint

16 oz = 1 lb

14 lbs = 1 stone

List of Useful Addresses

Eating Disorder Associations (Worldwide)

Eating Disorders Association
First Floor, Wensum House
103 Prince of Wales Road
Norwich NR1 1DW
Telephone Helpline: 01603 621414 (Open Mon-Fri 9.00 am – 18.30 pm)
Youth Helpline: 01603 765050 (Open Mon-Fri 16.00 to 18.30 pm)
E-mail: info@edauk.com
Website: www.edauk.com

National Association of Anorexia nervosa and Associated Disorders (ANAD)
P O Box 7
Highland Park
IL 60035
USA
Hotline: 847-831-3438
Fax: 847-433-4632
E-mail: info@anad.org
Website: www.anad.org

British Columbia Eating Disorders Association
526 Michigan Street
Victoria, BC
Canada V8V 1S2
Tel: 250.383.2755
Fax: 250.383.5518
Website: www.preventingdisorderedeating.org

Eating Disorders Association
P O Box 80 142
Green Bay
Auckland 7
New Zealand
Tel: 09 818 9561; 09 627 8493; 09 523 3531; 09 523 1308
E-mail: anorexia@health.net.nz
Website: www.everybody.co.nz/support/eating.html

The Eating Disorders Association

53 Railway Terrace
Milton
Queensland 4064
Australia
Tel: (07) 3876 2500
For after hours help - Lifeline: 131114
Kids Helpline: 1800 551800
Parents Helpline: 1300 301 300
Website: www.uq.net.au/eda/documents/start.html

Therapy and Counselling Organisations

The Institute of Family Therapy

24-32 Stephenson Way
London NW1 2HX
Tel: 020 7391 9150
Fax: 020 7391 9169
Website: www.instituteoffamilytherapy.org.co.uk

United Kingdom Council for Psychotherapy

167-169 Great Portland Street
London W1W 5PF
Tel: 020 7436 3002
Fax: 020 7436 3013
E-mail: ukcp@psychotherapy.org.uk
Website: www.psychotherapy.org.uk

United Kingdom Register of Counsellors

P O Box 1050
Rugby
CV21 5HZ
Tel: 0870 443 5232
Fax: 0870 443 5161
E-mail: alani@bacp.co.uk or helen@bacp.co.uk
Website: www.bac.co.uk

Other Useful Organisations

Childline
Freepost 1111
London N1 0BR
Tel: 0800 1111 (Open 24 hours a day, 7 days a week)
Website: http://www.childline.org.uk

The Samaritans
Tel: 0845 790 9090 or 0114 245 6789 (help 24 hours a day)
E-mail: jo@samaritans.org
Website: www.samaritans.org.uk

Kidscape
2 Grosvenor Gardens
London SW1W 0DH
Tel: 020 7730 3300
Fax: 020 7730 7081
Website: www.kidscape.org.uk

Rape Crisis Federation
7 Mansfield Road
Nottingham NG1 3FB
Tel: 0115 934 8474 (9.00 am - 5 pm Monday to Friday - answerphone at other times)
Fax: 0115 934 8470
Minicom: 0115 934 8473
E-mail: info@rapecrisis.co.uk
Website: www.rapecrisis.co.uk

Victim Support (England and Wales)
Cranmer House
39 Brixton Road
London SW9 6DZ

Supportline
Tel: 0845 30 30 900 (Low-call rate: 9.00 am - 9.00 pm weekdays, 9.00 am to 7.00 pm weekends)
Tel: 020 7735 9166
Fax: 020 7582 5712
E-mail: contact@victimsupport.org.uk
Website: www.victimsupport.org.uk

A new novel written by Anna Paterson to be published in 2002:

Running on Empty

"Useless! That's what you are! Totally useless! A waste of space!"

The words hit Julia like a slap in the face. She started to back away from her Father into the furthest corner of the room. His anger was frightening as the words continued to race from his mouth, his face growing a deeper red with every passing minute.

"Why can't you be more like your brother? He's a success, but you - YOU ARE JUST A FAILURE!"

Julia's feelings of failure started her off down a very dark road. Her strong desire to disappear led her to begin dieting but this was no ordinary diet. Julia was now slowly starving herself to death. However, although she didn't know it, she wasn't the only one in her class with problems. Susan and Linda also had eating disorders, which were different but just as dangerous. Will they all be able to find the courage to help one another before it's too late?